£40.00

D1642372

The Collected Papers of

Nevill Coghill

The Collected Papers of

Nevill Coghill

Shakespearian & Medievalist

Edited, with an Introduction by DOUGLAS GRAY

THE HARVESTER PRESS · SUSSEX

ST. MARTIN'S PRESS · NEW YORK

First published in Great Britain in 1988 by
THE HARVESTER PRESS LIMITED
Publisher: John Spiers
16 Ship Street, Brighton, Sussex
and in the USA by
ST. MARTIN'S PRESS, INC.
175 Fifth Avenue, New York, NY 10010

© Carol Martin, 1988

British Library Cataloguing in Publication Data
Coghill, Nevill
    The collected papers of Nevill Coghill,
    Shakespearian and medievalist.
    1. English literature—Middle English,
    1100–1500—History and criticism
    2. English literature—Early modern,
    1500–1700—History and criticism
    I. Title
    820.9   PR255

    ISBN 0-7108-1233-7

Library of Congress Cataloging-in-Publication Data
Coghill, Nevill, 1899–
    The collected papers of Nevill Coghill.

    Bibliography: p.
    Includes index.
    1. English literature—History and criticism.
2. Chaucer, Geoffrey, d. 1400—Criticism and interpretation.
3. Langland, William, 1330?–1400? Piers the Plowman.
4. Shakespeare, William, 1564–1616—
Criticism and interpretation.   I. Gray, Douglas.
II. Title.
PR99.C666 1988 820'.9'001   87-28859
ISBN 0-312-01672-7

Typeset in 11 on 12pt Plantin by C.R. Barber & Partners
(Highlands) Ltd, Fort William, Scotland

Printed in Great Britain by Mackays of Chatham, Kent

Contents

Introduction

He was a big man built on generous lines, his head was large, and brown hair, greying in middle life, curled and clustered on it as wiry as heather. He smiled easily, revealing somewhat battered teeth, and indeed his whole face had a slightly rough, knocked-about quality, like a chipped statue. But it was a noble statue, generous in expression and bearing. His voice was deep and strong, his speech soft and gentle, and this contrast was carried through everything. He was totally courteous, a gentleman by instinct as well as by tradition ...

With this memorable portrait John Wain began an affectionate memoir of Nevill Coghill. I recall it here because those who knew him will almost certainly, as they read through these papers, be reminded of his physical presence by some phrase which will call up a characteristic intonation or glance, and because that much larger group of readers who never saw him will almost certainly wish to know more about the strong personality which so obviously shines through all his written work. Nevill Coghill was a very remarkable person, famous in three 'spheres' – known first in Oxford, where he spent the whole of his working academic life, as a brilliant and inspiring lecturer and tutor ('a tutor in whom one could confide', as W.H. Auden said in his dedication to him of *The Dyer's Hand*); known there, and well beyond the walls of both University and city, also as a highly talented theatrical producer; and, finally, known throughout the whole English-speaking world as a translator, indeed as *the* translator, of Chaucer. These academic papers on Chaucer, Langland and Shakespeare are the product of the 'first' Coghill, the busy and devoted teacher, a member – though not exactly a typical member (he was never 'typical' in anything) – of a generation of Oxford dons in which the impulse to 'publish' was often felt faintly if at all, and in which the intellectual fruits of a wide and humane reading were set above the more dogged kinds of 'research', but the interests of the 'second' and 'third' Nevill Coghills can be seen just as clearly.

It seemed proper to give his Chaucerian papers the pride of place in this collection since it was as a Chaucerian translator that he achieved his greatest and most widespread fame. Like Dryden, he found that he had 'a soul congenial to his', and he too was a good translator of Chaucer partly because he sensed something in the poet's spirit and sensibility that was akin to something in his own. He brought Chaucer into the lives of many readers who, it may be suspected, would not have thought or dared to open an edition of that poet's works; and he did it with such effectiveness and gusto that it is not surprising to find some evidence that in the popular imagination he was beginning to be confused with Chaucer. A reviewer in *The Times Literary Supplement* (10.11.1982, p. 1364) made the point with some wit:

> There is a serious Indian shopkeeper in the Persian Gulf who once showed signs of wishing to kiss a lady's feet because she had once sat at the feet of the author of the Penguin *Canterbury Tales*; and the author himself recalls being asked solicitously, after the meeting of an East Anglian literary society, 'And how is *Mrs* Chaucer? We are so sorry you had to leave her at home!'

And, he continued, perceptively:

> If this confusion obtains in the minds of millions of the people Nevill Coghill has introduced to Geoffrey Chaucer, there is reason for it. Professor Coghill may not be the poet Chaucer was, though he can be pretty good; but he has become the *grand translateur* of Chaucer to this age because he sounds natural, because he has a good deal in common with his master besides the devotion of a disciple. He has the same quality of conveying delight in life that he attributes to Chaucer, a delight that is something more than mere jollity; they share, without embarrassment, that attitude to life which Professor Coghill pinpoints as 'Christian cheerfulness' ...

Modestly, he described his work as 'verse-paraphrase' rather than translation, although it is obvious that he thought long and hard about the problems involved in verse translation. He never pretended that his versions could ever be a substitute for Chaucer; they were simply 'chairs' for future Chaucerians: 'one way of learning to skate with ease is to lean on a chair pushed over the ice before one; clumsy as the chair is, it gives support to self-confidence and stills trepidation in the future skater.'

The translation of *The Canterbury Tales* was done originally to be broadcast on the BBC Third Programme. It was a new experiment in a new venture in radio, commissioned soon after the beginning of the Third Programme (*c.* 1946–7), and its great success undoubtedly had a part in the making of the Third Programme's distinctive ethos. Looking back on it (*Manuscripts* XXIII, 2 [1971], 93–4), Nevill Coghill, with characteristic modesty, preferred to describe it all as a 'fluke'. Stephen Potter, who had been told to 'put Chaucer on the air', was directed by David Nichol Smith to Coghill, then working on his book *The Poet Chaucer*:

> So Stephen called on me, and over a glass of sherry outlined his problem: *how was Chaucer to be put on the air?* I asked him, 'In the original?' 'What would it sound like?', he queried. I gave him a sample causing him to comment, 'I can just hear them switching off!' 'Then you want a translation; prose or verse?' 'Which do you recommend?' 'Prose is impossible, in my opinion; all the wit would evaporate.' 'Could you do a verse translation?' 'I don't know; I've never tried; give me a month and I'll see if I can.'

And so, the experimental sections approved, and a couple of programmes prepared ('You needn't worry too much,' said Potter, 'there won't be more than one or two thousand listeners, and they won't want more than one or two programmes at the most'), the first sections were eventually broadcast; he was astounded to be informed that 'listener research' had reported not two thousand listeners, but two million! In this success story there is a serious point which bears on Nevill Coghill's achievement as a critic of medieval literature. Well ahead of his time, he had realised that this 'literature', even as late as the days of Chaucer and Langland, was still often intimately involved with oral performance, and that modern readers could often understand it better if it was read aloud. Later, he was to produce a series of readings of Chaucer 'in the original' on gramophone records, and in his last years in Oxford he and a number of colleagues used to put on a reading of *Troilus and Criseyde* in Middle English which illuminated that poem in a remarkable way.

The Chaucerian papers reprinted here may all in one way or another be related to Nevill Coghill's book, *The Poet Chaucer*, which was published in 1949, and which remains one of the very best introductions to the poet's work. Nowadays, when introductory books on Chaucer abound, often repeating and reproducing themselves in an almost mechanical way, it requires an effort of memory to recover the sense of freshness and excitement that *The Poet Chaucer* brought with it. One of the most learned of twentieth-century Chaucerians, J.A.W. Bennett, welcomed it as one of the few 'oases in a great Salt-Lake Desert of dissertations':

> Thanks to Manly, Coulton, and their clans we now know doubtless more about the fourteenth century than Chaucer himself ever did. But there has lately been disconcerting evidence that when a social historian turns critic he may succeed only in making ten clichés grow where only one grew before.
>
> With what unwonted delight, then, do we come upon a book which captures the grace and gusto of both Chaucer's verse and a persuasive critic's talk ...

Closest to the book is the pamphlet 'Geoffrey Chaucer', which appeared in 1956 in that useful series 'Writers and their Work'. Intended to give a general view in short compass for the ordinary reader, this shows Coghill's liveliness and clarity of style at their best. With a delicate touch, he sets Chaucer in the context of his time and of his inherited literary and intellectual tradition. All that the reader needs to know about education or about rhetoric is deftly sketched in outline, with no trace of pendantry or heavy-handedness. Nevill Coghill was never one to grind away at a favourite axe: he does not exhaust us with tropes and figures; his use of parallels in the visual arts is invariably discreet as well as illuminating. He was equally at ease with Chaucer the poet of human experience as well as with Chaucer the poet versed in the 'auctoritee' of his books. This is nowhere more obvious than in his treatment of him as a poet of love, where he judiciously balances the poet's range of reading against his depth of understanding of ordinary people. He puts it memorably:

> But it is not only a question of range, variety and subtlety in his art of love; it is the sympathy. He is all things to all men and women in all their moods and modes of love, able to write as easily of the lowest as of the highest . . .
> The reason he can do so is that he takes joy in the created world, he grasps life affirmatively, and calls nothing that God has made unclean.

In 'Chaucer's Idea of What is Noble', the Presidential Address to the English Association in 1971, he returns to a strand in Chaucer's thinking which had long interested him, the notions of 'gentilesse', of 'courtesy', and of 'nobility'. 'Gentilesse' is, he sayd, 'the gold out of which the word *gentleman* was first minted.' And it is clear that this is something close to his heart: 'this word *gentleman* . . . is at the centre of our inheritance; it may be that the gold in it needs melting down and reminting into current coin, but it would be a pity to throw it away without knowing what gold there is in it.' It is refreshing nowadays to read a straightforward defence of Chaucer's Knight and his *gentilesse* instead of what purport to be 'ironical' readings showing him to be 'flawed'. (Coghill was not unaware of Chaucerian irony, but he knew that it was a subtle thing, and not necessarily always destructive.)

> . . . there is another, more fundamental answer to those who want to think the Knight's moral nature, as depicted by Chaucer, was too good to be true, and so can be no better than a romantic illusion. People who think thus can never have thought about Christianity at all; that we cannot live up to the moral demands that it makes on us, and that at any moment we may fall into the pit that opens beneath us, does not lessen the love we are taught to have for them, and which Chaucer's Knight too was taught to have, and to attempt.

He is quite certain that it is Christianity which is at the heart of Chaucer's idea of nobility – 'it is God who sends us grace to exercise our virtue in attempting to be perfect, by the pure simplicity of the *Imitatio Christi*, undertaken in that grace' – although he sets it firmly in the daily life of the secular world (where one of the qualities of *gentilesse* is 'a certain intellectual grandeur, a capacity to think a high thought'). In Coghill's view, this ideal depends on Christianity, and indeed on medieval Christianity:

> This concept of a gentleman was too high to hold long; it went down very quickly after Chaucer, and my impression of Castiglione and his famous book, *The Courtier*, some two centuries later, is always one of a downfall, however elegantly sophisticated.

There the Lord Julian rebukes a disputant for alluding to the Bible; the Wife of Bath, says Coghill, 'would have made short work of that kind of double-talk!'

Langland, the great contemporary of Chaucer, was a life-long interest of Nevill Coghill's, and although he never wrote a critical book devoted to him, we are fortunate in having a number of extensive and distinguished papers and articles. (It is to be hoped that one day his translations of selected passages from Langland, *Visions from Piers Plowman* [1949], which to my mind are even better than his Chaucer translations, will be republished.) In the pamphlet written for the 'Writers and their Work' series (1964, dedicated to Przemysław Mroczkowski, now the *doyen* of Polish scholars of medieval English literature) he gives an excellent succinct account of the poet and his work ('the greatest Christian poem in our language'), noting the extraordinary range of Langland's imagination – no sensitive reader

> can ... fail to wonder at the spiritual range and intensity of a mind that can generate a ferociously satirical laughter, a comparison as humane as Lear's upon the heath, and a mystical sense of glory in God's love in the passion and resurrection of Christ –

and singling out the essentials of Langland's thought:

> Love seen as Truth is the rock of his morality, and in the first visions of the poem, by this unanswerable criterion, he measures the actual, contemporary world presented in them.
> ... Truth is not only in his heavenly tower, but also in our hearts, for we are made in His image, and it is He who teaches us how to love.

We are taken carefully through the central part of the poem (which most readers at first find rather bewildering) and shown how out of the wilderness of disputation a number of important questions arise concerning the implications of the injunction to 'do well', and the nature and meaning of three good lives, and how 'gradually their meaning is felt to accumulate into a quite unsystematic yet feeling body of Christian wisdom.' We are introduced to the unique quality of Langland's poetry, combining a sublimity of vision with an earthy colloquialism of language, seen at its best in his vision of Christ's Passion – 'this triumph of eye-witness poetry' – and shown how at the climax of his poem Langland 'was not celebrating a victory but a desolation.' If he shares with Chaucer (an 'early modern' writer) the faculty for irony, Langland (essentially a 'late medieval' writer) has a characteristic urgency, which is only matched in *The Pilgrim's Progress*.

The earliest of the Langland papers, on 'The Character of Piers Plowman' (1933), argues that the character of Piers is 'intended as an emblem or personification of Dowel, Dobet, and Dobest successively'. The next sentence is a significant one: 'It was formerly believed that Langland's poem lacked a preconceived logical form.' With the solitary exception of an article by H.W. Wells, earlier literary criticism (and there was very little of it) had assumed that the poem was 'formless'. Whether or not the form of the poem is 'logical' and how far it is 'preconceived' are still questions that can be argued over, but there is no doubt that this article of Nevill Coghill's guided criticism in the direction of assuming a (more or less) coherent structure. Coghill's argument, based on an analysis of the various 'entries' Piers Plowman makes in the poem, is conducted with clarity and good sense, with a sensitivity to Langland's curiously indirect manner of working towards a meaning – 'Langland was a poet who liked to be seen feeling for his ideas; he tries out successive notions, and noses his way among opinions before the reader's eyes' – and with an honest confrontation of the many difficult passages (such as the notorious 'Pardon Scene' in B. VII). He had to defend the poem against the prevailing low opinion of allegory – 'Allegory, once believed to be the life of poetry, is now commonly thought the death of it' – and not only did he do this, but he described Langland's distinctive use of allegory, contrasting his poem, where 'the allegory is organic, the bone in the body', with the carefully crafted allegory of Spenser.

In his British Academy lecture of 1945, 'The Pardon of Piers Plowman', Coghill returned to that difficult scene, but his detailed treatment of the differences between the A and B texts led him on to a much wider discussion. The two texts, he argues, 'belong to separate species of poetry, to different orders of the imagination ..., and therefore call for different kinds of response from their readers, as they called for different kinds of treatment by their poet.' The A text 'is the anatomy of England'; Langland 'has a surgeon's eye and his scalpel is Christianity' – it is 'a topical narrative allegory about the moral condition of England'. In the B text, Langland 'found himself committed to a poem not about England but about Salvation and the Three Ways that led to it.' Here we have a 'more touching sense of the enfolding and creative love of God the Father', and Langland moves towards 'a poetry that has moments of lyrical contemplation, suggestive of a mystical rather than a moral vision, in so far as these can be distinguished.'

Finally, we have 'God's Wenches and the Light that Spoke' (1962), which he wrote for the Festschrift to celebrate the seventieth birthday of J.R.R. Tolkien. This is subtitled, 'Some Notes on Langland's Kind of Poetry', and in it he attempts to isolate those unique elements in the 'stunning-power' Langland shares with other great poets. Coghill distinguishes a 'huge fluidity' in his handling of allegory. Although his poem is usually called an allegory, it is 'so exceptional in its modes of vision that when we look at it closely we are forced to revise this general account of it and consult our definitions.' He contrasts it with the orderly, indeed mechanical, allegory of the *Psychomachia*: 'gone the notion of the soul as an orderly battlefield of the passions, where decisive victories in epic style smash, rather than probe, its problems.' He shows how Langland fused allegory and symbol, and how he deliberately mixed kinds. Comparing the parable in *The Castle of Love* in which four daughters of a king plead for a sinful thrall in prison with Langland's treatment of the Four Daughters of God, he points out how Langland blends 'a homely naturalism with mystery' – 'he simply thinks of them as "wenches", while creating for their appearance an atmosphere of darkness pierced by supernatural light.' Profoundly characteristic of Langland is his treatment of that odd character, 'Book': it is 'a perfect illustration of the grotesque in medieval art: partly ridiculous, partly sublime, even a little mad, by our standards, perhaps . . .' In Langland, we have 'a sense of the union of opposites, whether in space and time, allegory and symbol, familiar and fantastic, comic and sublime.' Although Coghill never wrote a book about *Piers Plowman*, any prospective student of Langland who reads through these papers will have been given an incomparable introduction to that brilliant and tantalising poem.

A number of the Shakespeare papers in this collection are obviously related to Nevill Coghill's long practical interest in the theatre, and to his book, *Shakespeare's Professional Skills* (based on his Clark Lectures given in 1959), published in 1964 by the Cambridge University Press. In the first chapter of this, 'Visual Meaning', he says: 'my starting-point is how to tell a story on a stage, and this was also Shakespeare's primal starting-point, so far as one can tell.' His insistence (expressed in his teaching long before this book) on the visual element in Shakespeare, now often – but still not always – taken for granted, was again something of a novelty. Shakespeare plays were usually studied exclusively as literary texts; eminent Shakespeareans sometimes deliberately avoided productions of the plays, and in some quarters in Oxford Nevill Coghill himself was regarded with suspicion because of his connections with 'amateur theatricals'. His paper on 'Six Points of Stage-Craft in *The Winter's Tale*' (1958) is an excellent example of how he could apply his own professional skills in the theatre to the elucidation – and to the defence – of Shakespeare's, and of how the keen eye of a producer-reader could pick up things which eluded the eye of a more traditional literary scholar. It is a careful defence of the dramaturgy of that play against the strictures of editors and critics. Such points as the supposed suddenness of Leontes' jealousy, the notorious '*Exit pursued by a bear*' etc., are taken up and examined with precision and sympathy. The sudden jealousy is 'a little miracle of stage-craft', a shock prepared for by a deliberate use of 'the technique of prepared surprise' in the conversation of Archidamus and Camillo; the bear not a piece of crude or antiquated stage-craft, but 'a dazzling piece of *avant-garde* work; no parallel can be found for what, at a stroke, it effects: it is the transformation of tragedy into comedy . . .', a scene in which 'the terrible and the grotesque come near to each other in a *frisson* of horror instantly succeeded by a shout of laughter.' Yet it is worth stressing also that Coghill was emphatically not one of those producer-critics who are convinced that the producer has a totally free hand and may do what he will with Shakespeare's text; in *Shakespeare's Professional Skills* the 'distortions' of Shakespeare are not just those of over-literary literary critics, but include those 'imposed by those directors whose pitiable ambition is to be "different" (to use their phrase) whereas the true virtue and fountain of all originality in production is to be finely perceptive.'

The two longer Shakespearian papers included here treat more general questions of Shakespeare's comic techniques, but they are none the less closely related in subject-matter and method to the other papers in the collection. In 'Wags, Clowns and Jesters', originally a lecture given at the Shakespeare Memorial Theatre Summer School, which with great zest and merriment runs through the actual jesters of the sixteenth century, and contrasts their wares with the superior quality of Shakespeare's fools, from Touchstone and Feste to the Fool in *Lear*, there is a moment of fine visual observation, when in analysing the 'master–boy' relationship he points to the comic disparity between the enormous Falstaff and his tiny page (whom he addresses as 'you giant'). And when in noting that 'most of the great clowns in Shakespeare are highly individual; they are among the most humanly perceived of all the members of their little worlds', he touches on their innocence, his interest in earlier literature emerges, and he thinks of 'the aphorism of St Augustine that Langland quotes in *Piers Plowman* . . . "See! very fools take Heaven by assault, where we, the wise, are sunk into the pit." ' Similarly, in his earlier 'The Basis of Shakespearian Comedy' (notable, among other things, for a brief but sympathetic and persuasive section on *The Taming of the*

Shrew), it is not surprising to find him arguing strongly for the existence of underlying medieval patterns:

> Shakespeare was not simply following the chances of temperament in designing his Comedies, but ... was following a tradition that evolved during the Middle Ages.

and not only in his conception of comedy but also in his comic treatment of evil:

> It is only with the existence of evil as a real presence in the world that a Comedy on the medieval pattern becomes difficult; it is not so easy to solve in joy the problem of sin. But medieval ways of thinking had an answer for that too, a Christian answer, like Shakespeare's. If there were a breach in nature there was also the power of charity and repentance, of mercy and forgiveness, with laughter on the way. *The Winter's Tale* follows a like pattern; so does *Measure for Measure*.

We are reminded of what he says of Chaucer (in 'Geoffrey Chaucer'), that

> it is the mortal world that most exercised his poetical gift, and there he is nearest to Shakespeare as the poet of humane understanding; like him he begets a caritas in the imagination of his readers.

Nevill Coghill was a genuinely modest man: he would not have presented his writings as those of a scholar of profound learning, but simply as the reflections of a well-read, cultivated, and intelligent reader and teacher, which he hoped would be helpful guides to other readers. And that is what these essays are, distinguished by their range, their intelligence and fine perceptiveness, as well as by their lightness of touch and elegance of style. In his essay on Shakespeare's comedies, Coghill remarks that hardly a single character in them 'is lacking in, or incapable of, a generous impulse.' The remark is typical, and significant, and helps us to see what it was in Coghill himself that drew him to the most *humane* writers in English. He himself was 'totally courteous, a gentleman by instinct as well as by tradition', and every line of his critical writing is pervaded by his own 'gentilesse'.

D. G.

BIOGRAPHICAL NOTE

Nevill Coghill was born on 19 April 1899, and was educated at Haileybury School and Exeter College, Oxford. He saw military service during the First World War. He was for many years Fellow and Tutor of Exeter College, and in 1957 became Merton Professor of English Literature. He retired in 1966, and died on 6 November 1980. (*Times Educational Supplement* 24.12.1982, p. 20)

I

Geoffrey Chaucer*

I. LONDON-BORN

> A shilling life will give you all the facts.
> W.H. Auden

In what his father and mother would have regarded as his career – for it was they who had the wit, and the luck, to launch him upon it – Geoffrey Chaucer did remarkably well. His successive appointments, missions and awards, achieved in the administrative service of three kings, was something better than a mediocre success; and who could have foreseen that his marriage, prudent and suitable as it was, romantic too, for all we know to the contrary, would ultimately make him brother-in-law to his own best patron, John of Gaunt, that is to the fourth son of Edward III, the uncle of Richard II and the father of Henry IV, the poet's chief employers?

But it was not as a poet that they employed him; his poetry was an extra, so far as they were concerned. His career was that of a courtier, as his father and mother had intended, and it was that career that gained him his place in the official records of the time; except for them, we should probably know as little about him as we do of the other great poets of his age, the authors of *Piers Plowman* and of *Sir Gawain*.

Yet the recorded facts of this courtier's life, remote from poetry as they may seem, are those upon which the styles of

---

Writers and their Work. No. 79. Published for The British Council and The National Book League (London: Longmans, Green, 1956).

his poetry turn; they mark its progress from his first beginnings, step by step, to his maturities. Being a courtier made a European of him, and more than that; he became the first great English poet in the general tradition of Christendom, the heir of Ovid, of Vergil, of Boethius; of St Jerome, of de Lorris and de Meun, of Dante and Boccaccio.

He was not our first great Christian poet; Langland was before him. But he was our first poet in the high culture of Europe, then breaking out all over England in glorious profusion of creative power. There are moments in the lives of nations when they declare their genius: the life of Geoffrey Chaucer fell in the middle of our first such moment.

In every art then known, and in some now lost, in architecture, sculpture, carving and stained glass; in the work of goldsmiths and armourers and of the makers of robes for ceremonial and daily use, in manuscript illumination, painting and portraiture, music and dancing, sudden perfections were being achieved all over the country. Moreover, they were harmonious with each other, as if there were a general sense of a particular style, and a very free flowering of it in every field. Grace, strength, freshness of invention, clarity, richness, and a sense of the humane as well as of the divine characterise this breeding-time of our first civilisation.

Out of a multitude of masterpieces, I will name a few to show these qualities: the central tower of Wells Cathedral and the breathtaking inverted arch that supports it, the work of William Joy about the year of Chaucer's birth (c. 1340): the great octagonally-fashioned vault over the transept of Ely Cathedral, the work of Alan of Walsingham and William Hurley not long before, miracles, both of strength and ingenuity: the nave of Westminster Abbey, grove of slender stone, built by the greatest English architect before Wren, Henry Yevele. Chaucer, late in his life, knew and worked with him. It was Yevele who, with Hugh Herland, Master-Carpenter, also gave us Westminster Hall (1394).

In portraiture, an art then dawning and of which Chaucer too became a master, we may think of the tragic alabaster face of Edward II that haunts the visitor to Gloucester Cathedral, or the knowingly practical visage of Henry IV, carved in

Canterbury; less tragic than Edward, more humane than Henry, the painted effigy of Edward, Lord Despenser, kneeling in his chantry-roof in Tewkesbury Abbey. Illumination and painting could show pieces as fine as these: instance the Wilton Diptych that presents the young Richard II to the Blessed Virgin and a host of angels, himself hardly less angelical in beauty; or the greater portrait of him that hangs in Westminster Abbey and shows him against a gold background in a robe the colour of dry blood. From his face, he seems to be thinking Shakespearian thoughts.

In glass the ante-chapel windows of New College by Thomas of Oxford, with their canopied saints and patriarchs in soft greens and porphyries and blues, seem a silent reproach to the baroque-souled figures and inharmonious tints of a neighbouring window by Sir Joshua Reynolds, that was somehow allowed to be put there in an age that knew no better. In the same chapel is the crozier of William of Wykeham, a master-work of the goldsmiths, silversmiths and enamellers of the fourteenth century.

Harp and flute and social song were part of a gentleman's education (as we shall see) and song was gracefully combined with dance in the 'carol'; the art of conversation was so much esteemed that Andreas Capellanus gives it third place among the requirements for a girl worthy to be loved, and Chaucer, in his first considerable poem, ensures that it shall be known to have graced the dead patroness he is celebrating, Blanche, Duchess of Lancaster:

> And which a goodly, softe speche
> Had that swete, *my lyves leche*![1]
> So frendly, and so wel ygrounded,
> *Up*[2] al resoun so wel yfounded
> And *se tretable*[3] to alle goode

In poetry (our chief concern in this essay) the age was richer than in all else, except architecture. There were the three great poets I have mentioned, of whom Chaucer was chief; there was John Gower too, and the makers of our Miracle Cycles, then coming to their first fullness in York and elsewhere. *Troilus & Criseyde, The Canterbury Tales, Piers Plowman, Sir Gawain, Pearl,* and *The Wakefield Miracle*

Cycle may speak for the great achievements of those times in poetry, but there was also a first pouring forth of lyrical writing, by many anonymous hands and one-poem men, of whose work here is a fragment:

> Bytuene Mersh and Aueril,
>   When spray biginneth to springe,
> The lutel foul hath hire wyl
>   On hyre lud to synge.
>   Ich libbe in loue-longinge
>   For semlokest of alle thynge:
>   (S)he may me blisse bringe;
> Icham in hire bandoun.
>   *An hendy hap ichabbe yhent;*
>   *Ichot from heuene it is me sent;*
>   *From alle wymmen mi loue is lent,*
>   *And lyht on Alysoun.*
>   (Sisam, *Fourteenth Century Verse and Prose*)

[Between March and April, when the spray begins to spring, the little bird has its pleasure to sing in its language. I live in love-longing for the seemliest of all things; may (s)he bring me joy; I am in her power. I have grabbed a lucky chance, I know it has been sent me from Heaven; from all women my love has turned away, and lights on Alison.]

and here another, in a more 'metaphysical' vein:

> Gold & al this werdis wyn
> Is nouth but cristis rode;
> I wolde ben clad in cristis skyn,
> That ran so longe on blode.
> & gon t'is herte & taken myn In –
> There is a fulsum fode.
>   (Carleton Brown, *Religous Lyrics of the Fourteenth Century*)

[Gold and all the glory of this world is nought, save Christ's cross; I would be clad in Christ's skin, that ran so long with blood, and go to his heart and make my Inn there, where there is a bounteous food.]

This was a mystical age, the age of Richard Rolle and Julian of Norwich; her writings are like the writings of a lover:

I saw his sweet face as it were dry and bloodless with pale dying. And later, more pale, dead, languoring; and then turned more dead unto blue: and then more brown-blue, as the flesh turned more deeply dead.

For his Passion shewed to me most specially in his blessed face, and chiefly in his lips: there I saw these four colours, though it were afore fresh, ruddy, and liking, to my sight.

It was also an age that loved learning, a founding-time of colleges. Eight new ones were added within the century, four at Oxford and four at Cambridge.

Paradoxes are to be understood as best they can. This same age of our first, and in some ways our finest, culture, was also an age pre-eminent for plague, poverty, rebellion, war (both international and civil), political murder, heresy and schism. Fissures seemed to be opening in the Catholic Church with the 'Babylonish' captivity of the Popes at Avignon, followed by a great schism and war between Pope and Anti-Pope. To Langland it seemed like the Day of Antichrist. Heresies were also raising their terrible heads; the chronicles tell the story of a knight who snatched the consecrated host out of his priest's hand and fled away with it, to devour it with oysters and mustard, thinking (in some obscure way) that this disproved transubstantiation.

There were secular terrors too: the Black Death began its repeated visitations in 1348, when Chaucer was a child.

> Ther cam a privee theef, men clepeth Deeth,[4]
> That in this contree al the peple sleeth.
>
> (*The Pardoner's Tale*)

The tyrannies of nature were matched by the tyrannies of man. Mob-madness and xenophobia filled London with the shouts and shrieks of massacre when the rebels of The Peasants' Revolt, entering London, fell upon the Flemings there in 1381; Chaucer, in later years, passed it off as a joke, a farmyard flurry:

> Certes, he Jakke Straw and his meynee[5]
> Ne made nevere shoutes half so shrille,
> Whan that they wolden any Flemyng kille,
> As thilke day was maad upon the fox ...
>
> (*Nun's Priest's Tale*)

This revolt, which was also an attack upon Church and Law, was suppressed as savagely as it had arisen, with hanging in chains for many a deluded peasant. Their betters were also liable to liquidation; the intrigues that stewed within and seethed outside the Court and government led often enough to the scaffold:

> The ax was sharpe, the stokke was harde
> In the xiii yere of Kyng Richarde.
> (Sisam, *Fourteenth Century Verse and Prose*)

As a sort of ground-bass to all these disturbances, there was an unstaunched issue of blood, bitter, barbarous and futile, in the feuds with France that are now called The Hundred Years' War. No doubt it was conducted with great panache and had moments of thrilling, heraldic heroism; it certainly dazzled the eyes of its chronicler, Froissart, who could write of it with the kind of romantic feeling that stirs in us when we read Chaucer's *Knight's Tale*:

> Thus the knights and squires sparkled abroad in the plain and fought together ... (Froissart, 1364)

> It was great joy to see and consider the banners and the penons and the noble armoury ... the Prince himself 'was the chief flower of chivalry of all the world, and had with him as then right noble and valiant knights and squires ... (1367)

> The men of arms beat down the Flemings on every side ... and as the Flemings were beaten down, there were pages ready to cut their throats with great knives, and so slew them without pity, as though they had been but dogs ... (1382)

What with Jakke Straw and the men of arms, the Flemings met with small mercy, but nationalism knows no restraint and soldiers cannot expect a ransom from a Flemish burgher.

Into this age of extremes, which in every direction forces superlatives from its astonished student, Geoffrey Chaucer, most equable of men, was born.

He was born in the middle of the century and in the middle of society, towards the year 1340, in a middle-class cockney home. No record was kept of the event. Round the corner and half a street away from his father's house, flowed the Thames; a little above towered old St Paul's, whose chapter-house and cloister, the work of William Ramsey, stood in their brand new perpendicular beauty. A new style had been born.

II. EDUCATION IN RHETORIC

The noble rethor poete of brytayne
(John Lydgate: *Life of Our Lady*, referring to Chaucer)

Not far away, in the Vintry, stood St Paul's Almonry; and if it is not a fact, it is likely conjecture that young Geoffrey was sent there daily to learn his letters and his Latin, through the medium of French:

Children in scole, ayenst the vsage and manere of alle othere naciouns beeth compelled for to leue hire owne langage, and for to construe hir lessouns and here thynges in Frensche, and so they haueth seth the Normans come first to Engelond. Also gentil men children beeth i-taught to speke Frensche from the tyme that they beeth i-rokked in here cradel ... And vplondisshe men wil likne hym self to gentil men, and fondeth with greet besynesse for to speke Frensce, *for to be i-tolde of.*
(Higden, *Polychronicon*, 1363)

As might be expected from the above, Chaucer's *Squire* in *The Canterbury Tales*, being of 'gentil' birth, was accustomed to speaking French, and confesses:

Myn Englissh eek is insufficient

and the *Franklin*, an 'vplondisshe' or country-bred man if ever there was one, loudly regrets that his own son lacks the gentle breeding of the *Squire*, in such a way as to unleash the mockery of the Host, who could see at a glance that there was a penny short in the shilling of the *Franklin's* gentility:

'Straw for youre gentillesse!' quod oure Hoost.

What was it like to be at school in those days? Children were sent very young: *enfantz*, they were called, and their instruction began like that of Chaucer's 'litel clergeon' in *The Prioress's Tale*, with the singing of Latin hymns, the easiest way into the difficult language of Heaven:

I lerne song, I kan but smal grammeere.
(*Prioress's Tale*)

At Westminster School, and probably at St Paul's too, a boy

who knew Latin and presumed to speak English or even
French, had a cut of the cane for every word so spoken. Rod
and birch were frequently applied to the seat of learning and
accepted as a rueful joke by the little victims. There is, for
instance, a late fifteenth-century poem by – or, at least, about
– a boy who had tried to excuse himself for being late for
school on the grounds that his mother had told him to go out
and milk the ducks:

> My master lokith as he were madde:
> 'wher hast *thou* be, thow sory ladde?'
> 'Milked dukkis, my moder badde:'
> hit was no mervayle thow I were sadde.
>   what vaylith it me thowgh I say nay?
>
> My master pepered my ars with well good spede …
> he wold not leve till it did blede.
> Myche sorow haue he for his dede!
> *(Babees Book*, ed. F.J. Furnivall)

Discipline, if rough, was ready, The day began with prayer,
then a recitation of the Creed, the Lord's Prayer, a Salutation
to the Blessed Virgin and some psalm-singing, which was
called 'dinging on David'. And so to class to learn your letters,
to do sums with counters, to Grammar, to Logic, to Rhetoric
and to the Classic authors, Ovid, Vergil, Lucan, Cicero,
Statius, Dionysius Cato and the rest.

Rhetoric has come to mean a windy way of speech, marked
by a pompous emptiness and insincerity, and trotted out as a
trick on any occasion calling for solemn humbug. It did not
mean this to the Middle Ages. To them it meant the whole
craft of writing, the arts and devices by which whatever you
had to say could best be varied, clarified and elaborated; it
even included the study of appropriate gesture.

> And, for his tale sholde seme the bettre,
> Accordant to his wordes was his cheere,
> As techeth art of speche hem that it leere.
> *(The Squire's Tale)*

[He suited his action to his words, as the art of speech teaches those that
learn it, to do.]

The word *rhetor* had come to be used as the simple

equivalent of 'good poet'; so Chaucer used it in *The Squire's Tale*, to underline the skill needed to describe the beauty of his heroine:

> It moste been a rethor excellent ...
> If he sholde hire descryven every part.
> I am noon swich, I moot speke as I kan.

So it was used of Chaucer by Lydgate and other poets:

> O reverend Chaucere, rose of rethoris all,
> As in oure tong ane flour imperiall ...
> (William Dunbar, *The Goldyn Targe*)

The rules of rhetoric are now, for the most part, forgotten, and the enormous effect they had on the formation of Chaucer's style is therefore often not perceived, even by good Chaucerists. Every educated person in the fourteenth century knew them and admired those who knew how to use them, of whom Chaucer was chief. It would be fair to say that an anthology of the finest things in Chaucer could be used as a means of demonstrating the nature and use of these rules.

They had come down from Roman times and reached a second flowering in the twelfth and thirteenth centuries. The scholars of that time, notably Matthieu de Vendôme (*c.* 1170) and Geoffrey de Vinsauf (*c.* 1210) had assembled all the traditions of rhetoric in a number of prose treatises and illustrative verses; the general heading under which particular devices of style were recommended, was that of *Amplificatio*, the art of enlarging and embellishing your matter. There were eight or ten principal ways of doing so, each with its high-sounding name, and some with as many as four subdivisions. To take a few examples, there was *Circumlocutio*, the art of making a simple statement in a roundabout and decorative way:

> The bisy larke, messager of day,
> Salueth in hir song the morwe gray,
> And firy Phebus riseth up so bright
> That al the orient laugheth of the light,
> And with his stremes dryeth in the greves[7]
> The silver dropes hangynge on the leves.
> (*The Knight's Tale*)

The simple statement underlying this lovely and lively passage is 'The sun rose brightly'. That Chaucer was perfectly conscious of this, and sometimes also amused by it, can be seen from:

> But sodeynly bigonne revel newe
> Til that the brighte sonne loste his hewe,
> For th'orisonte hath reft the sonne his lyght –
> This is as muche to saye as it was nyght.

The first twelve, magical lines of the *Prologue* to *The Canterbury Tales* is a simple *circumlocutio* for 'In mid-April, people go on pilgrimage'.

Another figure of rhetoric, much used by Chaucer, was *Interpretatio*; this consisted in repeating an idea in other words: *varius sis et tamen idem.*[8]

A plain example of this would be:

> Soun ys noght but eyr ybroken,
> And every speche that ys spoken,
> Lowd or pryvee, foul or fair,
> In his substaunce ys but air ...

> (*House of Fame*, II)

The last three lines are an *Interpretatio* of the first. But the figure could also have a subtler form, as when the idea was not only repeated, but given a new twist, for instance:

> Ful swetely herde he confessioun,
> And plesaunt was his absolucioun:
> He was an esy man to yeve penaunce,
> Ther as he wiste to have a good pitaunce.

> (*The Prologue*)

The last two lines repeat the sense of the first with a dagger-thrust of meaning added.

In like manner examples of every figure of rhetoric can currently be found in Chaucer: of *Digressio* in its two forms, namely when you digress to matter outside your story in order to illuminate it (as when the *Wife of Bath* tells the story of Midas to illustrate a point in her own tale) or when you digress by developing an idea within your story, in a manner directly arising from it (as when the *Merchant* in describing the garden that Old January had made, digresses to thoughts of the *Romance of the Rose*, Priapus and Proserpina). Or of *Occupatio*, when you explain that you are too busy to go into details; this can be used, either to shorten your tale:

> I coude folwe, word for word, Virgile,
> But it wolde lasten al to longe while.
>
> (*Legend of Good Women*)

or to lengthen it, by saying you have no time to describe the things which you then proceed to describe:

> ... And eek it nedeth nat for to devyse
> At every cours the ordre of hire servyse.
> I wol nat tellen of hir strange sewes,[9]
> Ne of hir swannes, ne of hire heronsewes.[10]
> Eek in that lond, as tellen knyghtes olde,
> Ther is som mete that is ful deynte holde,
> That in this lond men recche of it but smal;[11]
> Ther nys no man that may reporten al.
>
> (*The Squire's Tale*)

The *Squire's* use of *Occupatio* is tame, however, compared to that of his father the *Knight*, who performs a dazzling cadenza of some 50 lines towards the end of his tale, enumerating all the features of Arcite's funeral which (he says) he has no time to mention. It is a real *tour de force*.

But Chaucer's favourite rhetorical device was certainly *Apostrophatio*. This figure had four subdivisions, of which the commonest was *Exclamatio*, a simple exclamation of feeling, of whatever kind; the second and third, *Subjectio*, and *Dubitatio*, were forms of rhetorical question, and the last, *Conduplicatio*, a series of exclamations each beginning with the same phrase; this Chaucer only uses in his most serious invocations:

> Lo here, of payens corsed olde rites,[12] Lo here, what alle hire
>   goddes may availle!
> Lo here, these wrecched worldes appetites!
> Lo here, the fyn and guerdoun for travaille[13]
> Of Jove, Appollo, of Mars, of swich rascaille!
>
> (*Troilus & Criseyde*, V)

Chaucer sparkles with apostrophes; he is ever ready to

exclaim in sympathy, wonder, indignation, pathos, prayer and irony, to address his audiences personally with a question not meant to be answered, but which brings them into the story:

> Woot ye nat where ther stant a litel toun
> Which that ycleped is Bobbe-up-down,
> Under the Blee, in Caunterbury weye?
>
> (*The Manciple's Prologue*)

or to picture an incident in a tale by reminding them of something similar in their own lives, as when he asks them to imagine the plight of his heroine by recalling the sight of some unhappy criminal on his way to execution:

> Have ye nat seyn somtyme a pale face,
> Among a prees,[14] of hym that hath be lad
> Toward his deeth, wher as hym gat no grace,
> And swich a colour in his face hath had,
> Men myghte knowe his face that was bistad,[15]
> Amongse all the faces in that route?
> So stant Custance, and looketh hire aboute.
>
> (*The Man of Law's Tale*)

These are rhetorical questions, not exactly of the kinds named above, but of a kind to vary, by an apostrophe to his hearers, his means of engaging their attention. Often he will pause in mid-story to ask what sort of a universe it can be where such things happen, or to make a general comment on life:

> Allas, allas, that ever love was sinne!
>
> (*Wife of Bath's Prologue*)

These were things which Chaucer began to learn in his schooldays, and in his hands the rules of the pedants became the instruments of a living and natural style; as with any great virtuoso, the technical rule or accomplishment, artificial and laborious as it may seem, can become the means of greater freedom of expression, can even prompt a thought that might have been lost without it, for

> ... Nature is made better by no mean
> But Nature makes that mean: so, over that art

Which you say adds to Nature, is an art
That Nature makes.

(*The Winter's Tale*)

Above all, Chaucer's training in rhetoric sharpened his perception of character; no one was his equal in this, because no one had his touch with the rhetorical figure of *Descriptio*. This is a figure to which we must return later. At the moment let us pass on from St Paul's Almonry (if that indeed was where he had his early schooling) and follow him into the next phase of his up-bringing. It was the decisive phase, the true beginning of his career as a courtier, and as a poet.

III. EDUCATION IN COURTESY

Let me see if Philip can
Be a little gentelman.

(Heinrich Hoffman: *Struwwelpeter*)

At some unknown date, but certainly when he was still a boy, Geoffrey was taken from school and put out to service in the household of Elisabeth, Countess of Ulster. She was the wife of Lionel, third son of Edward III and later Duke of Clarence. For Geoffrey this was an almost unimaginable stroke of good fortune; his parents, no doubt through their slender court connections, had somehow pulled it off.

The Countess kept household books, on parchment. These books were later torn up and the parchment was used to line a manuscript of poems by Lydgate and Hoccleve. A nineteenth-century scholar, examining the manuscript, discovered the lining. It was found to contain the first known reference to Geoffrey Chaucer. It is dated April 1357 and records that the Countess laid out seven shillings on a cloak and a pair of red-and-black breeches for the lad. He had taken the first step in courtiership and was a page in a royal household.

This did not mean that his education was interrupted; on the contrary, it was widened, intensified and given a practical turn. We know almost exactly what it consisted of, thanks to another household book, the *Liber Niger* of Edward IV, in which is laid down the traditional curriculum for lads in his position, rising from page to squire. They were known as henxmen or henchmen, a word derived from the older word *hengest* meaning a horse; for all chivalry (to which Chaucer was now apprenticed) arises from the cult of the horse as the word *cheval* implies; it tamed and civilised the lust of battle much in the way that courtly love tamed and civilised the lust of the body; the tournament was the meeting-place of both, and it did what it could to impart to the natural Yahoo some qualities of the Houyhnhnm.

Edward IV arranged for 'young gentylmen, Henxmen, VI Enfauntes or more, as it shall please the Kinge' to be placed under the tuition of a Maistyr of Henxmen

> to shew the schooles[16] of urbanitie and nourture of Englond, to lerne them to ryde clenely and surely; to drawe them also to justes [*jousting*]; to lerne them were theyre harneys [*to teach them how to wear their equipment, armour etc*]; to have all curtesy in wordes, dedes and degrees [*i.e. to know who ranks above or below whom, as Griselda did in the Clerk's Tale, welcoming her lord's guests 'everich in his degree'*] ... *Moreover to teche them sondry languages, and othyr lerninges vertuous, to harping, to pype, sing, daunce, and with other honest and temperate behaviour and patience* ... *and eche of them to be used to that thinge of vertue that he shall be moste apt to lerne* [*i.e. to be encouraged in any persoanl talent*], with remembraunce dayly of Goddes servyce accustumed. This maistyr sittith in the halle, next unto these Henxmen ... to have his respecte unto theyre demeanynges [*attend to their behaviour*], and to theyre communication [*conversation*] ...

The best results of such a system can be seen in Chaucer's *Knight and Squire*; and, as I think, in Chaucer too.

Courtesy, it will be noticed, is the first thing to be stressed in this schedule of breeding, after the military essential of horsemastership. Courtesy is behaviour proper to a Court, and the masters in courtesy fixed their standards by the highest Court they knew of, which was the Court of Heaven. That was the Court, they claimed, in which courtesy had its origin:

> Clerkys that canne the scyens seuene,
> Seys that curtasy came fro heuen
> When gabryell owre lady grette,

And elyzabeth with here mette.
All vertus be closyde in curtasy,
An Alle vyces in voliny.

(The Young Children's Book)

[Learned men that know the seven sciences say that courtesy came from
Heaven when Gabriel greeted Our Lady and Elizabeth met with her. All
virtues are included in courtesy, and all vices in rusticity. *Vilony* is a
difficult word to translate. It is here intended to mean a condition of
primitive rustic malice, ignorance and crudity, to be presumed of a
countryman in a savage semi-animal state. *Villanus* means someone
living in the wilds as opposed to *civis*, a city-dweller versed in 'urbanitie'
(*urbs* = a city).]

Of all our poets, Geoffrey Chaucer is the most courteous to
those who read or listen to him; he seems ever-conscious of
our presence and charmed to be in such perceptive company.
He never threatens or alarms us, as Milton can, intent upon
his great theme; nor ignores us, as Wordsworth can, intent
upon himself. He addresses his readers as if he could wish for
none better, he exchanges experiences with them, consults
them, and begs them not to take offence at what he is about to
say, touching his show of courtesy with an elegant but ironic
wit:

But first I pray yow, of youre curteisye,
That ye n'arette[17] it nat my vileynye
Thogh that I pleynly speke in this mateere,
To telle yow hir wordes and hir cheere ...
Whoso shal telle a tale after a man,
He moot reherce as ny as evere he kan
Everich a word, if it be in his charge,
Al speke he never so rudeliche and large,
Or ellis he moot telle his tale untrewe,
Or feyne thyng, or fynde wordes newe.
He may nat spare, althogh he were his brother;
He moot as wel seye o word as another.
Crist spak hymself ful brode[18] in hooly writ,
And wel ye woot no vileynye is it.

(Prologue to the Canterbury Tales)

Chaucer learnt his manners not only from those with
whome he came into contact, but also from cautionary
rhymes, of which there survive a great number, specially
written for the education of children. They are too long to

quote in full, for they enter into details of table-manners, right down to versified instructions for the washing of spoons and the laying of cloths, freely intermingled with moral advice:

> ... Loke thyne hondis be wasshe clene,
> That no fylthe on thy nayles be sene.
> Take thou no mete tylle grace by seyde,
> And tylle thou see alle thyng arayede ...
> And at thy mete, yn the begynnyng,
> Loke on pore men that thow thynk,
> For the fulle wombe without any faylys[19]
> Wot fulle lytyl what the hungery aylys.
> Ete not thy mete to hastely,
> Abyde and ete esily ...
>   (*The Lytylle Childrenes Lytil Boke or Edylls be*[20])

Perhaps the best of these poems is the one called *The Babees Book*; it is addressed to children of the blood royal, and like other poems in this vein, gives precise instructions how to behave:

> Youre heede, youre hande, your feet, hold yee in reste
> Nor thurhe clowyng your flesshe loke yee nat Rent;[21]
> Lene to no poste whils that ye stande present
> Byfore your lorde ...

and so forth; and thus it ends:

> And, swete children, for whos love now I write,
> I yow beseche withe verrey lovande herte,
> To knowe this book that yee sette your delyte;
> And myhtefulle god, that suffred peynes smerte,
> In curtesye he make yow so experte,
> That thurhe your nurture and youre governaunce
> In lastynge blysse yee mowe your self avaunce!

In opening a window upon the Middle Ages, there is always the danger that it may turn into a stained glass window, nevertheless I am forced by all these cautionary verses to believe that the reason for being courteous was a religious reason, namely that it was pleasing to God and would advance your soul; it was the application of Christianity to social behaviour, a practical way of learning to love your neighbour as yourself. *Manners makyth Man.*

The simple piety of this approach to courtesy was no doubt dinned into the little bourgeois boy from the moment he entered the Ulster household. Although there were rules of thumb for courtesy, the underlying theory had been worked out by the philosophers and poets. Indeed, when he grew up, Chaucer himself, as we shall see, made a significant contribution to it.

The problem was one with which the age was profoundly concerned. What is nobility? How does one become noble? Has it to do with wealth or heredity?

> Whan Adam dalf and Eve span
> Who was tho the gentilman?

This watchword of The Peasants' Revolt had come to them (though they knew it not) from Dante, who had devoted an entire treatise to the subject:

> If Adam himself was noble, we are all noble, and if he was base, we are all base.
>
> *(Convivio, Treatise IV, Ch. xv)*

Dante was arguing that nobility was not inherited. In this he was echoing Boethius some eight hundred years before

> yif thou ne have no gentilesse of thiself ... foreyn gentilesse ne maketh thee nat gentil.
>
> (Boethius: *De Consolatione Philosophie* III prose vi, translated by Chaucer)

Nor, said Dante, had nobility anything to do with wealth. It was wholly a matter of virtue, he argued, following Aristotle in his argument:

> ... this word 'nobleness' means the perfection in each thing of its own proper nature ... everything is most perfect when it touches and reaches its own proper virtue ... So the straight path leads us to look for this definition ... by way of the fruits; which are moral and intellectual virtues whereof this our nobleness is the seed ...
>
> *(Convivio, IV. xvi)*

Chaucer had read and alludes to this discussion in the

Convivio, but in giving his own account of 'gentilesse' (or as we would say, 'nobility') he appeals to higher authority than Dante, or Aristotle either. To be 'gentil', he says, is to imitate Christ, for that is the perfection of our proper natures.

> But, for ye speken of swich gentillesse
> As is descended out of old richesse,
> That therfore sholden ye be gentil men,
> Swich arrogance is nat worth an hen.
> Looke who that is moost vertuous alwey,
> Pryvee and apert,²² and moost entendeth ay
> To do the gentil dedes that he kan;
> Taak hym for the grettest gentil man.
> Crist wole we clayme of hym our gentillesse,
> Nat of oure eldres for hire old richesse ...
>
> (*Wife of Bath's Tale*)

This, the root of all things, was for Chaucer the root from which the flowers of charity and courtesy both sprang, and, like sainthood, they might be met with in every rank of society. The rough-mouthed Host himself was capable of it:

> ... And with that word he sayde,
> As curteisly as it had been a mayde,
> 'My lady Prioresse, by youre leve,
> So that I wiste I sholde yow nat greve,
> I wolde demen that ye tellen sholde
> A tale next, if so were that ye wolde.
> Now wol ye vouche sauf, my lady deere?'

But the finest figure of courtesy in *The Canterbury Tales* is the *Knight*. Chaucer was very careful to make this noble figure as realistic as any of his rogues; half the details of his career, as it is epitomised in the *Prologue*, were fresh in Chaucer's mind from the Scrope-Grosvenor trial of 1386, in the course of which the Scrope family, bearing the disputed arms (*azure a bend or*), had been seen in 'the great sea', at Satalye, at Alexandria, in Spain, Prussia and Lithuania (Lettowe). All these place-names occur in the *Prologue*, written in the same year, in the description of the *Knight's* military career; nothing said of him could have sounded more likely or authentic to Chaucer's first hearers; his 'character' would have sounded equally so, formed as it was on the principles of Christian courtesy dinned into everyone day in and day out from childhood. The entire knightly caste had been brought up that way for some two centuries and was to be brought up so for at least a century more.

Chaucer's *Knight* is the embodiment of a whole way of life, a creation whose importance I cannot measure or state; for it is the first image of the idea of a gentleman, in the language that has given that idea to the world. The *Knight* is to the *Plowman* as a fourteenth-century cathedral is to a fourteenth-century parish church, and all four of them were the products of the same great style and civilisation.

Many things are mocked in Chaucer, but never courtesy; it was the great ideal of his age, upheld by every writer. The poet of *Sir Gawain* builds his poem upon it, to maintain in honour the Court of Arthur and the order of chivalry. If the idea was, in its origins, aristocratic, it spread outwards and downwards through society to a universal acceptance, so that the peasant Langland could think and speak of the Incarnation as the courtesy of Christ.

IV. COURTIER–SOLDIER–SCHOLAR–POET

The courtier's, soldier's, scholar's eye, tongue, sword ...
                                                        (*Hamlet*)

Like many another henxman before and since, Chaucer was presently sent to the wars. It was a foul campaign, bitterly cold, utterly inept, a military fiasco; but it had one important result, it struck a blow for civilisation by putting the young genius into direct touch with France and her poetry. For Chaucer's luck held; he was taken prisoner almost at once. We get a glimpse of this over his shoulder, as it were, for he tells us about it in the Scrope–Grosvenor trial already mentioned; he was one among the many witnesses. Indeed, so many and so distinguished were those called on to give evidence, a *Who's Who* for 1386 could easily be compiled from them. Chaucer deposed:

GEFFRAY CHAUCERE ESQUIER del age de xl ans & plus armeez p xxvii ans pduct pr la ptie de mons Richard Lescrop

jurrez & examinez demandez si lez armeez dazure ove und bende
dor appteignent ou deyvent appteigner au dit mons Richard du
droit & de heritage. dist q oil qar il lez ad veu estre armeez en
Fraunce devant la ville de Retters ...&... p tout le dit viage tanq
le dit Geffrey estoit pris ...[23]

His captivity did not last long; he was no Flemish burgher,
only fit to have his throat cut, but a negotiable prize. On the
first of March, 1360, the King paid sixteen pounds towards
his ransom. It is an old joke among the biographers of
Chaucer that this was slightly less than he paid to ransom Sir
Robert de Clinton's charger.

From now on Chaucer led three interweaving kinds of life,
a courtier's, a scholar's and a poet's. Some chronological
shape can be given to at least the first of these, the events of
which help to date some of his poems, and the accessions of
strength, style and subject to be discerned in them. Many are
the subjects he handles; we have already touched upon one,
the idea of a gentleman, and I mean to restrict myself in this
essay to two more, his greatest as I think, for somewhat
detailed consideration, rather than attempt in so small a
space, to touch on every aspect of his genius. The subjects I
have chosen are those of *Love* and *Men and Women*; but
before I may come to them, there is the outline of a triple life
to be sketched.

For the next seven years there is no record of him as a
courtier, save that he carried letters for the King to Calais at
least once. But his poet's life was beginning; he was at work on
a translation of the *Roman de la Rose*, transplanting an
aristocratic and French philosophy of love and a French way
of poetry to our native soil. He was also engaged in formal
studies, too, at the Inner Temple, if we may believe a late
tradition reported by Speght in his edition of Chaucer (1598)
which also asserts that he was 'fined two shillings for beatinge
a Franciscane Fryer in fletestrete'.

He was growing to manhood; all of a sudden we find him
married, to a lady-in-waiting to Queen Philippa, her god-
daughter perhaps, Philippa de Roet; she became Philippa
Chaucer in 1366. Were they in love? We do not know; he has
left us no poem to her, though he once refers to her in jest. He

compares her voice awakening him in the mornings to the scream of an eagle.

In 1369, Queen Philippa died, and the Chaucers went into service with Blanche, Duchess of Lancaster, first wife of John of Gaunt. With that began (if it had not begun even earlier) the firm friendship and steady patronage that the Duke gave Chaucer ever after. Philippa Chaucer's sister, Catherine, was to become the governess of the Duke's children, then his mistress and at last his wife; so the Duke ended brother-in-law to the poet.

If the Duke did much for Chaucer, Chaucer did more for him. He made him a central and romantic figure in his first masterpiece, *The Book of the Duchess*, an elegy on the lady Blanche, who died in this very year (1369).

It is the first elegy in our language, drenched in a leisured melancholy that begins with a dream and moves out into a great forest, to the sound of far-off hunting horns; under a tree the poet meets with a sorrowful figure in black, singing a lament for his dead lady. It is John of Gaunt, mourning the loss of Blanche, his wife. Though the poem is an elegy, it is imagined as a love-story; narrative instinct and a feeling for sexual passion (let it take what form it may) are things we learn to expect in Chaucer. This slow and dreamy poem keeps the memory of Blanche in her living grave, heroine of a tale of courtship and untimely death; the courtier and rhetor had put forth all his young art for his patron and sometime patroness.

His career as a man of affairs was now beginning; he was being used as something between a King's Messenger and a royal nuncio to France in 1370, but the great events of this kind were his missions to Italy in 1372 and 1378, for it was from these that his poetry took on much of its greatest strength.

It is worth pausing on the voyage of 1372; he went to Genoa and Florence *in nuncio regis in secretis negociis*. He was away for six months, and it is a reasonable conjecture (doubted, however, by some scholars) that he spent a part of them on a private poetical pilgrimage of his own, to visit Francis Petrarch, the most famous living poet of the day, in Padua. It would have been a rough journey, 150 miles off-course, across the Apennines in the cold and windy month of March, through a war-stricken countryside. But all that would have been nothing to a young poet (in his early thirties) eager to snatch a chance of meeting the greatest literary figure of his time.

What prompts all readers to believe he did are the lines that Chaucer was later to put into the mouth of the *Clerk of Oxford*, as he broaches the Tale of Griselda:

> I wol yow telle a tale which that I
> Lerned at Padowe of a worthy clerk,
> As preved by his werdes and his werk.
> He now is deed and nayled in his cheste,
> I prey to God so yeve his soule reste!
> Fraunceys Petrak, the lauriat poete,
> Highte this clerk, whos rethorike sweete
> Enlumyned al Ytaille of poetrie ...

Now it is a question whether what an imaginary character says in imagined circumstances is evidence of anything that happened to his imaginer in the actual world. So many authors can be shown to have used their own lives to create the lives of their characters, that it is not unreasonable to believe that Chaucer did so on this occasion, that he did indeed hear the story of Griselda from Petrarch's lips, and recorded the occasion in this oblique manner. The text of the tale, from which he came to fashion his own version, must have been subsequently acquired by him in some other way, for its date has been established as June 1374, the year of Petrarch's death. For all these possibilities, we have no proof that the two poets ever met, and it may be wisest to say, with the Sage of Cambridge:

Wovon man nicht sprechen kann, darüber muss man schweigen.[24]

In between these Italian journeys Chaucer was promoted; he became Comptroller of the Customs and Subsidies of Wools, Skins and Tanned Hides in London, and had to keep the books in his own fair hand.[25] It was a busy life and all his recreation was to read:

> For when they labour doon al ys,
> And hast mad alle thy rekenynges,

In stede of reste and newe thynges,
Thou goost hom to thy house anoon,
And, also domb as any stoon,
Thou sittest at another book
Tyl fully daswed is thy look.[26]

So spoke the admonishing eagle (with a voice like his wife's) in *The House of Fame*, and what the bird said need not surprise us, for Chaucer read enormously – smatteringly, perhaps, but rememberingly. Almost everything that he read seems to have left its trace upon his poetry, for he delighted in allusion and quotation (whether acknowledged or not) from his favourite authors. He drew easily on the Latin classics, Ovid, Vergil, Statius, Boethius; he was at home in the poetry of France, Deguilleville, Machault, Froissart, Deschamps and the authors of the *Roman de la Rose*. In Italian he was a reader of Dante and of Petrarch; above all he had met with at least two of Boccaccio's poems, *Il Filostrato* and the *Teseide*. Of these he made two of his own noblest works, *Troilus & Criseyde* and *The Knight's Tale*.

He was also a considerable student of the sciences, especially of astronomy and mathematics; he was read in medicine, psychology and other natural sciences, including the pseudo-science of alchemy. His theology he did not so readily parade, though there is an amusing passage on God's uses for fiends in the *Friar's Tale*. He read St Jerome and St Bernard and could quote from almost every book in the Bible and Apocrypha. Though he may not have been the most learned, he was perhaps the most widely-read man of his day; he seems never to have lost the habit and delight of reading:

On bokes for to rede I me delyte
                    (*Prologue to the Legend of Good Women*)

There is a passage in Boswell's *Life of Johnson* describing the special powers of mind enjoyed by the Doctor; they describe Chaucer's equally well:

... His superiority over other learned men consisted chiefly in what may be called the art of thinking, the art of using his mind; a certain continual power of seizing the useful substance of all that he knew and exhibiting it in a clear and forcible manner; so that knowledge, which we often see to be no better than lumber in men of dull understanding, was, in him, true, evident and actual wisdom. His moral precepts are practical; for they are drawn from an intimate acquaintance with human nature. His maxims carry conviction; for they are founded on the basis of common sense, and a very attentive and minute survey of real life ...

It will not surprise us that Boswell adds

His mind was so full of imagery that he might have been perpetually a poet.

To return to Chaucer's life as a courier: he had had a windfall in the Customs in 1376; he caught out a man called John Kent evading duty on an export of wool to Dordrecht, and the culprit was fined for it to the tune of £71 4s 6d. The whole of this sum (worth many thousands of pounds of modern money) was paid over to Chaucer as a reward. He was becoming almost affluent. Foreign missions continued now and then to come his way, civil appointments also; in 1382 he was made Comptroller of Petty Customs, in 1385 he was allowed to appoint a deputy and was made a Justice of the Peace. In October, the following year, he sat in Parliament at Westminster as Knight of the Shire for Kent.

Then, suddenly, in 1386, fortune deserted him,

For whan men trusteth hire, thanne wol she faille,
And covere hire brighte face with a clowde.

(*Monk's Tale*)

John of Gaunt was out of the country, and Chaucer, deprived of his patron, was deprived of his offices. He must live on his pension and on his savings until better times. In the next year Philippa dies; he was now a widower with nothing to do; if this was sad for him, it was lucky for us. He began to compose *The Canterbury Tales*.

To take brief stock of his career as a writer up to the time of his wife's death, it had been fruitful of several long or fairly long poems, ambitiously different from anything ever written before in English, as well as a prose translation of Boethius's *Consolations of Philosophy* and a work of instruction in mathematics – A treatise on the Astrolabe – for 'Lyte Lowys, my sone'. There is no agreement among scholars about the dating, and little agreement about the order in which his poems were composed. We may be certain that *The Book of the Duchess* was written in 1369–70 and *The Legend of Good Women* in 1385–86; it is also sure that *Troilus & Criseyde* and such parts of his translation of the *Roman de la Rose* as have survived were written before the *Legend of Good Women*, because it mentions them; it also mentions *The Parliament of Fowls*, 'al the love of Palamon and Arcite' (later *The Knight's Tale*), the translation of Boethius, and the *Life of St Cecilia* (later *The Second Nun's Tale*).

The Canterbury Tales (it is agreed) were begun as such towards 1386–87, and remained his 'work in progress' until the end of his life, never completed. It would seem that towards the end he tired of writing:

> For elde, that in my spirit dulleth me,
> Hath of endyting al the subtilte
> Wel nygh bereft out of my remembraunce
> > (*The Complaint of Venus*)

We need not, however, take this confession too seriously; it had always been his way to make fun of himself.

Of his longer poems, it only remains to mention *The House of Fame*, of which it can only be said with certainty that it was written after Chaucer had read the *Divine Comedy*; that is, at some time after his first or second visit to Italy.

His very last poem, perhaps, was a poem addressed, on the accession (1399) of the new King: it was a complaint to Chaucer's empty purse:

> I am so sory, now that ye been lyght.

It need not be taken too tragically; the poem is almost as light as the purse.

According to the inscription on his tomb, put there by a Tudor admirer, Nicholas Brigham, in 1556, Chaucer died on 25 October 1400. He was buried in Westminster Abbey; it is not known why. St Margaret's, Westminster, was his parish church, and that would have been his natural resting-place; perhaps they put him in the Abbey because he had been Clerk of the Works, or perhaps he slipped in by some oversight, when the tumult of the new reign dwindled to a calm, much as King George III, according to Lord Byron, slipped into Heaven. It was anyhow not Chaucer's fame as a poet that made him Head of the Poets' Corner; it was not until the late sixteenth century that a corner in the Abbey began to belong to the poets.

V. THE POET OF LOVE

> For I, that God of Love's servantz serve ...
> (*Troilus & Criseyde*, I)

From the beginning, as we have seen, Chaucer revealed himself as a love-poet and a teller of tales; to commemorate the Duchess Blanche he imagined a story about her death, told by her mourning lover in a dream-forest.

Now, in truth, this 'lover' represented John of Gaunt, Blanche's widower; they had been married ten years. In the poem, however, they are seen as courtly lovers and 'The Man in Black' voices his desire on that ideal courtly plane, in full troubadour style,

> To love hir in my beste wyse,
> To do hir worship and the servise
> That I koude thoo, be my trouthe,
> Withoute feynynge outher slouthe[27]

Troilus was later to delcare his passion in the same key:

> And I to ben youre verray, humble, trewe,
> Secret, and in my paynes pacient,
> And evere mo desiren fresshly newe
> To serve, and ben ay ylike diligent ...
> (*Troilus & Criseyde*, III)

For a long time, true to the convention, the Man in Black dares not confess his love, and when he at least summons the courage to say the hard word, he uses the favourite in the whole vocabulary of courtly love:

> I seyde 'mercy!' and no more.

and he is refused; it is only after a conventional year of 'service' that she understands and is willing to reward his sufferings:

> So whan my lady knew al this,
> My lady yaf me al hooly
> The noble yifte of hir mercy,
> Savynge hir worship, by al weyes.[28]

All that was young and romantic in Chaucer had swallowed the dream-allegories of France and the philosophy of courtly love in long draughts from the *Roman de la Rose*, the *Fontaine Amoureuse*, the *Jugement du Roi de Behaingne* and other poems of the sort, and he was trying to do extreme honour to this ordinary Christian marriage by representing it is an idealised amour; all the conventions are beautifully there, the golden hair, the gentle eyes, the neck like a tower of ivory, the long body, the white hands, the round breasts, the tints of her cheek:

> But thus moche dar I sayn, that she
> Was whit, rody, fressh, and lyvely hewed,
> And every day hir beaute newed.

It was this way of imagining love and of writing poetry that Chaucer brought back from France. Much has been written about 'courtly love' and of its sudden appearance in the courts of the nobles of Languedoc in the eleventh and twelfth centuries; some have explained it as a degenerate form of Plato's ideal affection, passed on through Arab hands to France from Africa, and, in the process, heterosexualised and allowed the gratification of the body. Be that as it may, this elegant, illicit amorism took all Christendom for its province, and our world began to ring with ballades, rondels, virelays, aubades and complaints, such as the Man in Black was singing when Chaucer came upon him in the dream-forest.

If in his youth he thought it a compliment to a bereaved husband to speak of his wife as if she had been a mistress, he came ultimately to change his perspective, and his maturest expression of courtly love, *Troilus & Criseyde*, ends in the knowledge of its insufficiency.

Troilus & Criseyde was the greatest yield of his Italian journeys; he learnt from Boccaccio how to abandon dream and build a story of the waking world with clarity and realism, and yet retain within it the delicacies of feeling and convention that prevailed in the visionary, allegorical world of the *Roman de la Rose*; the new poem was undergirt by the philosophy of Boethius, who taught him the shape of tragedy and filled him with thoughts of Fortune and Free Will. For the lovers (and their mentor Pandarus) so human-free as they may seem in a thousand decisions and indecisions, move to the calls of courtly love as surely as they move under fatal stars. On the way to their still-distant doom, they pass through an ecstasy of high sexual passion, and Chaucer rises effortlessly to the great poetry of their long night of first union, which I do not know where to find equalled, except in Shakespeare, for intimacy, tenderness and noble quality; he reveals himself as *engaged* by the love he is describing:

> O blisful nyght, of hem so longe isought,
> How blithe unto hem bothe two thow weere!
> Why nad I swich oon with my soule ybought,
> Ye, or the leeste joie that was there?[29]

Yet he retains his attitude of spectator, so typical of him:

> this Troilus in armes gan hir streyne,
> And seyde, 'O swete, as evere mot I gon,[30]
> Now be ye kaught, now is ther but we tweyne!
> Now yeldeth yow, for other bote is non!'[31]
> To that Criseyde answerde thus anon,
> 'Ne hadde I er now, my swete herte deere,
> Ben yold, ywis, I were now nought heere!'
>
> O, sooth is seyd, that heled for to be
> As of a fevre, or other gret siknesse,
> Men moste drynke, as men may ofte se,
> Ful bittre drynke; and for to han gladnesse,[32]
> Men drynken ofte peyne and gret distresse;
> I mene it here, as for this aventure,
> That thorugh a peyne hath founden al this cure.
>
> And now swetnesse semeth more swete,
> That bitternesse assaied was byforn;
> For out of wo in blisse now they flete;

Non swich they felten syn that they were born.[33]
Now is this bet than bothe two be lorn.
For love of God, take every womman heede
To werken thus, if it comth to the neede.

Criseyde, al quyt from every drede and tene,[34]
As she that juste cause hadde hym to triste,
Made hym swich feste, it joye was to seene,[35]
Whan she his trouthe and clene entente wiste;
And as aboute a tree, with many a twiste,
Bytrent and writh the swote wodebynde,[36]
Gan ech of him in armes other wynde.

And as the newe abaysed nyghtyngale,
That stynteth first whan she bygynneth to synge,
Whan that she hereth any herde tale,
And after siker doth hire vois out rynge,
Right so Criseyde, whan hire drede stente,[37]
Opned hire herte, and tolde hym hire entente ...

... Hire armes smale, hir streghte bak and softe,
Hire sydes longe, flesshly, smothe and white
He gan to stroke, and good thrift bad ful ofte[38]
Hir snowisshe throte, hire brestes round and lite;
Thus in this hevene he gan hym to delite,
And therwithal a thousand tyme hire kiste,
That what to don, for joie unnethe he wiste ...[39]

... Benigne Love, thow holy bond of thynges,
Whoso wol grace, and list the nought honouren,[40]
Lo, his desire wol fle withouten wynges ...

(*Troilus & Criseyde*, Book III)

But from this exaltation the poem has to turn; the fatal
moment must come, the lovers must part; once parted from
her lover, Criseyde lacks the strength to return to him, lacks
the strength to resist Diomed, is faithless. Chaucer does not
reproach her; he says he would excuse her, 'for routhe', that
is, for pity. At last Troilus is killed by the fierce Achilles.

Swich fyn hath, lo, this Troilus for love!
Swich fyn hath al his grete worthinesse!
Swich fyn hath his estat real above,[41]
Swich fyn his lust, swich fyn hath his noblesse!
Swich fyn hath false worldes brotelnesse!

It is the insecurity of human love in a world ruled by chance
that made Chaucer see the brittleness of the courtly code.

Fortune can untie the holy bond of things in human affairs, and if we seek a lasting love we must look elsewhere, to a region beyond her power:

> O yonge, fresshe folkes, he or she,
> In which that love up groweth with youre age,
> Repeyreth hom fro worldly vanyte,
> And of youre herte up casteth the visage[42]
> To thilke God that after his ymage
> Yow made, and thynketh al nys but a faire,
> This world, that passeth sone as floures faire.
>
> And loveth hym, the which that right for love
> Upon a crois, oure soules for to beye[43]
> First starf, and roos, and sit in hevene above;
> For he nyl falsen no wight, dar I seye,
> That wol his herte al holly on hym leye.
> And syn he best to love is, and most meeke,
> What nedeth feynede loves for to seke?

What the Court held to be love, the Church held to be sin. It had a contrary love-system of its own. Of absolutely sovereign value in the Church's scale of sex was virginity; there was no higher kind of life than to be a virgin for the love of God. St Jerome expressed the idea in one of his startling epigrams:

> Nuptiae terram replent, virginitas paradisum.
>
> (*Epistola adversus Jovinianum*)
> [Marriages replenish the earth, virginity replenishes Paradise.]

The pre-eminence of virginity is asserted by Chaucer in *The Parson's Tale*:

> Another synne of Leccherie is to bireve a mayden of hir mayden-hede; for he that so dooth, certes, he casteth a mayden out of the hyeste degree that is in this present lyf ... And forther over, sooth is that hooly orde [Holy Orders] is chief of al the tresorie of God, and his especial signe and mark of chastitee ... which that is the moost precious lyf that is.

It is again asserted by the *Prioress*, in her apostrophe to the martyred chorister of her tale:

> O martir, sowded to virginitee,[44]
> Now maystow syngen, folwynge evere in oon[45]
> The white Lamb celestial – quod she –

> Of which the grete evaungelist, Seint John,
> In Pathmos Wroot, which seith that they that goon
> Biforn this Lamb, and synge a song al newe,
> That nevere, flesshly, wommen they ne knewe.[46]

It is even asserted by the *Wife of Bath*:

> Virginitee is greet perfeccion
> (*Wife of Bath's Prologue*)

and again,

> Crist was a mayde, and shapen as a man,
> And many a seint, sith that the world bigan;
> Yet lyved they evere in parfit chastitee.
> I nyl envye no virginitee.

Next to virginity, the Church esteemed the condition of wedded chastity, that Shakespeare was later to celebrate allegorically in the *Threnos* of his most metaphysical poem, *The Phoenix and the Turtle*; it is a condition to which the Wife of Bath refers to, with approval, as

> continence with devocion.

and one of the first stories Chaucer ever wrote, the story of St Cecilia (later *The Second Nun's Tale*) celebrates her sanctity in having persuaded her young and noble husband, on their wedding night and for ever after, to forgo the consummation of his love. The same idea is at the back of Chaucer's mind when, in *The Man of Law's Tale*, he feels it incumbent on him to defend his holy-hearted heroine for yielding her body to her husband; the passage rings in my ear with a note of comedy, but I am not sure if Chaucer intended it so, for it comes from his most pious period as a writer:

> They goon to bedde, as it was skile and right;[47]
> For thogh that wyves be ful hooly thynges,
> They moste take in pacience at nyght
> Swiche manere necessaries as been plesynges
> To folk that han ywedded hem with rynges,
> And leye a lite hir hoolynesse aside,
> As for the tyme – it may be bet bitide.[48]

Griselda is another chaste and patient wife; her story, enormously popular in the Middle Ages, found its fullest eloquence in Chaucer's telling of it. It was an earlyish work of his, and when he came back in later life to shape it for inclusion in *The Canterbury Tales*, he modified the effect of this marriage-sermon by adding an ironic tail-piece

> It were ful harde to fynde now-a-dayes
> In al a toun Griseldis thre or two ...

Still, virginity and chastity and married love of the kind approved by the Church, were approved in these and other of Chaucer's poems, and with no less poetry than he had celebrated courtly love. It is true that there is no sexual ecstasy recorded of the unions of Griselda or of Constance with their husbands; but then, sexual ecstasy, even in marriage, was held suspect:

> And for that many man weneth that he may nat synne for no
> likerousnesse that he dooth with his wyf, certes that opinion is fals.
> *(Parson's Tale)*

Over against what the Church taught and what the Troubadours taught about women, there were the opinions of the Celibate Misogynists. They reached in a long tradition of St Jerome to Walter Map, and the extremes to which they went in vilifying the fair sex almost outdistanced the extremes of the gynecolaters in the opposite direction; as I have said before, it was an age of extremes.

The *Wife of Bath* knew all about these Children of Mercury, the natural enemies of the Children of Venus:

> the clerk, whan he is oold, and may noght do
> Of Venus werkes worth his olde sho,
> Thanne sit he doun, and writ in his dotage
> That wommen kan nat keepe hir mariage!

But, for all her low opinion of them as lovers, she admired them as debaters, and put on the whole armour of their abuse to subdue her first three husbands; her method was to anticipate the worst that could be said of women – and here she helped herself freely to St Jerome – and fling it back scornfully at her men:

> ... Thou seist to me it is a greet meschief
> To wedde a povre womman, for costage;
> And if that she be riche, of heigh parage,[49]
> Thanne seistow that it is a tormentrie
> To soffre hire pride and hire malencolie.
> And if that she be fair, thou verray knave,
> Thou seyst that every holour wol hire have ...[50]
> ... And if that she be foul, thou seist that she
> Coveiteth every man that she may se,
> For as a spanyel she wol on hym lepe,
> Til that she fynde som man hire to chepe.[51]
> Ne noon so grey goos goth ther in the lake
> As, seistow, wol been withoute make ...[52]
> Thus seistow, lorel, whan thow goost to bedde;[53]
> And that no wys man nedeth for to wedde,
> Ne no man that entendeth unto hevene.
> With wilde thonder-dynt and firy levene
> Moote thy welked nekke be tobroke![54]

All this, and much more, that she had to say, came, almost word for word, from St Jerome's *Epistola adversus Jovinianum* and from other 'celibate' sources.

She met her match in her fifth husband, a pretty-legged lad half her age called Jankyn (Johnnykin), with whom she was reckless enough to fall in love; this lost her the initial advantage and it was soon he, not she, that was studying the Misogynists; they became his favourite reading.

> he hadde a book that gladly, nyght and day,
> For his desport he wolde rede alway ...
> At which book he lough alwey ful faste.

It was a composite volume full of anecdote, proverb and abuse against women, and the *Wife* gives us long extracts from it; here, for instance is an anecdote borrowed from Walter Map:

> Thanne tolde he me how oon Latumyus
> Compleyned unto his felawe Arrius
> That in his gardyn growed swich a tree
> On which he seyde how that his wyves thre

Hanged hemself for herte despitus.[55]
'O leeve brother,' quod this Arrius,
'Yif me a plante of thilke blissed tree,
And in my gardyn planted shal it bee!'

It was in these ways that Chaucer chose to voice the views of the Tertium Quid.

If the wonderful *Wife of Bath* seems, when we first meet with her, to have drawn her philosophy from some Cartesian well of *Copulo ergo sum*, we soon get to know her better and appreciate the complexities of her character; she can hold contradictory beliefs without the slightest inconvenience to herself, such as that virginity is a great perfection, and celibacy a thing contemptible; her bullying methods with her husbands seem at first a matter of mood and idiosyncrasy, but turn out to be employed on principle, and it is this that puts her in a central position in the Great Sex War of *The Canterbury Tales*. It is fought on the issue 'Who is to have the mastery in marriage, husband, or wife?'

How she handled her husbands is a lesson to every knowing woman (as she says herself) and to every man about to marry, as Chaucer said in a poem to his friend Bukton, in that momentous situation:

The Wyf of Bathe I pray yow that ye rede ...

In her view, it was right and proper that husbands should submit to their wives; this is not only the moral of her long preamble (the *Prologue* to her *Tale*) but also of the tale itself. The point of the story is to discover what it is that women most wish for, and the surprising answer is

Wommen desiren have sovereynetee
As wel over hir housbond as hir love,
And for to been in maistrie hym above.

Women, that is, wish for the same sovereignty over their husbands that they exercise over their lovers; a tall order.

The challenge thus flung down by the *Wife of Bath* is taken up first by the *Clark of Oxford* with his tale of patient Griselda, and her exemplary obedience to her husband; other aspects of marriage come before us too: *The Merchant's Tale*

of January and May shows what can happen between
husband and wife when an old man marries a young girl. *The
Shipman's Tale* presents us with the well-known truth that
there are always half a dozen things a woman absolutely
needs, to keep up with the neighbours, that she cannot very
well tell her husband about:

> And wel ye woot that wmmen naturelly
> Desiren thynges sixe as wel as I ...
> For his honour, myself for to arraye.

and so she is driven to tell someone else:

> Thanne moot another payen for oure cost,
> Our lene us gold, and that is perilous.[56]

Perhaps the liveliest domestic scene is that between
Chanticleer and Pertelote, when with husbandly self-
importance he debates the prophetic meaning of a dream he
has had, which his wife ascribes to constipation.

These are the variations on the theme proposed by the *Wife
of Bath* to which we return for a final statement by the
Franklin; his story voices that wise equability and kindliness
that is so great an attribute of Chaucer's mind. *The Franklin's*
hero and heroine are married lovers; they had begun their
attachment by falling in love in the best courtly manner

> And many a labour, many a greet emprise[57]
> He for his lady wroghte, er she were wonne ...
> ... But atte last she, for his worthynesse,
> And namely[58] for his meke obeysaunce,
> Hath swich a pitee caught of his penaunce,
> That pryvely she fil of his accord
> To take hym for hir housbonde and hir lord.

This fourteenth-century Millament and her Mirabell had,
however, laid down certain provisos and counter-provisos
before they agreed to marry; he was to exercise no 'maistrie'
over her,

> But hire obeye, and folwe hir wyl in al

and she was to allow him 'the name of soveraynetee', so that he should not in public suffer the disgrace of his surrendered authority.

> That wolde he have for shame of his degree.

And, on this happy compromise, the *Franklin* stops his story for a moment to address the company with a Chaucerian wisdom suiting with his sanguine temperament:

> For o thyng, sires, saufly dar I seye,
> That freendess everych oother moot obeye,[59]
> If they wol longe holden compaignye.
> Love wol nat been constreyned by maistrye.
> Whan maistrie comth, the God of Love anon
> Beteth his wynges, and farewel, he is gon!
> Love is a thyng as any spirit free.
> Wommen, of kynde, desiren libertee[60]
> And nat to be constreyned as a thral;
> And so doon men, if I sooth seyen shal.

There was still one other ambient attitude to love-making in those times for Chaucer to voice and grace, namely the attitude of the *fabliau*, the low-life oral tale of animal grab that in all ages circulates from mouth to mouth, like a limerick. In the typical *fabliau*, copulation seems to thrive in its cold-blooded way, borne along on strong undercurrents of guilt and hatred. Priests and Millers (the most powerful and therefore the most to be humiliated men in the village) are generally the victims, and the very sexuality of the story, which, at one level, they are supposed to enjoy, at another level, seems to be a part of their vileness, of their punishment, even. The laugh at the end is bitter with triumphant malice.

Chaucer took two such sows'-ear stories and turned them into the silk purses of *The Miller's Tale* and *The Reeve's Tale*. Here, at the bottom of the social scale, the clerical students of Oxford and Cambridge, happy go luckies of a saucy sexuality, are seen aping the adulteries of the aristocracy with all the cant of courtly love on their tongues. *Nicholas* in *The Miller's Tale* woos *Alison* with a

> '. . . Lemman, love me al at ones,
> Or I wol dyen, also God me save!'

It is the argument that Pandarus uses on behalf of Troilus. *Absalom*, in the same story goes on his knees (as Troilus did) to receive a kiss. That he got more than he bargained for cured him for ever, we are told, of love *par amour*, that is of courtly love. But Chaucer does more than this to rescue his *fabliaux* from their beastly dullness; the whole life of the village springs up before us, the rustic conversation, the superstition, the cunning; the impudence and bravado of the young in their gallantries, the rascality of the Miller, the gullibility of the Carpenter, the cottages they live in, and the vivid wenches,

> With buttokes brode, and brestes rounde and hye

of whose portraits, Alison's is the most convincingly fresh and seductive that Chaucer, or anyone else, ever painted.

If, then, we ask ourselves what this 'servant of the servants of Love' knew about his masters, and about their Master, a short answer would be that he knew everything; everything that was known and felt on the subject at that time in Christendom. He voiced the whole thought of the Middle Ages, speaking as eloquently for Courtly as for Christian love, and as much an expert in marriage as in misogyny; everything came within the power of his pen, right down to the antics of John and Alan, Nicholas and Absalom and their 'popelotes'. No other English author has a comparable range in such matters. But it is not only a question of range, variety and subtlety in his art of love; it is the sympathy. He is all things to all men and women in all their moods and modes of love, able to write as easily of the lowest as of the highest:

> O mooder Mayde! O mayde Mooder free!
> O bussh unbrent brennynge in Moyses sighte,
> That ravyshedest doun fro the Deitee,
> Thurgh thyn humblesse, the Goost that in th'alighte,
> Of whos vertu, whan he thyn herte lighte,
> Conceyved was the Fadres sapience . . .

[O bush unburnt, burning in the sight of Moses, though that didst ravish down, from the deity, the Spirit that alighted in thee, by thy

humbleness; by whose power, when He illumined thy heart, the
Sapience of the Father was conceived . . .]

The reason he can do so is that he takes joy in the created
world, he grasps life affirmatively, and calls nothing that God
has made unclean.

VI. MEN AND WOMEN

> For the eye altering alters all
>
> (William Blake: *The Mental Traveller*)

Chaucer thought the work of a writer to be something like
that of a reaper, and it is with a wondering smile that we hear
him say that all the corn of poetry has been reaped already and
that only the gleanings are left for him after the great poets
have done their word:

> For wel I wot that folk han here-beforn
> Of makyng ropen, and lad awey the corn;[61]
> And I come after, glenynge here and there,
> And am ful glaf if I may fynde an ere[62]
> Of any goodly word that they han left.
>
> (*Prologue to the Legend of Good Women*)

The fields that he is thinking of are the fields of 'auctoritee'
that is, of the ancient writers that he loved so much, for their
poetry, philosophy and learning, whence all new learning
came:

> For out of olde feldes, as men seyth,
> Cometh al this newe corn from yer to yere,
> And out of olde bokes, in good feyth,
> Cometh al this newe science that men lere[63] . . .
>
> (*The Parliament of Fowls*)

But there was another immense field, the field of
Experience, which he himself was wont to contrast with
'Auctoritee'. It was the 'fair field full of folk' of which his
great contemporary, Langland, had written, the busy
London world of men and women, with whom, whether he
was at Court or in the Customs House, it was his profession
and his pleasure to deal.

No one had ever before looked at people in the way Chaucer did; it was his eye that altered everything, It knew what to look for. His was not only an observant, but an instructed eye through which he looked out on to the world of Experience. The instruction had, however, come to him from Authority.

There are at least three kinds of book that we can observe directing his discovery of human nature; books on *Rhetoric*, books on *Medicine*, and books on *Astrology*. From each of these he learnt something that helped to train his eye. To demonstrate (as I shall now try) is not to offer an explanation of his genius, but *to show it at work*.

Other men may perhaps have known as much as he about rhetoric, medicine and astrology; but Chaucer knew how to use his knowledge, how to put his knowledge (so to speak) at the disposl of his eyes and ears. The result can be seen in the descriptions of the characters in the *Prologue* to *The Canterbury Tales*.

The Rhetoricians were perfectly clear on the subject of how to present a human being; it was a technique or figure known to them as *Descriptio*, of which there were at least three doctrines, equally explicit, which were current in the Middle Ages. The first was Cicero's.

> Ac personis has res attributas putamus; nomen,
> naturam, victum, fortunam, habitum, affectionem,
> studia, consilia, facta, casus, orationes.
>
> (*De Inventione*, I. xxiv)

[We hold the following to be the attributes of persons: name, nature, manner of life, fortune, habit, feeling, interests, purposes, achievements, accidents, conversation.]

As Cicero goes on to paraphrase these eleven attributes, we are able to gloss them, where necessary, as follows:

Name.
Nature. Includes Sex, place of origin, family, age, bodily appearance, whether bright or dull, affable or rude, patient or the reverse, and all qualities of mind or body bestowed by nature.
Manner of Life. Includes occupation, trade or profession and the character of the person's home-life.
Fortune. Includes whether rich or poor, successful or a failure, and rank.

Habit. Includes some special knowledge or bodily dexterity won by careful training and practice.

Feeling. A fleeting passion, such as joy, desire, fear, vexation, etc.

Interests. Mental activity devoted to some special subject.

Purposes. Any deliberate plan.

Achievements. What a person is doing, has done or will do.

Accidents. What is happening to a person, has happened, or will happen.

Conversation. What a person has said, is saying, or will say.

I suppose many readers will agree that the most strikingly described character in the *Prologue* is that of *The Wife of Bath*. In some thirty natural, easy lines of seemingly casual observation, she appears in startling completeness. For all that air of unconcern, Chaucer has worked his miracle by remembering his Cicero:

A good Wif was ther of biside Bathe	*Nature* (sex, place of origin)
But she was somdel deef, and that was scathe.	(bodily quality)
Of clooth-makyng she hadde swich an haunt,	*Manner of Life* (trade)
She passed hem of Ypres and of Gaunt.	*Habit* (dexterity)
In al the parisshe wif ne was ther noon	*Fortune* (rank)
That to the offrynge bifore hire sholde goon;	
And if ther dide, certeyn so wrooth was she,	*Feeling* (vexation)
That she was out of alle charitee.	
Hir coverchiefs ful fyne weren of ground;	*Nature* (appearnce)
I dorste swere they weyeden ten pound	
That on a Sonday weren upon hir heed.	
Hir hosen weren of fyn scarlet reed,	
Ful streite yteyd, and shoes ful moyste and newe.	
Boold was hir face and fair, and reed of hewe.	
She was a worthy womman al hir lyve:	*Fortune* (rank)
Housbondes at chirche dore she hadde fyve,	*Manner of Life* (home-life)
Withouten oother compaignye in youthe –	
But therof nedeth nat to speke as nowthe.	*(Occupatio)*
And thries had she been at Jerusalem;	*Achievements* (past doings)
She hadde passed many a straunge strem;	and *Accidents*
At Rome she hadde been, and at Boloigne.	
In Galice at Seint Jame, and at Coloigne.	
She koude muchel of wandrynge by the weye.	*Habit* (special knowledge)

Gat-tothed was she, soothly for to seye.	*Nature* (bodily quality)
Upon an amblere esily she sat,	*Achievements* (what doing)
Ywympled wel, and on hir heed an hat	*Nature* (appearance)
As brood as is a bokeler or a targe;	
A foot-mantel aboute hir hippes large,	
And on hir feet a paire of spores sharpe.	
In felaweshipe wel koude she laughe and carpe.	*Conversation*
Of remedies of love she knew per chaunce	*Interests*
For she koude of that art the olde daunce.	

The only points demanded by Cicero that are left out are her name and purposes. We learn later that her name was Alison; as for her purposes, one of them could go without saying – to seek the shrine of St Thomas with the other pilgrims. We may perhaps infer another:

> Yblessed be God that I have wedded fyve!
> Welcome the sixte, whan that evere he shal.
>
> *(Prologue* to her *Tale)*

Ciceronian as is her portrait, Cicero cannot claim it all. There is the hint of something learnt from Geoffrey de Vinsauf in it too. De Vinsauf's teaching was that a description must start at the top of the head and inch its way downwards, detail by detail, to the feet – *poliatur ad unguem*, let it be polished to the toe-nail. To follow this counsel slavishly would lead to what, in another context, Chaucer calls the 'fulsomness of his prolixitee'; but he follows it selectively, beginning with the ten-pound head-dress. His eye is then drawn for an instant from the boldness of her face to her all-too-striking hose, but returns to her face and wimple, glides to her hips and falls to her spurs.

A third doctrine of *Descriptio* was that of Matthieu de Vendôme, who held that a writer must first describe the moral nature and then the physical appearance of his subject. Chaucer moved easily among all these prescriptions, allowing each to point in some direction where the discerning eye could pause, the attentive ear listen. So it comes about that the account of the *Prioress* in *The Prologue* begins in the Ciceronian manner (name, sex, profession, social position, special skill and her prevailing study, 'to been estatlich of manere'), then follows Matthieu with an account of her moral sensibilities, her amiable carriage, her charity and tenderness of heart, her charming sentimentality over her pets (which, as a nun, she had of course no business to own) and at last comes to her appearance; here he follows Vinsauf, starting with her wimple and thence to nose, eyes and mouth, moving downward to the tell-tale wrist with its ambiguous brooch, inscribed *Amor Vincit Omnia*. Her portrait is a perfect example of how rules obey a genius.

There was also a medical approach to character. Medicine had evolved a theory that the human constitution was fashioned of the Four Elements, earth, air, fire and water. *Earth* had the quality of being cold and dry; *air*, hot and moist; *fire*, hot and dry; *water*, cold and moist. Now according to the particular proportion and mixture of these elements in the individual man, he was thought to have a predominating 'complexion' or temperament. Too earthy, he would be *melancholy*: too airy, he would be *sanguine*: too fiery, he would be *choleric*: too watery, he would be *phlegmatic*.

To each of these 'complexions' or 'humours' were attached a number of subsidiary qualities and predispositions, so well-known as to be enshrined in popular mnemonic verses, Latin and English. Here, for instance, is a popular rhyme to remind you what to expect of a *Sanguine* man:

> Of yiftes large,[64] in love hath grete delite,
> locunde and gladde, ay of laughyng chiere,
> Of ruddy colour meynt somdel with white;[65]
> Disposed by kynde to be a champioun,[66]
> Hardy I-nough, manly, and hold of chiere.
> Of the sangwyne also it is a signe
> To be demure, right curteys, and benynge.
> (Robbins, *Secular Lyrics of the 14th and 15th centuries*)

The Prologue tells us that the *Franklin* was a sanguine man, and that one word is intended to carry all the qualities listed in the rhyme. They fit him very well, not only as we first see him, but as we see him later on during his colloquy with the *Squire*, and in the tenor of his tale. The *Reeve*, we are told, was a choleric; all that he says and does is in keeping with what medical lore asserted of such men, who were held to be refractory, deceitful, given to anger, full of ruses, lustful, hardy, small and slender, dry of nature, covetous and solemn. Indeed the Host rebukes him for solemnity in the prelude to his tale. The *Pardoner*'s moral and physical nature are described in terms from which any Doctor (as Professor Curry has made clear) could at once have diagnosed him as a eunuch from birth, and this fact about him explains much in his subsequent adventures on the pilgrimage. Chaucer helped himself to medical lore in much the way a modern novelist might use his knowledge of Freud or Jung.

Astrology offered yet another approach to the imagining of a character. Professor Curry has also shown that the characters of King Emetrius and King Lycurgus in *The Knight's Tale* are imagined as 'personal representatives, in the lists, of the astrological forces' that are involved in the story, namely of Saturn and of Mars respectively, and he quotes Claudius Ptolemaeus to show that the description of these kings by Chaucer follows almost exactly the physical details attributed to men born under those planets. Horoscopy is explicitly invoked by the *Wife of Bath* to account for the contradictions in her character; they were dictated by the position of the heavenly bodies at her birth:

> For certes, I am al Venerien
> In feelynge, and myn herte is Marcien.
> Venus me yaf my lust, my likerousnesse,
> And Mars yaf me my sturdy hardynesse;
> Myn ascendent was Taur, and Mars therinne.
> Allas, allas, that ever love was syme!

Instructed in such ways as these by *auctoritee*, Chaucer looked out with sharpened eyes upon *experience*, and saw not only how to grasp the essentials of a personality posed for a portrait, but also how to make use of what is latent in other ways within a given personality and to draw it forth with a surprising touch of individual or local colour. For instance, in *The Miller's Tale*, one of the characters is a superstitious old carpenter, living at Osney, just outside Oxford. When, peeping into the room of his lodger, Nicholas, to find out what is wrong with him, he sees Nicholas lying gaping on his back on the floor:

> This carpenter to blessen hym bigan,
> And seyd 'Help us, seinte Frydeswyde!'

In other words, he crossed himself and invoked St Frideswide, the local Osney Saint. One could tell that the carpenter was an Osney man, simply from that.

In like manner, in *The Reeve's Tale*, the Miller's wife, awoken by the battle between Alan and the Miller, and feeling the sudden weight of her husband's body falling on top of her, cries out:

> 'Help! hooly croys of Bromeholm!'

This relic, the Holy Cross of Bromeholm, was preserved in East Norfolk, where the Reeve came from, not very far from Cambridge, where the Miller's wife lived. No one else in Chaucer invokes St Frideswide or the Cross of Bromeholm; they are pin-points of local colour, latent in the people he was creating, and perceived by him.

This power of seeing the implications in a character or a situation, so as to give a sudden twist or flavour, depth or tone of his tale, is one of the important things that make Chaucer immeasurably superior as a story-teller to his friend and contemporary John Gower, and indeed to all writers of English narrative poetry. The perceptiveness of which I am speaking is continuously, sensitively, present throughout *Troilus & Criseyde*, in which there is never a false move or impulse of feeling, and the whole is sensed to be deploying humanly, freely and yet inevitably, under the compulsions latent in the characters, in their struggle with destiny.

On a small scale, we may see the operation of this kind of insight in *The Merchant's Tale*, perhaps his most masterly short story. It is characterised by Chaucer's usual moral lucidity. Nothing could be clearer than the never-stated motive of rebellious lust present in its three main characters. These are Old January, whose senile sexuality is hallowed by matrimony and encouraged by aphrodisiacs; young Damian with his treacherous animalism; and the 'faire fresshe May' who is ready to climb a tree for it.

With rarest comment by the narrator, all three are presented through their own eyes, that is, with all the

sympathy and self-approval that they all separately feel for
the fantasy lives latent within them, which Chaucer elicits.
January sees himself as a dear, kind, wise old gentleman,
penitent for his past, eager to sin no more, and seeking the
delicious safety and sanctity of wedlock; his earnest care in
consulting his friends in the choice of a wife (but insisting that
she be under twenty), his tender apprehensions lest she be too
delicate to endure his amorous heats, his solicitude for the
sick squire Damian (who is about to cuckold him) and for his
wife's soul (about to collaborate with the squire), are all
presented from the old man's point of view; in his own
opinion he is a generous, romantic figure; his wife will wear
mourning for ever after his death. We even hear his doting use
of troubadour-language to entice his wife into the Priapic
Garden of the Rose which he had designed for their summery
encounters; like Absalom and Nicholas, he would be a courtly
lover too:

> 'Rys up, my wyf, my love, my lady free!
> The turtles voys is herd, my dowve sweete;
> The wynter is goon with alle his reynes weete.
> Com forth now, with thyne eyen columbyn,[67]
> How fairer been thy brestes than is wyn! ...

At the end of this dithyramb, Chaucher (or his *persona*, the
Merchant) permits himself the remark:

> Swiche olde lewed wordes used he.

But the irony does not consist in the bare contrast between
this fantasy of courtly love and the nastiness of the old lecher
who utters it; he is nothing so simple as a rich, dirty old man;
perhaps no one is. He *is* considerate, affectionate and
generous – humble, even ready to admit his dislikable
qualities to his girl-wife:

> '... And though that I be jalous, wyte me noght.[68]
> Ye been so depe enprented in my thoght,
> That, whan I considere youre beautee,
> And therwithal the unlikly elde of me,[69]
> I may not, certes, though I sholde dye,
> Forbere to been out of youre compaignye
> For verray love; this is withouten doute.
> Now kys me, wyf, and lat us rome aboute.'

In all the irony, there is pathos; and in the pathos, irony. That January should go blind (as he does in the course of the story) is pathetic, but it is ironic, too. He had been blind all along.

> O Januarie, whay myghte it thee availle,
> Thogh thou myghte se as fer as shippes saille?
> For as good is blind deceyved be
> As to be deceyved whan a man may se.[70]

In like manner, Young Damian, the seducer, is, in his own esteem, a lover-poet; he wears the verses that he writes to May in a silk purse upon his heart, and May, who reads and memorises his lines in a lavatory (to which, for safety, she consigns them) is a heroine of romance to herself:

> 'Certeyn,' thoghte she, 'whom that this thyng displese,
> I rekke noght, for heere I hym assure
> To love hym best of any creature,
> Though he namoore hadde than his sherte!'

Again the ironical narrator allows himself to intrude:

> Lo, pitee renneth soone in gentil herte!

No moral is pointed at the end of this story; by a perfection of irony, they all lived happily ever after.

There is one character in Chaucer that neither realistic observation nor the authority of ancient books can wholly account for. He comes from some unknown half-world, a visiting presence that some have thought to be the figure of Death, some the Wandering Jew, some the Old Adam, seeking renewal. It may be better to leave him wholly mysterious and unexplained; it is the ancient, muffled man who directs the three rioters of *The Pardoner's Tale* to the heap of gold, when they ask him if he knows where Death is to be found. To their rough language, and the question why he is so old, he gives this strange reply:

> 'For I ne kan nat fynde
> A man, though that I walked into Ynde,
> Neither in citee ne in no village,
> That wolde chaunge his youthe for myn age;

And therfore moot I han myn age stille,
As longe tyme as it is Goddes wille.
Ne Deeth, allas! ne wol nat han my lyf.
'Thus walke I, lyke a restelees kaityf,[71]
And on the ground, which is my moodres gate,
I knokke with my staf, bothe erly and late,
And seye 'Leeve mooder, leet me in!
Lo how I vanysshe, flessh, and blood, and skyn!
Allas! whan shul my bones been at reste? ...'

It is an unexpected shock to meet with so haunting a figure
in the bright Chaucerian world, a figure so loaded with
suggestions of supernatural meaning. With slow gravity, he
rebukes the three rioters for their discourteous behaviour:

'But, sires, to yow it is no curteisye
To speken to an old man vileynye.'

and that is the reader's link with this strange phantom and the
shadowy world to which he belongs – the huge importance of
courtesy. We are never told who are instructor is, nor has he
been found in any book that Chaucer studied, save for a few
hints in the obscure Latin poet Maximian; the essential
creation is all Chaucer's and it was his 'cyclopean eye' that
discerned this eerie figure, tap-tapping his invisible way
through the crowds at Queenshithe or by the Custom House,
and among the courtiers of Richard II at the palaces of
Eltham or of Shene.

VII. ENVOY

'... I am sure you are become a good Chaucerist ...'
(Ralph Winwood, in a letter to
Sir Thomas Edmondes, 1601)

I have tried to present Chaucer's career as a courtier and to
suggest its effect on his career as a poet, rather than write an
all-embracing 'honeysuckle life'. If this approach leaves
much unsaid that needs saying, there are many other studies
to supply my deficiencies. More can always be said of any
great poet.

His greatness has been a little impugned by Matthew

Arnold, in a celebrated passage, where Chaucer is accused of lacking 'high seriousness'. It is clear, however, that Arnold knew very little about Chaucer; he only shows a light acquaintance with *The Canterbury Tales* and does not appear to have read *Troilus & Criseyde* at all. It need not, therefore, surprise us that he did not perceive Chaucer's moral stature, or that he could not find high seriousness in high comedy; he did not know where to look for it.

There is so much fun in Chaucer, and so little reproof, that his appeal to moralists (who are seldom quite happy about pleasure) is not immediate. Yet he is one of those rare poets who can strongly affect, not only our passions and intelligence, but our wills too; he creates generosities in them. A sense of welcome to the created world, to men and women, and to the experience of living, flows from his pen.

He can reach out to a supernal world too; and if, to do so, he has borrowed a little from Dante, he knew what to borrow and how to borrow it:

> Thow oon, and two, and thre, eterne on lyve,
> That regnest ay in thre, and two, and oon,
> Uncircumscript, and al maist circumscrive,
> Us, from visible and invisible foon,
> Defende ...
>
> (*Troilus & Criseyde*, V)

[Thou One and Two and Three, that livest eternally and reignest ever in Three and Two and One, uncomprehended, and yet comprehending all things, defend us from visible and invisible foes ...]

or

> Withinne the cloistre blisful of thy sydis
> Took mannes shap the eterneel love and pees.
>
> (*Second Nun's Prologue*)

[Within the blissful cloister of thy womb, the eternal love and peace took human shape.]

or

> Victorious tree, proteccioun of trewe,
> That oonly worthy were for to bere

The Kyng of Hevene with his woundes newe,
The white Lamb that hurt was with a spere ...

[Victorious Tree, the protection of all true (souls), that alone wert
worthy to bear the King of Heaven ...]

(Man of Law's Tale)

But it is the mortal world that most exercised his poetical
gift, and there he is nearest to Shakespeare as the poet of
humane understanding; like him, he begets a *caritas* in the
imagination of his readers. His vision of earth ranges from
one of amused delight to one of grave compassion; these are
his dawn and his dusk. His daylight is a lively April of fresh
good will and kindly common sense, and if, here and there,
there is a delicate frost of irony, warmth is his great
characteristic. He takes deep joy in what we think of as the
simple things of nature – birdsong, sunlight, gardens, daisies
in the grass, the 'ayerissh bestes' of the sky (the ram, the bull
and other signs of the zodiac zoo) and even in a chance, timid
hound-puppy:

And as I wente, ther cam by mee
A whelp, that fauned me as I stood,
That hadde yfolowed, and koude no good.
Hyt com and crepte to me as lowe
Ryght as hyt hadde me yknowe,
Helde doun hys hed and joyned hys eres,
And leyde al smothe doun hys heres;
I wolde have kaught hyt, and anoon
Hyt fledde, and was fro me goon ...

(The Book of the Duchess)

The joy he seems to experience, he can communicate, or
create in others, and that is to create a kind of goodness, or a
mood that makes goodness easier; he forges a basic sense of
and desire for harmony. His universe is not off-course, but on
the way to a perhaps distant but a happy and christian
fulfilment, in which men and women have their generous
share. There are plenty of rascals among them, to be sure; he
gazes at them evenly with unembarrassed, uncondemning
delight, limiting his aspirations to *tout comprendre*, and
leaving *tout pardonner* to Higher Authority.

All this is done with laughter not left behind, nor music

either. If Matthew Arnold was a little blind where Chaucer
was concerned, at least he was not deaf, and has written with
wonderful discernment and eloquence on the sound of
Chaucer's verses:

> ... of Chaucer's divine liquidness of diction, of his divine fluidity of
> movement, it is difficult to speak temperately. They are irresistible, and
> justify all the rapture with which his successors speak of his 'gold dew-
> drops of speech' ...

Chaucer's music was not unrelated to that courtiership of
his that we have been studying. The *Liber Niger* of Edward
IV ordains that young henxmen shall be encouraged to
'harping, to pype and sing'. Squires of his household

> of old be accustomed, winter and summer, in afternoons and eveninges,
> to draw to Lordes Chambres within Court, there to keep honest
> company after there Cunninge, in talking of Cronicles of Kinges and
> other Pollicies, or in pipeing or harpeing, songinges and other actes
> marcealls, to helpe to occupie the Court, and accompanie estrangers ...

In afternoons and evenings, Chaucer's music would be
heard in his own voice (after his cunning), when he read out
his poems. In winter, in a Lord's chamber, or in the great hall;
in summer, in the garden below, where he would 'help to
occupie the Court' and 'accompanie estrangers', Jean
Froissart, perhaps, among the others.

The College of Corpus Christi, Cambridge, owns a
fifteenth-century manuscript of *Troilus & Criseyde*; in this
there is a full-page illumination of just such a scene. Against a
sky of afternoon gold, rise the trees and towers of a royal
palace, Shene, it may be, or Windsor, or Eltham; a company
of young lords and ladies in the richly simple robes of those
times are moving down the garden slopes towards a dell,
where a small pulpit has been set up. It is surrounded by the
gathering Court; the Queen is seated on the grass before it,
with her ladies about her. King Richard stands in cloth of
gold, a little to the left of her; to the right there stands an older
man in blue, with a gold girdle. It might be John of Gaunt. In
the pulpit, at which this older man is gazing, Geoffrey
Chaucer is reading from a book; he seems to be a youngish

man, the hair and the eyes are brown; young as they are, they have something of the same sad look.

He is reading from his greatest completed poem, the first tragedy in our language, *Troilus & Criseyde*:

Go, litel bok, go, litel myn tragedye,
Ther God thi makere yet, er that he dye,
So sende mygħt to make in some comedye!
But litel book, no makyng thow n'envie,
But subgit to be alle poesye;
And kis the steppes, where as thow seest pace
Virgile, Ovide, Omer, Lucan and Stace.

[Go, little book, go my little tragedy, to that place whence God may likewise yet send thy maker power to make something in the manner of a comedy, before he dies. But, little book, envy no other poetry, but be subject to all poesy, and kiss the steps where thou seest Virgil, Ovid, Homer, Lucan and Statius pacing.]

NOTES

1. My life's physician.
2. Upon all reason.
3. So tractable.
4. There came a secret thief that men call death.
5. And his gang.
6. The Black Prince.
7. Groves.
8. Be various and yet the same (de Vinsauf: *De Poetria Nova*).
9. Strange broths.
10. Their young heron (like the swans, a dish to eat).
11. In this country people think little of it.
12. Behold the accursed, ancient rites of pagans.
13. Behold the end and the reward for your labours (given by Jove, etc.).
14. Crowd.
15. Set round (with enemies).
16. Scholars?
17. Impute it not.
18. Very broadly.
19. For the full stomach, without fail, knows very little of what the hungry one is suffering.
20. 'Ere they become noble'?
21. See that you do not tear yourself by scratching.

22. In private and public.

23. Geoffrey Chaucer Esquire, of the age of forty years and more, having borne arms for twenty-seven years, produced by Sir Richard Le Scrope's party, sworn and examined, asked if the arms of *azure with a bend or* belonged or should belong to the said Sir Richard by right and inheritance. Said that yes, for he had seen them being armed in France before the town of Retters (Rhetel, near Rheims, probably) ... and ... during the whole campaign when the said Geoffrey was taken prisoner ... (*The Scrope and Grosvenor Roll*, Vol. 1, edited by Sir N.H. Nicolas, 1879.)

24. Ludwig Wittgenstein, *Tractatus Logico-Philosophicus*: 'What one cannot speak about, one has to keep quiet about.'

25. And a fair hand it was, if Dr D.J. Price is right in conjecturing that a late fourteenth-century manuscript, *The Equatorie of the Planetis*, recently brought to light by him at Peterhouse, Cambridge, is a Chaucer holograph.

26. Till thy look is fully dazed.

27. That I then could, by my truth, without pretence or sloth.

28. My lady gave me all wholly the noble gift of her mercy, saving her honour, of course.

29. Why had I not bought one such night at the price of my soul, yes, or the least joy that was there?

30. As ever I may go (thrive).

31. There is no other remedy.

32. To have gladness.

33. None such they felt since they were born.

34. Quite free of fear and distress.

35. Made such a feast (welcome) for him.

36. The sweet honeysuckle engirdles and writhes about.

37. And as the newly abashed nightingale, that stops, as she begins to sing, when she hears any shepherd speak, and afterwards rings her voice out, just so Criseyde, when her fear ceased.

38. And begged a blessing on her snowy throat, her breasts, round and small.

39. He hardly knew what to do for joy.

40. Whoso desires grace, and cares not to honour thee.

41. His royal estate, above earth (after death).

42. Repair home (i.e. to Heaven) from worldly vanity and cast up the countenance of your heart to that God that made you after His image.

43. To buy our souls, first died and rose, and sits in Heaven above.

44. O martyr, soldered to virginity.

45. Continually following.

46. That never knew women after the manner of the flesh.

47. As it was reasonable and right.

48. That is the best that can happen.

49. High lineage.

50. That every lecher will have her.

51. Some man to make a bid for her.

52. Will be without a mate.
53. Thus you say, you wretch.
54. With a wild thunderbolt and fiery lightning, may your withered neck be dashed in pieces!
55. Hanged themselves, out of the spite in their hearts.
56. Lend us gold.
57. Enterprise.
58. Especially.
59. Friends must obey one another.
60. Women, by nature, desire liberty.
61. For well I know that folk before now have reaped (the field of) poetry and carried away the corn.
62. Find an ear (of corn).
63. Learn.
64. Large in his giving.
65. Mingled somewhat with white.
66. Disposed by nature.
67. With thy dove's eyes.
68. Blame me not.
69. My dislikable old age.
70. For it is as good to be deceived when blind as when you have your sight.
71. Like a restless captive.

2

Chaucer's Idea of What is Noble*

In Professor W.H. Auden's most recent and entirely delightful book, *A Certain World*, he makes the ironical remark: 'Today gentlemen are no longer in demand.' It is the wry dismissal of a word and an idea now almost universally denigrated, jeered, smeared and sneered at by three centuries of playwrights, novelists and class-warriors, as the huge, slow juggernauts of social evolution crush out our older life-styles, and move on towards some bourgeois or proletarian epiphany. Meanwhile to recommend a man as a Christian gentleman is virtually to lose him the job.

A curious corroboration of Professor Auden's remark came to me recently from a non-literary source. An enormous young man, standing at the side of the road, thumbed a lift from me. I stopped and picked him up. As we drove off together, he settled himself into his safety-strap and airily remarked:

'I'm just out of prison.'
'Indeed? What for?'
'Larceny.'
'How long did they give you?'
'Nine mumfs.'
'O dear . . . that was a heavy sentence; what did you do all that time?'
'O, I improved me mind. I read a book.'
'A book? Indeed! What book?'

---

*The English Association, *Presidential Address 1971*.

'*Lady Chatterley's Lover.*'

'You don't say! And what did you think of it?'

'Oh, I enjoyed it. That game-keeper having that Ladyship! It properly cut her and her class down to size!'

This was an entirely new light for me on that unreadable though fuss-worthy novel; my learned Theban's remark revealed that he took it for an essentially social and political manifesto, not a sexual one; it was a shrewd blow struck for the righteous-minded Left, though admittedly a little below the belt. It reminded me of a similarly emblematic use of sex as an instrument of hatred in the class war, to be found in that masterly and moving novel *Radcliffe* by Mr David Storey, which greatly impressed and shook me. These things are signs of the times.

Now we, in twentieth-century England, having inherited a great part of the wealth of Christendom, are among Time's millionaires, and it is as well to notice this word *gentleman* of which I began to speak, for it is at the centre of our inheritance; it may be that the gold in it needs melting down and reminting into current coin, but it would be a pity to throw it away without knowing what gold there is in it; we must not be Time's spendthrifts to throw away a civilisation for the sake of a political sneer.

I have therefore thought it might be worth an hour of the Association's time to reconsider this word and what it stood for, when it was still fresh-minted in the fourteenth century, in the age of our first great civilisation after the Conquest. Even then there were those who sneered at it and picked on it with a question to which Dante had already supplied one answer, as we shall see. But the question, to those who knew not Dante, was popularly taken as a piece of unanswerable wit:

> Whan Adam dalf and Eva span,
> Who was then the gentil man?

Chaucer was to supply another and even better answer than Dante's; nevertheless it was a powerful question about a powerful idea, an idea, as I have claimed, at the centre of the civilisation of Christendom.

The impregnation of a society by a civilising idea is a long and painful process, for what is tender, civilising and (as we may say) *humane* in it, has to fight, in all its naked sensitiveness, against embattled brutalities. Nature both creates and resists improvements upon herself and within herself, for

> nature is made better by no mean
> but nature makes that mean.

So, in our own days, we hear of sensitive writers and poets sent to exile, prisons and lunatic asylums, yet still the green tendrils of their thought and passion push through the political concrete walls built to resist them; much as I have seen a rambler rose force its way through stone and mortar walls to declare a blossom on the far side; but the agony may take a great while. William Blake has a strange poem, called *The Mental Traveller*, which I only partly understand, but it seems to describe the process of which I am speaking, by which an idea enters and, in the end, possesses an ancient society, to renew and enrich it.

> I travel'd thro' a Land of Men,
> A Land of Men & Women too,
> And heard & saw such dreadful things
> As cold Earth wanderers never knew.
>
> For there the Babe is born in joy
> That was begotten in dire woe;
> Just as we reap in joy the fruit
> Which we in bitter tears did sow.
>
> And if the Babe is born a Boy
> He's given to a Woman Old,
> Who nails him down upon a rock,
> Catches his shrieks in cups of gold.
>
> She binds iron thorns around his head,
> She pierces both his hands & feet,
> She cuts his heart out at his side
> To make it feel both cold & heat.
>
> Her fingers number every Nerve,
> Just as a Miser counts his gold;
> She lives upon his shrieks & cries,
> And she grows young as he grows old.

Till he becomes a bleeding youth,
And she becomes a Virgin bright;
Then he rends up his Manacles
And binds her down for his delight.

He plants himself in all her Nerves,
Just as a Husbandman his mould;
And she becomes his dwelling place
And Garden fruitful seventy fold.

An aged Shadow, soon he fades,
Wand'ring round an Earthly Cot,
Full filled all with gems & gold
Which he by industry had got.

And these are the gems of the Human Soul,
The rubies & pearls of a lovesick eye,
The countless gold of the akeing heart,
The martyr's groan & the lover's sigh.

They are his meat, they are his drink;
He feeds the Beggar & the Poor
And the wayfaring Traveller:
For ever open is his door.

After this the poem passes into a realm of Blakean visions which I am not sure I understand, and will not attempt to gloss; but, as far as I have read it to you, I understand it in this way: the Old Woman is an ancient society into which a new idea – the Babe – is born. The ancient society attempts to torture and repress it, but instead begins to be rejuvenated by it, as the idea gains strength. Finally the idea masters society and produces a new wealth, an enriched society or civilisation, which pours out its benefits to all and sundry, though the idea that originated them with such agony is gradually forgotten and fades out.

I do not know, but I fancy that Blake had the idea of Liberty, Equality and Fraternity in mind when writing his poem – a prophetic or emblematic vision of the French Revolution; however, the poem will do just as well to describe the first and early second millennia of the Christian idea, the efforts to suppress it, its gradual triumphs, the gems and gold of its best achievements, the groans of its martyrdoms, and the sighing of its love. At the heart of this crucifixion, the heart of this rose that thrust its way through the brutish oppositions of paganry, is the idea of *gentilesse* – the essential idea that we intend when we speak of *gentle Jesus*. More than any other English poet, Geoffrey Chaucer has created the images by which we know this idea, especially in its secular context; there are many ways of describing it, but he calls it *gentilesse*. It is the gold out of which the word *gentleman* was first minted. It has a long history, out of which I would like to put a few points before you. I must begin at the Incarnation.

The life-redeeming core of Christianity comes before our imaginations most readily in the Sermon on the Mount and at the Crucifixion; taken together, they mark out the way for the individual Christian soul, and assert God's inestimable love for each and every one of them. So firmly central became this concept of a universal, personal salvation as the aim and goal of the entire universe that Thomas of Celano, if it was he that wrote the *Dies Irae*, could make the following astounding claim on his Saviour:

> Recordare, Jesu pie,
> Quod sum causa tuae viae;
> Ne me perdas illa die.

The claim is that the single soul that sings this hymn is the *cause* of the Incarnation; the sheep has caused the shepherd's journey, the lone and single sheep; and the fear is, not that the sheep will be lost, but that the Shepherd may lose it.

> *Ne me perdas illa die*
> Lest thou lose me on that day.

This paradox of arrogance and humility is the rock on which the infinite importance of the individual soul is built, namely the clear claim that every single human creature is infinitely loved by God, and has an everlasting and infinite destiny entrusted to it for fulfilment under God's grace.

Now this is the vision we see proclaimed in the poetry of *Piers Plowman* and of the great drama-cycles of England of the late fourteenth century. These cycles were written for the secular but Catholic public, city-dwellers for the most part, and they demonstrate how the whole Creation moves towards a final judgement of grief or glory for the individual, personal, single soul. It was left for Geoffrey Chaucer to transfer this

religious vision of individuality to its earthier counterpart in
the secular world, where it appears less as a soul than as a
personality, and has secular idiosyncrasies like warts on
noses. This, of course, is no denial of its religious aspects. A
soul is the immortal part of a personality, they coexist until
death. So in Chaucer the religious background to the secular
foreground is there as a matter of course, and is sufficiently
indicated at the end of both of Chaucer's greatest poems; we
are shown the soul of pagan Troilus ascending, after his
death, under the guidance of Mercury, to a point at which he
is aware of 'the pleyn felicitee that is in hevene above' after
which he is taken where Mercury 'sorted him to dwelle'; it is
then that Chaucer turns to remind the 'young, fresshe folkes,
he or she' that they are made in the image of God, and are
bidden to love him

> which that right for love
> Upon a crois, oure soules for to beye,
> First starf, and roos, and sit in hevene above.

So, too, at the conclusion – in so far as Chaucer can be said to
have reached it – of the *Canterbury Tales*, the pilgrims are
exhorted to remember the still more perfect pilgrimage upon
which they all are set, namely to the heavenly Jerusalem,
Jerusalem celestial.

Chaucer, as everybody knows, has given us the exact
physiognomies of the salient figures in his poem, that have for
ever embalmed – no, not embalmed, *embodied* – the type
within the individual; and first among such individual
representatives he puts the *Knight* and his son the *Squire* in
their proper social order, each recognisably himself and no
one else, yet each a representative of the quality that Chaucer
most deeply admired – *gentilesse*.

Let me here break off for a brief foray into philology, to
reach the root-meaning of this word. It is one of a familiar
cluster that stems from and begins with the letters G-E-N –
*gen*tle, *gen*erous, *gen*erative, *gen*ius, *gen*eric, *gen*der,
*gen*ealogical, and so forth that are all related to the Latin word
gens, a family.

Here, then, at its philological origins lay the popular fallacy
that there was something *hereditary* in being a *gentil* and that

there was such a thing as gentle blood, a mystical thing, that showed through all efforts to disguise it; we see it in the sons of Cymbeline, or in Perdita; it is a faith proper to romances, inextricably interwoven with the stuff of language, and even of poetry; the Squire is the Knight's *son*. Also popularly connected with the idea of heredity is the idea of wealth. One of the qualities proper to a man of great family was *largesse*; he must give in a large way; he must be *gen*erous with his wealth; and therefore he must be wealthy. *Generosus*, which in classical Latin meant *eminent* or *distinguished*, is the normal word in medieval chronicle Latin for a gentleman, as we would have to translate it; it implied wealth and hereditary station.

These confusions of thought thus buried in the language were almost irresistible, and so arose the popular revolutionary counter-claim I have mentioned as to who was a gentleman in the days of Adam and Eve. Clear-thinking Dante put the whole question of heredity into a nutshell; we are all descended from Adam. 'If then Adam was noble, we are all noble; if base, then base.' It was a telling point made in his discussion of *gentilesse* in the Fourth Treatise of his *Convivio* (ch. xv), a treatise in which he seeks to refute the Emperor Frederick of Swabia, who put forth the opinion that *gentilesse* was a matter of 'ancient wealth and gracious manners' (ch. iii). Having eliminated heredity, Dante proceeds to eliminate wealth; riches, he says, cannot ennoble or be a cause of nobleness, for riches in themselves are base. Then he turns to define true nobleness, basing his thought on Aristotle, so he tells us. 'This word *nobleness*', he says, 'means the perfection of each thing in its proper nature' (ch. xvi); 'so the straight path', he continues, 'leads us to look for this definition by way of the fruits, which are moral and intellectual virtues, of which nobleness is the seed'.

Dante then reads off a list of virtues, that sound a little strange in our ears, which he claims to have taken from 'the philosopher', i.e. Aristotle, as appropriate to nobility of nature – Courage, Temperance, Liberality, Munificence, Consciousness of Greatness, Proper Pride, Serenity, Affability, Frankness, Pleasantness, and Justice.

'No one', says Dante, 'because he can say "I am of such and

such a race" should believe that he has nobleness, unless these fruits are in him ... for the divine seed falls not upon the race, that is the stock, but falls upon the several persons; and, as will be shown below, the stock does not ennoble the several persons, but the several persons ennoble the stock.'

This is as far as we need to follow Dante for the moment; let us turn to the Catalan, Ramon Lull. Ramon Lull, the Catholic mystic and martyr, was born in 1235, a whole generation before Dante; his book, which Caxton later translated under the title of *The Order of Chivalry*, was a seminal work and set the tone for the nature and duties of a Knight or Squire about a hundred years before Chaucer's Knight came into being. I cannot prove that Chaucer read Lull as I can prove that he read Dante, but the general type delineated by Lull was well enough known to colour Chaucer's picture. He could not have escaped it.

Lull's *Order of Chivalry* makes no mention of Aristotle; it is wholly grounded in the New Testament and the feudal system. Knighthood, he declares, is an office of dedication, if need be to the death, in the service of God, and is only less sacred than priesthood; they are the two noblest offices in the world. The first duty of a Knight is to defend the Catholic faith, the second to defend his territorial overlord; he is at all times and in all places to maintain justice; he must keep himself exercised in arms by attending battles and tournaments, and in spirit by practising wisdom, charity, loyalty and humility. He must above all be courageous, but temper his courage by discretion; he is pledged to defend women, especially the helpless, the sick and the weak; and children too; he is to undertake words of mercy and pity.

To him are given a number of weapons and accoutrements with an allegorical as well as a practical significance – the spear of Truth, the pennon of Faith, the helmet of modesty (Caxon calls it *shame-fastness*), the spurs of speed and diligence, the cross-hilted dagger that betokens mercy, the saddle of courage, the bridle of restraint, the gauntlets of gratitude, and, above all, the horse, the *cheval*, from which chivalry derives, which Lull – or rather, Caxton – says signifies the '*nobleness* of courage'. Having said all this, and more in the same strain, Caxton's version concludes this section with

> And yf in a knyght were not charyte / how myȝt he be in thordre of
> chyualry / Charite is a vertu aboue other vertues for she departeth euery
> vice / Charite is a loue of the which euery knyȝt ouȝt to haue as moche as
> nede is to mayntene his offyce / & charite also maketh a man to bere
> lyȝtly the peisāt burthēs of chyualry / for al in lyke wyse as an hors
> withoute feete may not bere the knyght / Ryght soo a knyght maye not
> without charyte susteyne the grete charge and burthen of his ordre.

It is clear that this kind of thinking lies behind the vivid image
of Knighthood Chaucer pictures for us in the *Prologue*; a
phrase like Caxton's 'Courtesy and chivalry concorden
togyder, for villainous and foul words been against the Order
of Chyvalry' recalls the Chaucerian lines:

> He nevere yet no vileynye ne sayde
> In al his lyf, unto no maner wight.

It is sometimes said by the sneering critic that this portrait is
an ideal, nostalgic, romantic hankering for an institution,
already on its way out, indeed already being blown up by
gunpowder, and we are not to trust to it as we trust the
portraits of the drunken, thieving, bawdy-minded Miller, or
the carbuncular Summoner. This kind of criticism shows
complete misunderstanding of the entire subject. In the first
place it ignores the absolutely pin-pointed realism of the
Knight's history and appearance, his war-worn clothes, his
many expeditions, all of which can be paralleled from the
facts of the Scrope-Grosvenor case of 1386, at which Chaucer
was present and gave evidence; or we may take the fact of the
Knight's having campaigned in Lithuania; it may sound
incredible, a piece of idealisation; but no; it was sober fact that
young knights were sent to Lithuania to gain military
experience at that time; Henry Bolingbroke himself was one;
he went there in 1390, only a few years after Chaucer wrote
the description of the Knight.

   The careful accuracy Chaucer shows in all matters of fact –
I do not believe he was ever found wrong on any point of
detail – gives a kind of guarantee that we can trust him in
spiritual matters too; but there is another, more fundamental
answer to those who want to think the Knight's moral nature,

as depicted by Chaucer, was too good to be true, and so can be no better than a romantic illusion. People who think thus can never have thought about Christianity at all; that we cannot live up to the moral demands that it makes on us, and that at any moment we may fall into the pit that opens beneath us, does not lessen the love we are taught to have for them, and which Chaucer's Knight too was taught to have, and to attempt. Christianity plainly tells us to be perfect, impossible as it seems, impossible as it proves; but this does not make that demand less real, or even less realistic; it cannot be blown up by gunpowder. Coming to the aid of human imperfection there is grace.

We are not told of any imperfections in the Knight and his *gentilesse*; we are told that he loved Chivalry, Truth, Honour, Freedom and Courtesy. Let me pause on these words a moment. Chivalry is the mystique of the horse, the totemic animal of Knighthood, that horse-mastery and control of power in the saddle that gives an edge to human eminence; we see it not only in Christendom, but also in the horse-culture that grew up at much the same time in Japan, and is called *Bushido*; in Japan, too, the first necessity for a member of this class was always to tell Truth. There was a saying 'A Bushi has no second word'; but perhaps it is as fanciful to find a connection between horse-mastership and a regard for the truth, as it is in our own times to find a connection between scarlet cars and dangerous driving. It may be mere coincidence. Honour is another attribute of Knighthood loved by the Knight, another way of describing that total of integrity sought by the young hero of Salinger's *Catcher in the Rye*; it means the opposite of disgrace, the earning of a good fame, the virtue which in *Beowulf* is called *lof*, perhaps, for which Beowulf was most eager. Good *renomee* in Malory.

Truth and freedom are the most interesting and deepest in meaning of these knightly attributes. To understand the full meaning of Truth we must turn from Chaucer to Langland, who tells us that God is Truth, and that he proves it by the text that God is Love:

> Whan alle tresores aren tried, trewthe is the best;
> I do it on *deus caritas*, to deme the sothe.

Now we are made in God's image, as both Langland and
Chaucer remind us, and that means that we too are capable of
those perfections, not only if we are high-born knights, but
also if we are simple farmers. Piers Plowman tells us that he
digs and he delves and does as Truth commands him and that
he will be Truth's pilgrim at the plough, for poor men's sakes.

Chaucer with his secularising imagination sees Truth as
the highest thing a man may seek in his daily life, and that it is
akin to freedom, that is to generosity. This is the substance of
The Franklin's Tale where these qualities are seen in action;
you may recall that it tells of Dorigen who is happily married,
love for love, to an excellent Knight, who leaves her for a
while in Brittany while he enters for a tournament in
England; she suffers terror from the rocks of Brittany which
she fears may wreck him on his return. Unknown to her, a
young man called Aurelius has fallen in love with her, and
seeing that her husband is away, he declares himself to her;
she is horrified and disgusted, but in the end makes a joke of it
and says she will yield to him if he will remove the rocks of
Brittany – thinking this impossible; but she had reckoned
without magic. Aurelius promises a magician a thousand
pounds if he will cause the rocks to vanish; the magician
agreed, and when his calculations have been completed, the
rocks disappear. Aurelius in high delight reminds her of her
promise, saying that he asks nothing as of right, but he would
not have her break her word. She goes in despair to her
husband, who has returned, and tells him all; he sternly tells
her that if that is what she has promised, she must perform it,
for his *love* for her demands her *truth*:

> I hadde wel levere ystiked for to be
> For verray love which that I to you have,
> But if ye sholde youre trouthe kepe and save.
> Trouthe is the hyeste thyng that man may kepe.

So Dorigen keeps her word, weeping as she does so, and
offers herself to Aurelius, at her husband's command. But
when Aurelius learns this to be the case, the astounding
nobility her husband has shown in preferring his wife's Truth
to his own disgrace — the disgrace of cuckoldry – he finds it
something greater than he can accept, and he is moved to

release Dorigen from her foolish vow, saying:

> Thus kan a squier doon a gentil dede
> As wel as kan a knyght, withouten drede.

So Dorigen and her husband are reunited, their truth and honour vindicated, and poor Aurelius is left disconsolate in his generosity, not having enjoyed the lady, and wondering where he was going to find a thousand pounds to pay the magician with. He determines to beg the magician for time to get the money together:

> My trouthe wol I kepe, I wol nat lye!

The magician, however, worms the whole story out of him; when the tale was told

> This philosophre answerde 'Leeve brother,
> Everich of yow dide *gentilly* til oother.
> Thou art a squier, and he is a knycht,
> But God forbede, for his blisful myght,
> But if a clerk koude doon a gentil dede
> As wel as any of yow, it is no drede!'

And he releases Aurelius of his debt. So the *Franklin* ends his tale, and turns to his pilgrim-audience to ask this question:

> Lordynges, this question, thanne, wol I aske now:
> Which was the mooste *fre*, as thynketh yow?

Which was the freest, in the sense in which the *Knight* of the *Prologue* loved freedom? The story shows Truth and Freedom at their best in *gentilesse*; and shows that, in respect of *gentilesse*, philosophers, knights, and squires have equal opportunity and, perhaps, capacity. Neither birth nor wealth have anything to do with it. This thought had been with Chaucer ever since he translated the *Roman de la Rose*; here again was a poem as democratic in its understanding of nobility as even G.K. Chesterton could have wished; according to the *Roman* your capacity to show *gentilesse* depends on your capacity for friendship or love: to have no such capacity is to be 'vilein':

> Thise vilayns aren withouten pitee,
> Frendshipe, love and al bountee.
> But undirstonde in thyn entent
> That this is not myn entendment
> To clepe no wight in noo ages
> Oonly gentill for his lynages;
> But whoso is vertuous,
> And in his port nought outrageous; ...

To be outrageous, pitiless, friendless, loveless, to have no givingness, these things make villainy in any lineage. Such villains appear in the peerage as well as in the peasantry, bourgeoisie and proletariat.

There is another quality in *gentilesse* which Chaucer seems to discern, namely a certain intellectual grandeur, a capacity to think a high thought. We see it particularly in *The Knight's Tale*, where Duke Theseus, Palamon and Arcite are all given great speeches to utter, which Chaucer has taken from his reading in Boethius; so we listen to the great outcries against Fortune transferred from the tongue of Boethius to the tongues of these young lovers, and we hear the great Duke speak of the grand design of the universe; he accepts, or rather asserts, that this our world is only a thoroughfare and full of woe, nay more, it is a 'wrecche world', and he speaks of the 'foule prison of this lyf'. But that, we must understand, is in comparison with another world and life above the moon, in the region beyond corruption; and he asserts the greatness and purpose of the First Mover, the First Cause of all, that made the fair chain of love in which all is bound together. This it is noble to believe:

> The Firste Moevere of the cause above,
> Whan he first made the faire cheyne of love,
> Greet was th' effect and heigh was his entente;
> Wel wiste he why, and what thereof he mente.

We, he tells us, are a part of this great whole, and so it is wise to make a virtue of necessity. Wisdom too is an attribute of *gentilesse*; the Knight himself is wise, as we are told in the Prologue.

Chaucer made another attempt to speak of this star-cluster

of words that he used to describe the Knight in the Prologue –
the truth, honour, knighthood, wisdom, humility and
freedom or generosity, that are embodied in *gentilesse*; they
are indeed more like the several facets of a well-cut diamond
than a cluster or galaxy. It comes in the dying speech of Arcite
in *The Knight's Tale*, which is among the most beautiful
speeches in romantic narrative poetry, at least in my opinion.
It is noteworthy that this speech is purely Chaucer's
invention; much of *The Knight's Tale* follows closely on his
original in Boccaccio; but here and there, as in his *Troilus and
Criseyde*, also taken from Boccaccio, he diverges and invents,
in order to enlarge the spiritual or psychological scope of his
characters or thrust in a piece of Boethian wisdom, as a rule;
the character of Pandarus, as Chaucer paints it, is a wonderful
illustration, in a comic vein, of this way of idiosyncratic
enlargement; the dying speech of Arcite is a melancholy but
heroic lightening before death, that redeems his character
from its ferocity, its care for nothing but to win, its utter
dedication to Mars; his death shows him capable of love and
friendship as well, requisites of *gentilesse*, according to the
code of the *Roman de la Rose*, a real *largesse*.

Imagine Arcite, carved out of his armour, and lying on his
death-bed, by which stands his beloved, that Emelye for
whom he and his blood-brother and cousin Palamon have so
long contended, and have twice faced each other in mortal
combat. And now, after a seeming victory for Arcite, victory
is snatched from him by a mortal accident, devised by the
malignant wit of Saturn, and death is dividing him from both
victory and love; and thus he speaks:

> Naught may the woful spirit in myn herte
> Declare o point of alle my sorwes smerte
> To yow, my lady, that I love moost;
> But I biquethe the service of my goost
> To yow, aboven every creature,
> Syn that my lyf may no lenger dure;
> Allas, the wo! Allas, the peynes stronge,
> That I for yow have suffred, and so longe!
> Allas, the deeth! Allas myn Emelye!
> Allas departynge of oure compaignye!
> Allas, myn hertes quene! Allas my wyf!
> Myn hertes lady, endere of my lyf!

What is this world? What asketh men to have?
Now with his love, now in his colde grave,
Allone, withouten any compaignye!
Farewel my swete foo, myn Emelye!
And softe taak me in youre armes tweye
For love of God, and herkneth what I seye.

I have heer with my cosyn Palamon
Had strif and rancour many a day agon,
For love of yow, and for my jalousye.
And Juppiter so wys my soule gye
To speken of a servaunt proprely,
With alle circumstances trewely,
That is to seyn, trouthe, honour, knyghthede,
Wysdom, humblesse, estaat and heigh kinrede,
Fredom, and al that longeth to that art,
So Juppiter have of my soule part,
As in this world, right now, ne knowe I non
So worthy to ben loved as Palamon,
That serveth yow, and wol doon al his lyf.
And if that evere ye shul been a wyf,
Foryet nat Palamon, the gentil man.'

We have seen how all these qualities of which I have been speaking have been identified in the character of the Knight in the Prologue and in his Tale of Palamon and Arcite, with Chivalry, and the Froisartian world, and Truth is their first element; we have seen how Truth is identified in Langland's vision of Holy Church with divine love. Here, in the death of Arcite, Chaucer associates all that he knows of *gentilesse* with *human* love, the love of a man for a woman and the love of a man for his friend; chivalry and romantic love, often called courtly love, were the two great victories of the spirit in the secular civilisation of Christendom over the two most powerful male impulses, aggression and an omnivorous sexuality; these basic impulses were much beautified, and perhaps a little tamed, by these great inventions: chivalry and romance: both have survived if only as the Aged Shadow of Blake's poem, but the gems and gold are there.

I have tried to indicate how Aristotle, the New Testament, Boethius, Ramon Lull, Guillaume de Loris and Dante have helped, over a thousand years and more, to apprehend and give meaning to this word *gentil*; they all shine in the penumbra of Chaucer's use of it, as it flowers in his images and stories; I have tried to show how it is central in the moral concept of Christendom, stemming from the Sermon on the Mount and the Crucifixion, and is in the equal reach of all men and women, whatever their birth, breeding, rank or wealth. It is like courtesy – which is yet another aspect of the same thing – a thing within our human reach to some extent in that it is no more than the application, which all are told to attempt, of Christianity to normal everyday social behaviour. But the final, finest, simplest statement Chaucer has to make on it has still to be told. At a single step, Chaucer strides out beyond all that had been said about it by the other poets and philosophers of Christendom. He has put his summing up of this high matter into the mouth of the *Wife of Bath*.

Before I quote from her, let me first say that the experience of trying to learn how to understand Chaucer, which has lasted me a lifetime, continually leads me back to the opinions of the *Wife of Bath*, whom, I believe, he created to be the mouthpiece or stalking-horse behind which he could deliver his most cherished and extreme opinions; you will remember her Tale, in which a young man is landed into a marriage, by a vow almost as rash as Dorigen's, to a hideous, ill-bred, penniless, ancient crone; a situation of purest Chaucerian comedy. He lies there beside her in bed upon their wedding night, sweating, groaning, writhing, turning and despairing; she lies, however, in patience, with a quiet smile on her face. At last she asks him what is the matter; is this what the Knights of King Arthur do on their wedding nights? What is troubling him? Then it all comes out with a rush: the Knight answers

> Thou art so loothly, and so oold also
> And therto comen of so lough a kynde
> That litel wonder is thogh I walwe and wynde.

The lady is so old and so loathsome and of so base a birth, what wonder is it if he wallows and twists? Though she has an answer to his accusations of her loathsomeness and her old age too, she keeps these in reserve, and goes straight to the accusation that she is of *base birth*; that she is not a gentlewoman. To this she replies with the most remarkable of all Chaucer's many sermons, and the most unexpected; here are some of the major points she makes:

> But for ye speken of swich gentillesse
> As is descended out of old richesse
> That therfore sholden ye be gentil men,
> Swich arrogance is nat worth an hen!
> Looke who that is moost vertuous alway,
> Privee and apert, and moost entendeth ay
> To do the gentil dedes that he can;
>   Taak him for the grettest gentil man.
> *Crist wole we clayme of hym our gentilesse,*
> Nat of our eldres for hire old richesse . . .
>
> For God it woot, men may wel often finde
> A lordes sone do shame and vileynie;
> And he that wole han prys of his gentrye,
> For he was boren of a gentil hous
> And hadde his eldres noble and vertuous,
> And nel himselven do no gentil dedis,
> Ne folwen his gentil auncestre that deed is,
> He nys nat gentil, be he duk or erl;
> For vileyns synful dedes make a cherl.
> For gentillesse nis but renomee
> Of thyne auncestres, for hire heigh bountee,
> Which is a strange thyng to thy persone.
> Thy gentillesse cometh fro God allone;
> Thanne comth our verray gentillesse of grace
> It was no thyng biquethe us with oure place.

And now the cat is really out of my bag. It is Christ who wills that we claim the right to be called gentlemen from Him, not from our ancestors and their wealth; it is God who sends us grace to exercise our virtue in attempting to be perfect, by the pure simplicity of the *Imitatio Christi*, undertaken in that grace.

So we may say that both for Chaucer and for Langland, in their different ways, the vanishing-point of their vision is the Incarnation, the union of God in Man; Chaucer sees the idea in secular terms:

> He was a verray parfit gentil knight

and Langland, in describing Christ's entry into Jerusalem and his crucifixion, also sees it as a piece of Knighthood, a piece of courtesy, of *gentrice*: he views him as a Jouster against sin and death, come to win his spurs:

> Thanne I frayned at Faith what al that fare bemente
> And who sholde jouste in Iherusalem? 'Jhesus' he seyde . . .
> 'This ihesus of his gentrice wole iuste in piers armes,
> In his helme and in his haberioun, *humana natura.*'

This concept of a gentleman was too high to hold long; it went down very quickly after Chaucer, and my impression of Castiglione and his famous book *The Courtier*, some two centuries later, is always one of a downfall, however elegantly sophisticated. It could be that at about this time the Prince of Darkness became a gentleman, as we all know he did: the Great First Cause for Castiglione seems to have been the Duke of Urbino, and the thought of him sets Pope's tremendous couplet ringing in my head:

> Philosophy that leaned on Heaven before,
> Shrinks to its second cause and is no more.

What are we to think, for instance, when in the Third Book of *The Courtier*, the Lord Julian rebukes a minor disputant in the dialogue for having dared to allude to the Bible, saying that we should not 'meddle holy matters with our fond reasoning'? The *Wife of Bath* would have made short work of that kind of double-talk! 'What', she might say, 'the Blessed Virgin too holy to be mentioned in polite society? So much the worse for polite society!' She would have had a twentieth-century sympathiser in J. Alfred Prufrock who did not dare ask his lady-love a question that called for Lazarus to answer, and so failed to ask it, and could only watch the ladies come and go, talking of Michael Angelo, with such cultivation.

I have now nearly finished what I intended to say in this paper, but am a little dashed to find I have here and there repeated things I have said of Chaucer and *gentilesse* before, and of Langland too. One cannot long read these authors without perceiving how profoundly at one they were (in spite of so many differences in style) on this central feature of the civilisation they have handed on to us. If I have repeated myself, it is because many rereadings have confirmed what I have tried to say before; but I hope I have also a little enlarged and strengthened the points I had in view, and that, taken as a whole, it may seem fresh to the Association, in the sense that grass is fresh to us in spring, however familiar it may seem to us from last year. It is the same grass with the same daisies, but perhaps more of them.

I will not drag you through the long downfall of *gentilesse*; what happened to it at the Restoration, for instance, among those gentlemen-scoundrels like Horner of *The Country Wife* or Lovelace of *Clarissa*, or the seedy shams of supposed gentry in so many of the novels of Charles Dickens, Mr Dorrit for instance; the whole concept of *gentilesse* and of its origin in the Incarnation seems lost there, utterly and for ever, together with the concept of Christendom. And yet in Dickens there are passages enough of strong Christian feeling and allusion, though I cannot at the moment recall one in this precise connection. Words go out of currency and change their significance, as Chaucer was well aware:

> Ye knowe ek that in forme of speche is chaunge
> Withinne a thousand yeer, and wordes tho
> That hadden pris, now wonder nyce and straunge
> Us thinketh hem, and yet thei spake him so,
> And spedde as well in love as men now do;
> Ek for to wynnen love in sondry ages
> In sondry londes, sondry ben usages.
>
> (*Troilus and Criseyde*, ii. 22–8)

It is a part of our business in the English Association to keep green the meaning of our more ancient texts, lest some precious part of our inheritance be negligently thrown away. The root idea of our civilisation of which I have been talking, that may be summed up as the imitation of Christ, still finds expression by some poets of our own time; it is to be heard in the words of some pop-singer poets, and in our younger novelists here and there, as it was in Dickens; the most moving expression I know of it I have quoted before, in a similar context, and take leave to quote it again; it comes in Mr Beckett's masterpiece *Waiting for Godot*. His two down-and-out tramps, Estragon and Vladimir, are, as usual, talking; Estragon has taken off his boots and placed them on the floor, downstage, near the audience:

Vladimir: Your boots. What are you doing with your boots?
Estragon: I'm leaving them there ... Another will come, just ... as ...
              me, but with smaller feet, and they'll make him happy.
Vladimir: But you can't go barefoot!
Estragon: Christ did.
Vladimir: Christ! What's Christ go to do with it? You're not going to
              compare yourself with Christ!
Estragon: All my life I've compared myself to him.

Yet in spite of sudden glimpses by poets, we are no longer in a biblical age, but in an economic one, and passing through an evolution, or revolution, such as I mentioned at first; it is a little ironical that as we seem to move away from Christendom and its gospel, we find ourselves on the point of re-entering Europe, for economic and political reasons. It is something that Chaucer, like Estragon, has left us his boots.

3

Langland: *Piers Plowman**

The writer of short studies, having to condense in a few pages the events
of a whole lifetime, and the effect on his own mind of many various
volumes, is bound, above all things, to make the condensation logical
and striking ... It is from one side only that he has time to represent his
subject. The side selected will be either the one most striking to himself,
or the most obscured by controversy.

Robert Louis Stevenson, *Men and Books*

I. AUTHORSHIP AND DATE: SUCH FACTS AS THERE ARE

Piers Plowman, the greatest Christian poem in our language,
comes to us from the second half of the fourteenth century
and is thought, though not unanimously, to be the work of an
unbeneficed cleric, probably in minor orders, called William
Langland. Nothing certain is known about him; even his
name comes doubtfully down to us by a late tradition. All we
know of his personal life is what he tells us of it in the poem,
and that is little enough and open to doubt. In these
uncertainties it is best to begin by setting out such facts as
there are, for they shed a light helpful to criticism on the
poem, on the man who wrote it and on how it was written and
received.

It has survived in 51 manuscripts of the fourteenth and
fifteenth centuries – a very large number, although *The*

Writers and New Work. Published for the British Council and the National Book
League (London: Longmans, 1964).

Canterbury Tales tops it with 83 – and in one early printed
text; the poem is cast in the form of a series of dream-visions
told in the first person, as if Dreamer and Poet were one, and
no sensitive reader can escape some impression of his
personality and genius, or fail to wonder at the spiritual range
and intensity of a mind that can generate a ferociously
satirical laughter, a compassion as humane as Lear's upon the
heath, and a mystical sense of glory in God's love in the
passion and resurrection of Christ. Here and there, among
these greater effects, there are other touches, telling us
something about the accidents, rather than the substance of
his life, and to these touches can be added a few marginal
comments with which later fifteenth-century hands have
annotated one or two manuscripts, and the brief jottings,
gathered by hearsay by Robert Crowley and set down in the
early printed text I have mentioned, of which he was the
editor, which first appeared in 1550; another version of the
same information, more garbled than before, appears in the
yet later catalogue of John Bale, *Scriptorum Illustrium
Maioris Britanniae Catalogus* (1559).

Before we can consider the author and what is said of him,
there is something further to be said of the texts, for they
present a complication which bears directly on the author's
methods and on the poem's date. The manuscripts fall into
three clear classes, offering three distinct versions of the
work; they are known as the A, B and C Texts. Seventeen
manuscripts support the first, fifteen and Crowley's text the
second, and nineteen the third. A study of these three
versions makes it abundantly clear that B is a revision of A,
and C of B. It has been doubted whether all three were the
work of one mind, and fifty years ago a number of scholars,
led by J.M. Manly of Chicago University, persuaded
themselves they had reason to believe that no less than five
different poets had had a hand in it. But reason that could
convince was never shown and critics have now ceased to saw
the poet asunder.

The A and B Texts can be dated with some certainty, from
references within the poem to contemporary events; the A
Text, for instance, refers unmistakably (A.V.14) to the
famous storm that started to blow on the evening of Saturday,

15 January 1362, which the chronicle-writers also record, and it follows that the first version of the poem was at least later than that. The B Text, which is three times as long as the A Text, described, with baleful satire, the coronation of Richard II (B. Prologue, 112-209), an event which took place in 1377. The date of the C Text cannot be so clearly established, but Sister Mary Aquinas has shown that it has strongly influenced another work of the late fourteenth century, *The Testament of Love* by Thomas Usk; as he was put to death in 1388, it follows that the C Text must have largely been in being by then. The picture which emerges from these datings is one of a life-time's work-in-progress, seen in its three major stages; they bridge a period of 25 years. The poet may have continued to work on it until his death, no date for which is known. He seems not to have written anything else; he was a one-poem man.

When we attack the problem who and what he was, we have to push forward through quagmires of even deeper uncertainty, for the records are late and conflicting. In his own day the poem was famous enough; there is reason to think it had some of the effect of a rallying-cry on the insurgents in the Peasants' Revolt of 1381, for John Ball's famous letter to his followers seems to allude to it; I have italicised the relevant phrases; Ball calls himself Schep (a shepherd) to signify his leadership:

Iohon Schep, som tyme Seynte Marie prest of York, and now of Colchestre, greteth wel Iohan Nameles, and Iohan the Mullere, and Iohon Cartere, and biddeth hem that thei bee war of gyle in borugh [tell them to beware of guile in town] and stondeth togidre in Godes name, *and biddeth Peres Ploughman go to his werk*, and chastise wel Hobbe the Robbere, and taketh with yow Iohan Trewman and alle his felawes, and no mo, and loke schappe you to on heved, and no mo [see that you form together under one head, and no more].

> Iohan the mullere hath ygrounde smal, smal, smal;
> The Kynges sone of hevene schal paye for al.
> Be war or ye be wo; knoweth your freend fro your foe;
> Haveth ynow, and seith 'Hoo'!
> *And do wel and bettre*, and fleth synne....
>
> [John the miller has ground fine, fine, fine;
> The Son of the King of Heaven shall pay for all.

Beware before you are sorry; know your friend from your foe;
Have enough and say 'Ho'!
And do well and better, and flee from sin....]

This would be enough to make a poet cautious in the use of his name and avoid blowing himself up with is own gunpowder; but in any case anonymity was then a common fate for poets; the author of *Sir Gawain and the Green Knight* is unknown, and even Chaucer, though careful to put himself by name into *The Canterbury Tales*, was only mentioned in the official records of his times, because he was a trusted servant of the Court, whose work and wages had to be set down in the accounts. William Langland also put his name into his poem, but under the veils of allegory and anagram. There is an ambiguity in the name *William* when it is shortened to *Will*, especially in poems that are involved in moral issues, and even the name Langland or Longland (for they are the same) can be played with:

'I have lyved in *londe*', quod I, 'my name is *longe wille*'[1]

(B.XV.148)

['I have lived in the country', said I, 'my name is long Wil'.]

The Laud manuscript, now in the Bodleian, bears a scribal comment at this line, '*Nota, the name of th'auctour*'. The fullest scribal note, however, is to be found in a Trinity College, Dublin, manuscript, in a late fifteenth-century hand:

Memorandum quod Stacy de Rokayle pater Willielmi de Langlond, qui Stacius fuit generosus, et morabatur in Schypton vnder Whicwode, tenens domini le Spenser in comitatu Oxon., qui predictus Willielmus fecit librum qui vocatur Perys ploughman.

[To be remembered that Stacy de Rokayle (was) the father of William of Langlond, and this Stacy was a gentleman, and lived at Shipton-under-Wychwood in the country of Oxford, a tenant of Lord Despenser, and this aforesaid William made the book called Piers Plowman.]

This seems circumstantial; the Rokayles are known to have been involved with the Despensers, who were Lords of Malvern Chase; business might easily have brought Stacy over from Shipton-under-Wychwood to Malvern. It is odd that his son William should have taken the name Langland if his father's name was de Rokayle, but in the fourteenth and fifteenth centuries 'there is abundant precedent for younger sons not taking the father's name', as R.W. Chambers reminds us; it is possible, too, that William Langland was illegitimate, and that he took his name from the place of his birth. This last possibility will be further considered in a moment, but let us first turn to the testimony of Robert Crowley and John Bale.

This was gathered 150 years and more after the poet's death, a long stretch for the linkages of human memory; a man born in (say) 1380 might have had personal knowledge of Langland and have lived on until (say) 1460; another born in 1450 might have met him in his last years and learnt from him of the author of *Piers Plowman*, then a famous poem, and have passed the information on in turn, to Robert Crowley in his old age. I have myself spoken to a lady who knew Charlotte Brontë's aunt, Miss Prunty, and who clearly recalled that old lady's contempt for the change of the family name from Prunty to Brontë, which she regarded as foreign and finical. And that linkage covers 150 years.

For whatever reason Langland changed *his* name, both Bale and Crowley assert him to have been called *Robert Langelande* and say he was a Shropshire man, born 'about eight miles from the Malvern Hills', at 'Cleybirie' says Crowley, at 'Mortymers Clibery' says Bale. Both these authorities, being valiants in the early days of Protestant propaganda, proclaim the poet to have been a champion of their new faith and a follower of Wycliffe: '*contra apertas Papistarum blasphemias adversus Deum*' trumpets Bale; one of those, declares Crowley, who were given the boldness of heart 'to open thir mouthes and crye out agaynste the workes of darckenes, as dyd John Wicklyfe'.

As Langland's poem shows him to have been one of the most orthodox Catholics that ever took a sacrament, this opinion is clearly an error; but then all that they say is erroneous. The poet's name was not Robert but William; he never calls himself anything else, and the manuscript note already mentioned confirms this; what is more, the reason for this error is easily found in the line which opens the ninth passus of the A Text: 'Thus, yrobid in rosset, I rombide aboute' which means 'Thus robed in russet', not 'Thus I, Robert, in russet', as no doubt Crowley and Bale conjectured. One manuscript has been found which incorporates this error. Neither Cleobury nor Cleobury Mortimer is eight miles from the Malvern Hills, but something over twenty. These topographical discrepancies can however be reconciled with what appears to be the truth, if we suppose that *Cleobury* was an aural or scribal blunder for *Ledbury*, which is at the right distance from Malvern. This conjecture was first made by A.H. Bright in an exciting book on our subject, *New Light on Piers Plowman*, published in 1928. The Bright family had long lived near Ledbury; local knowledge was their speciality.

We learn from this book that in the parish of Colwall, not far from Ledbury, there lies a great flat meadow called *Longland*; the name, says Bright, can be found to describe it in conveyances as far back as 1681. Anyone who takes the main road from Ledbury to Malvern will come upon it, immediately to the left of the road, just below the Duke of Wellington Inn and Chance's Pitch.

As Bright looked up from this field, he was able to see the Herefordshire Beacon towering above him; a little below and to one side, as his local knowledge told him, there lay the moat-like ditches belonging to a vanished Norman keep known as 'Old Castle'; from the Beacon ridge, there flowed several streams, the best of which was known as 'Primes-well'[2] and from this brook could be seen a fine stretch of fields between the site of Old Castle and the Herefordshire Beacon. One had only to go there, thought Bright, and stand by the Primeswell, to recognise instantly the whole landscape that unfolds into a magical allegory in the opening lines of *Piers Plowman*:

> In a somer sesoun whanne softe was the sonne
> I shop me into a shroud as I a shep were;
> In abite as an Ermyte, unholy of werkis,
> Wente wyde in this world, wondris to here.
> But on a May morwenyng on Malverne hilles
> Me befel a ferly, of fairie me thoughte;
> I was wery, forwandrit, and wente me to reste
> Undir a brood bank be a bourne side,

And as I lay and lenide and lokide on the watris
I slomeride into a slepyng, it swiyede so merye.
Thanne gan I mete a merveillous swevene,
That I was in a wildernesse, wiste I nevere where;
Ac as I beheld into the Est, an heigh to the sonne,
I saigh a tour on a toft triyely imakid;
A dep dale benethe, a dungeoun therinne,
With depe dikes and derke and dredful of sight.
A fair feld ful of folk fand I there betwene
Of alle maner of men, the mene and the riche,
Worching and wandringe as the world askith.

(A. Prologue. 1–19)

[In a summer season when the sun was soft, I got myself into clothes to look like a shepherd, in the habit of a hermit of unholy behaviour, I went abroad in the world, to hear of wonders. But on a May morning, on the Malvern Hills, a marvel befell me, it seemed from fairy-land; I was weary, having wandered too far, and I went to rest myself under a broad bank by the side of a brook, and as I lay and leaned and looked into the waters, I slumbered into sleep, it rippled so merrily. And then I began to dream a marvellous dream, that I was in a wilderness, I have no idea where, but as I looked towards the east, high up to the sun, I saw a tower on a hill-top, well and truly made; a deep dale beneath with a dungeon in it, with deep ditches and dark ones, and dreadful to see. A fair field full of folk I found between them, all manner of men, the middling and the rich, working and wandering as the world asks.]

In the sight of these texts and of this topography it is not unreasonable to believe, as many scholars now do, that *Piers Plowman* was written by William Langland, born in the parish of Colwall by the Malvern Hills, towards the end of the first half of the fourteenth century. We can even refine on this a little, for twice in the course of the B Text (B.XI.46 and B.XII.3) he hints in his allegorical way that he is five-and-forty, and as the date of the B Text cannot be earlier than 1377, Langland cannot have been born before 1332, if his hints are to be trusted.

At what date he left the Malverns for London we cannot know, but go to London he did to seek his fortune, for he tells us so; the A Text is full of a knowledge of London and its ways, so he had become a Londoner by the time he was thirty at least. It is likely, indeed, that he went there soon after finishing the education he may be presumed to have had at Malvern Priory, for he had not the physique for farm work, or so he tells us:

Ich am to waik to worche with sykel other with sythe,
And to long, leyf me, lowe for to stoupe,
To worchen as a workeman, eny while to dure.

(C.VI.23–5)

[I am too weak to work with sickle or with scythe
And too long in the back, believe me, to stoop low,
Or to last any length of time working as a workman.]

But if he could not work as a workman, he could work as a
cleric, for he had had a good education:

'Whanne ich yong was', quath ich, 'meny yer hennes,
My fader and my frendes founden me to scole,
Tyl ich wiste wyterliche what holy wryt menede,
And what is best for the bod, as the bok telleth,
And sykerest for the soule ...'

(C.VI.35–9)

['When I was young', said I, 'many years ago, my father and my friends
paid for my schooling until I assuredly knew what Holy Writ meant, and
what is best for the body, as the Book tells, and what surest for the
soul ...']

Such a young man would naturally enter Holy Orders, and
that Langland did so is a reasonable certainty, not only from
the deeply-instructed religious cast of the poem, but from
what he tells us of how he earned a living:

The lomes that ich laboure with and lyflode deserve
Ys *pater-noster* and my prymer, *placebo* and *dirige*,
And my sauter som tyme and my sevene psalmes.
Thus ich singe for hure soules, of suche as me helpen
And tho that fynden me my fode vouchen saf, ich trowe,
To be welcome whanne ich come otherwhyle in a monthe ...

(C.VI.45–50)

['The limbs I labour with and earn my living by are my *paternoster* and
(elementary religious) primer, *Placebo* and *Dirige*, and my psalter
sometimes and then my seven psalms. Thus I sing for the souls of such
as help me, and those that find me my food are kind enough, I believe, to
make me welcome when I come once or twice a month'. *Placebo* and
Dirige are phrases from Psalms 114 and 5 in the Vulgate version and are
used as antiphons in the Office for the Dead. The seven psalms in
question are those called the Penitential Psalms, 6, 32, 38, 51, 102, 130,
143.]

As no one would pay a layman to do these offices, it follows that Langland must have taken holy orders of some kind; yet it is almost equally certain he cannot have been a priest, for he tells us he had a wife called Kitty and a daughter called Calotte (C.VI.2 and B.XVIII.426) and I see no reason to disbelieve him. We may conclude he was a *tonsuratus*, an acolyte, who liked wearing the long robe of his profession in which he describes himself, and who went round from patron to patron, praying for them and for their cherished dead, and perhaps (if I may conjecture) reading to them from his poem now and then.

It is a continual source of wonder to any lover of Langland how such a spirit, so learned, so religious, so orthodox and fervent a son of the Church, escaped, or avoided, full priesthood. Perhaps he knew himself to lack the gift, if it is a gift, of continence; for he tells how in his wild youth he gazed into the mirror of middle-earth that Fortune held out before him, telling him to make up his mind what thing he wanted among the wonders of the world, and to go out and grasp it (B.XI.8–10), and instantly in his dream there appeared 'two faire damoyseles', one called *Concupiscencia Carnis*, who 'colled him about the neck' [necked him round the neck], and the other, *Pryde-of-parfyte-lyvynge*; and these:

> badde me, for my contenaunce, acounte clergye lighte

['And bade me, in respect of continence, to take little notice of holy orders.' 'Clergy' means 'learning' but in this passage it refers to holy orders, for the learned were generally ordained. As learning, by itself, is no bar to incontinence, Langland must here be thinking of Ordination.]

and so (he allows us to think) he gave himself over to the flesh and to the lust of the eyes drawn on by 'Fauntelté' [Childishness]. '*Concupiscentia Carnis* acorded alle my werkes' (B.XI.42) he confesses, as long as Fortune was his friend. And then he forgot his youth and hastened on into age, and Fortune became his foe, and poverty pursued him (B.XI.61); he lost his hair and his teeth, and was attacked by gout (B.XX.182,190, C.XXIII.191); he went deaf and lost his potency: eld (old age)

hitte me under the ere, unethe may ich here;
He buffeted me aboute the mouthe and bette out my tethe,
And gyved me in goutes, I may noughte go at large.
And of the wo that I was in, my wyf had reuthe,
And wisshed ful witterly that I were in hevene.
For the lyme that she loved me fore, and leef was to fele,
On nyghtes namely, whan we naked were,
I ne myght in no manere maken it at hir wille,
So elde and she sothly hadden it forbeten.

(B.XX.189–97)

[hit me under the ear, I can hardly hear; he buffeted me about the mouth
and beat out my teeth, and gyved me with gout, I could not walk about.
And my wife sorrowed for the woe I suffered and most certainly wished
I were in Heaven. For the limb she loved and was fond of feeling,
especially at night when we were naked, I could in no way make behave
in the way she wanted, old age and she, to tell the truth, had so utterly
battered it.]

This sardonic glimpse of his latter days is the last we get of
Langland the man, and so we may leave him to consider
Langland the poet.

II. THE FIRST VISIONS

It is reasonable and attractive to imagine the young cross-
grained poet, standing lankily in the big flat field from which
he had taken his name and looking up in the May sunshine at
the Malvern Beacon, overcome by a moment of great vision.
Suddenly he had seen the whole universe, as he knew it, in the
configuration of his parish and the hills about it. He had
perhaps been helped to this eye-opening instant by seeing
miracle plays; that he had seen some cannot be doubted, for
he uses their very language at moments. The triple world of
the medieval theatre, with the mansions of Heaven high on
one side and Hell's mouth below and on the other, with man's
middle-earth between them, suddenly had bodied itself forth
in the Beacon, the ditches of Old Castle and the intervening
fields. This was the setting for the first flight of his poem, his
first dream-series, known as the *Visio de Petro Plowman*;
when it burst upon him, he cannot have foreseen how three
further visionary tracts would open up before him and

demand to be explored, consequences or sequels to the first, and would be called the *Vita de Do-wel*, the *Vita De-Bet* and the *Vita de Do-Best*. Into these four large movements the texts are divided.

The first movement, then, gives the whole poem its name, *Visio de Petro Plowman*; but it is a long time before we meet with Piers in it; Langland had first to depict a world to be saved before he could show a saviour for it. The opening vision of the Field full of Folk is this world as he saw it; it has as much of London in it as of Herefordshire, for we open upon great crowds, busy about the maze of their lives, 'working and wandering as the world asks'. Chaucer shows us England through some thirty sharply individual pilgrims; Langland through surging crowds of shadowy self-seekers, differentiated by their ways of bullying, begging, thieving, tricking and earning a living out of the Tom Tiddler's Ground of the world; instead of one amiable and distinguished rogue of a friar, such as Chaucer chooses as his exhibit, Langland lumps all the Mendicants together, all the Four Orders, 'preaching the people for the profit of their bellies' (A.Prologue.56) and we see a swirl of parsons, pardoners and bishops, barons and burgesses, lawyers and businessmen, butchers, and brewers, weavers and workmen, with tinkers and tailors and the idle scum of beggars, sham hermits and common jugglers, while we hear the shouts of the tavern-keepers' apprentices advertising their masters' wares with 'Hot Pies! Good pork and goose! Come and Dine! White wine from Alsace, red wine from Gascony!' (A.Prologue.96–108)

In all this rout there are, however, some that quietly and straitly live by the criterion upon which all Langland's thought is based – the love of our Lord:

> In preyours and in penaunce putten hem manye,
> all for love of oure lord lyvede wel streite
> In hope for to have hevenriche blisse.

(B.Prologue.25–7)

[Many gave themselves to prayer and penance, and lived austerely enough, all for the love of our Lord, in hope to have the bliss of the Kingdom of Heaven.]

One may say that the whole poem is a search for the true nature of that love. In the last moments of the poem, after all that has been seen and said, when he finds himself beset by old age and death, after the attack of Antichrist, and left alone in the universal desolation of the world, the Dreamer turns once more to Kynde, that is, to Nature (and perhaps to God, whose works and will are seen in Nature) who passes by as he sits in helpless grief and terror:

> And as I seet in this sorwe, I say how kynde passed,
> And deth drowgh neigh me; for drede gan I quake,
> And cried to kynde out of care me brynge.
> 'Loo! elde the hoore hath me biseye,
> Awreke me, if yowre wille be, for I wolde ben hennes.'
> 'Yif thow wilt ben ywroken, wende into unité,
> And holde the there evere, tyl I send for the,
> And loke thow conne somme crafte, ar thow come thennes.'
> 'Conseille me, kynde', quod I, 'what craft is best to lerne?'
> '*Lerne to love*', quod kynde, '*and level of alle othre.*'
> (B.XX.198–207)

[And as I sat in this sorrow, I saw how Kynd passed by, and death drew near me; I began to quake for fear and cried to Kynd to bring me out of care. 'Look, Old Age the Hoary One has set eyes on me; avenge me if you will, for I would be out of this.' 'If you would be avenged, go into Unity (i.e. the Church) and keep yourself there till I send for you; and see that you learn some craft (trade) before you leave.' 'Advise me, Kynd', said I, 'what craft is best to learn?' 'Learn to love', said Kynde, 'and leave all other learning.']

His first lesson in love opens the poem, when the Prologue is over; it is that Truth and Love are the same, for God is both; this he learns of Holy Church, the Lady lovely of face, who comes down from the Tour on the Toft, Truth's Tower, in the opening vision already quoted:

> 'Whan alle tresores aren tried', quod she, trewthe is the best; I do
>   it on *deus caritas*, to deme the soth;
>
> For trewthe telleth that love is triacle of hevene;
> May no synne be on him sene that useth that spise,
> And alle his werkes he wroughte with love as him liste;
> And lered it Moises for the levest thing, and most like to hevene,
> And also the plente of pees, moste precious of vertues.
> For hevene myghte noghte holden it, it was so hevy of Hymself,

Tyl it hadde of the erthe yeten his fylle.
And whan it haved of this folde flesshe and blode taken.
Was nevere leef upon lynde lighter thereafter,
And portatyf and persant as the poynt of a nedle,
That myghte non armure it lette, ne none heigh walles.'

(B.I.85–6/146–156)

['When all treasures are tried', she said, 'Truth is the best; I prove it by the text "God is Love" ... For Truth tells that love is the treacle of Heaven; no sin may be seen on him that uses that spice. And all the works that He created, He created with love, as it pleased Him, and He taught it to Moses as the dearest thing, the thing most like Heaven, and also the plant of peace, most precious of virtues. For Heaven could not hold it, it was so heavy with Himself, till it had eaten its fill of earth; and when of this fold of earth it had taken flesh and blood, never was leaf on linden lighter than it thereafter, and it was portable and piercing as the point of a needle, so that no armour could keep it out, nor any high wall.']

Love seen as Truth is the rock of his morality, and in the first visions of the poem, by this unanswerable criterion, he measures the actual, contemporary world presented in them. Truth and Love are the strengths under the rage, under the irony, under the laughter, under the compassion of all his poetry. Opposite to Truth is Falsehood, and this is first pictured for us in the vision of Lady Meed, fountain of bribery and simony, surrounded by a route of governmental and ecclesiastical officials, Sherriffs, Deans, Archdeacons, Registrars, lawyers and liars; her portrait is drawn in language that suggests the notoriously venal and luxurious Alice Perrers, mistress of Edward III in his senility. She is a colourful figure, robed in scarlet and loaded with jewellery; her wedding present is the Lordship of the lands of the Seven Sins. But presently her wedding is challenged and all her grotesque followers are put to ignominious flight, riding on each other's backs. After this sardonic vision of officialdom and the political world has run its course, and Lady Meed has met with the reproof of Conscience before the King – this time an ideal King, certainly not a Plantagenet – Langland takes us once again to the Field of Folk, and shows us Reason, with a cross before him, preaching repentance to the common people. They weep and their Seven Sins come forward, one after the other, to make their confession, and are absolved.

These sins are no abstractions, but are seen in terms of shop and pub and fair, false weights, wicked words, watered beer, short measure, slander, ignorance, laziness and a generally sozzled condition. Of the many portraits of the Seven Sins that we have in our literature, these are the most lively, the most scrofulous, the most penitent; and, as they show Langland's satiric art at its best, let us pause over the most famous of them – Glutton on his way to church, to make his confession. Before he get there Betty the Breweress tempts him into the tavern and there he finds the whole village – Cissy the Shoemaker, Wat the Warrener, Tim the Tinker and two of his apprentices, Hickey the Hackneyman, Clarice of Cockslane, Daw the Ditcher and a dozen others:

> There was laughyng and louryng and 'let go the cuppe!'
> And seten so til evensonge and songen umwhile,
> Tyl Glotoun had yglobbed a galoun and a jille.
> His guttis gunne to gothely as two gredy sowes;
> He pissed a potel in a *paternoster* while,
> And blew his rounde ruwet at his rigge-bon ende,
> That alle that herde that horne held her nose after,
> And wissheden it had be wexed with a wispe of firses.
> He myghte neither steppe ne stonde, er he his staffe hadde;
> ... And whan he drowgh to the dore, thanne dymmed his eighen,
> He stumbled on the thresshewolde, an threwe to the erthe.
> Clement the cobelere caughte hym bi the myddel,
> For to lifte hym aloft, and leyde him on his knowes;
> As Glotoun was a gret cherle, and a grym in the liftynge,
> And coughed up a caudel in Clementis lappe;
> Is non so hungri hounde in Hertfordschire
> Durst lape of the levynges, so unlovely thei smaughte.

> (B.V.344–63)

[There was laughing and scowling and 'Let go the cup!', and they sat so till evensong, singing now and then, till Glutton had englobed a gallon and a gill. His guts began to grumble like two greedy sows; he pissed a pottle – two quarts – in the time it takes to say a paternoster and blew his little round horn at his back-bone's end, so that all who heard that horn, held their noses after and wished it had been wiped with a wisp of gorse. He could neither step nor stand until he had his staff ... and when he drew towards the door, his eyes dimmed and he stumbled on the threshold and threw to the earth. Clement the cobbler caught him by the middle, to lift him up, and laid him across his knees; but Glutton was a great big fellow, grim in the lifting, and he coughed up a caudel in Clement's lap. There is no hound so hungry in Hertfordshire that it would dare lap up those leavings, they tasted so unlovely.]

To the delinquent world thus pictured in the Seven Sins a
penance is given: the penitents are to make a pilgrimage to St
Truth. For Langland saw sin as a failure in truth and love, a
failure for which a sort of bloody-minded ignorance was
partly responsible, it would seem; but a change of heart could
change the bloody mind, and his sinners showed themselves
eager for their pilgrimage:

> A thousand of men tho throngen togideris,
> Wepynge and weylyng for here wykkide dedis;
> Criede upward to Crist and to this clene Modir
> To have grace to seke Treuthe; God leve that hy moten!
>
> (A.V.251–4)

[A thousand men then thronged together, weeping and wailing for their
wicked deeds; cried upward to Christ and to his clean Mother, to have
grace to seek Truth. God give them leave to do so!]

But their ignorance remained with them; few were so wise as
to know the way, and they 'blustered forth as beasts over hills
and streams' (A.VI.2), pretty well at random. Presently they
met with a palmer, one of those perpetually globe-trotting,
trophy-laden pilgrim-tourists, of the shrine-collecting type,
who seemed to have visited every holy place on earth; so they
ask him the way to St Truth. He is the last of Langland's
figures of satirical comedy in this part of the poem, and is here
introduced, with a technique typical of medieval art, to make
an explosion of derisive laughter immediately before a
moment of solemnity, thus creating the easy step from the
ridiculous to the sublime; for this is the moment for the entry
into the poem of Piers Plowman:

> 'Knowist thou ought a corseint,' quath thei, 'that men callen
>   Treuthe?
> Canst thou wisse us they wey where that wy dwellith?'
> 'Nay, so me God helpe', seide the gome thanne.
> 'I saugh nevere palmere with pik ne with scrippe
> Axen aftir hym, er now in this place.'
> '*Petir*', *quath a ploughman and putte forth his hed,*
> '*I knowe hym as kyndely as clerk doth his bokis.*'
> *Clene Conscience and Wyt kende me to his place,*
> *And dede me sure hym sithe to serve him for evere;*
> *Bothe sowe and sette while I swynke mighte.*
> *I have ben his folewere al this fourty wynter!*'
>
> (A.VI.21–30)

['Do you know a sainted body', said they, 'that people call Truth? Can you inform us of the way to where the creature lives?' 'No, so help me God', said the fellow then, 'I never saw a palmer with staff and scrip ask after him until now and in this place!' *'Peter!' said a plowman, and put forth his head,' I know him as naturally as a cleric knows his books! Clean Conscience and natural Intelligence told me the way and bound me afterwards to serve him for ever, both to sow and to plant as long as I could work. I have been his follower all these forty winters!'*]

Piers knows the way to Truth, first in the simplest sense of knowing and doing honest, faithful work; but he also knows the more spiritual way through meekness and obedience to the Commandments, that leads to Langland's grand criterion, the love of Our Lord. Piers says:

> 'Ye mote go thorugh meknesse, both men and wyves,
> Til ye come into consience that crist wyte the sothe,
> That ye loue hym levere thanne the lif in youre hertis;
> And thanne youre neighebours next in none wise apeire
> Otherwise thanne thou woldist men wroughte to thiselve.'
>
> (A.VI.48–52)

[You must go through meekness, both men and women, till you come into knowledge that Christ knows the truth, that you love him more dearly than the life in your hearts, and then your neighbours next, in no way to injure them, or do otherwise that you would wish people to do unto you.]

If you follow this way, says Piers, you shall come to a Court as clear as the sun, whose moat is mercy, who walls are wit to keep out evil will, whose crenellations are Christendom and whose buttresses are belief, roofed with love, guarded by grace; and the tower in which Truth is, is up towards the sun:

> He may do with the day sterre what hym dere likith;
> Deth dar not do thing that he defendith.
>
> (A.VI.80–81)

['He may do with the day-star what seems best to him; death dares do nothing that he forbids.' The day-star, I think, here means Lucifer.]

And if grace grants that you may enter this Court:

> Thou shalt se treuthe himself wel sitte in thin herte
> And lere the for to love, and hise lawes holden.
>
> (A.VI.93–4)

[You shall see Truth himself truly sitting in your heart, and he shall teach you how to love, and keep his laws.]

Truth is not only in his heavenly tower, but also in our hearts, for we are made in His image, and it is He who teaches us how to love.

The pilgrims find all this too difficult for them, and beg Piers to be their guide; and he consents, but asks them, before they set out, to help him plough his half-acre. So the poem turns from the problem of sin to the problem of hunger in a Christian world, for the 'half-acre' is an emblem of England under the threat of famine, as it was, after the Black Death; and the pilgrims are set to work to provide food for the community. Work is also prayer, and honest work is truth, feeding the hungry is love. As a reward for their work, Hunger is sent away, and Piers receives a Pardon from Truth Himself, for him and his heirs, 'for evermore aftir' (A.VIII.4), a pardon for sin perpetually available.

Then comes the climax, both in drama and significance, of this first great section of the poem; all critics agree as to its striking poetic force; no two wholly agree as to its significance. What happens is this. Piers is standing with the document containing Truth's pardon in his hand, not yet unrolled. A priest in the crowd, supposing him ignorant of Latin, offers to construe it for him into English:

> And Peris at his preyour the pardoun unfoldith,
> And I behynde hem bothe beheld al the bulle.
> In two lynes it lay and nought o lettre more,
> And was writen right thus in witnesse of truethe:
> *Et qui bona egerunt ibunt in vitam eternam;*
> *Qui vero mala in ignem eternum.*

(A.VIII.91–6)

[And Piers at his prayer unfolds the pardon, and I, behind them both, saw the whole bull. In two lines it lay, not a single letter more, and was written exactly thus, in witness of truth: Those who did good shall go into eternal life, but those who did evil into eternal fire.]

This baleful statement (which comes from the end of the Athanasian Creed) is no pardon, as the priest instantly points out; it demands an eye for an eye and a tooth for a tooth. So Piers tore it in pieces.

And Piers for pure tene pulde it assondir
And seide '*Si ambulavero in medio umbre mortis,*
Non timebo mala, quoniam tu mecum es'

(A.VIII.101–3)

[And Piers, 'for pure teen' tore it asunder and said 'Though I should
walk in the midst of the shadow of death, I shall fear no evil, for thou art
with me'.]

What is the meaning of '*pure teen*'? Why did he tear the
Pardon asunder? Here begin the enigmas, the inward
mysteries of this extraordinary poem, upon which hardly two
critics can be found perfectly to agree. '*Teen*' can mean almost
any shade of feeling of sorrow, distress, disappointment,
anger or lament. The tearing of the Pardon, which, as a piece
of imaginative story-telling, seems so superbly, so
unexpectedly fitting, as a piece of allegory bursts with
ambiguity. Was it a pardon or was it not? Had Truth really
sent it, or was it a cunning fraud, like the pardons of so many
Pardoners? And what did Piers think of it? His gesture of
tearing it has invited many explanations, and this may be the
reason why it is left out in the C Text; for the changes made by
Langland in his last revision seem to be made in order to
clarify his meanings. Be that as it may, in all three Texts a
dispute arises between Piers and the priest, and the noise of it
awakes the Dreamer, who finds himself 'meatless and
moneyless in the Malvern Hills', wondering, like his readers,
what his vision can have meant.

III. DO-WEL, DO-BET AND DO-BEST

The poem now leads us through a wilderness of disputation
that seeks to solve the overwhelming question posed by the
Pardon. If our salvation depends on our 'doing well' (*bona
agere*), what does 'doing well' involve? On this quest the
Dreamer-poet now sets out, but has no Piers to guide him; for
Piers vanishes with his first vision and does not return to
comfort and instruct him for many a long Passus.

The first disputants the Dreamer meets with are a couple of
Friars, and they remind him, quoting the *Book of Proverbs*,

that even the just man sins seven times a day. If he sins, how can he be 'doing well'? If the just are lost, who then can be saved? So what can be the efficacy of the Pardon of Truth? Where is the catch? In his triadic mind the Dreamer's first question now multiplies itself by three, and the quest continues not only for doing well, but also for doing better and doing best. Many are the allegorical phantoms and figures he consults, and his triple question proliferates in their answers and his own conjectures into tissues of theological speculation. What are the merits of the Active, what of the Contemplative Life? Can Learning save the soul? Does not Predestination foredoom us from everlasting to election or to damnation? What are the relative values of Faith and Works? Are the Righteous Heathen (like Aristotle and Trajan) saved? Why? How is it that all Nature obeys Reason, except Mankind? And, as he marvels at the natural world, the tediums of disputation (so fascinating to medieval clerisy) are lifted for a moment, and we hear a kind of poetry that Wordsworth, had he known it, might have envied:

> Briddes I bihelde that in buskes made nestes;
> Hadde nevere wye witte to worche the leest.
> I hadde wonder at whom and where the pye lerned
> To legge the stykkes in whiche she leyeth and bredeth . . .
> Moche merveilled me what maister thei hadde,
> And who taughte hem on trees to tymbre so heighe,
> That noither buirn ne beste may her briddes rechen.
> And sythen I loked upon the see, and so forth upon the sterres . . .
> I seigh floures in the fritthe, and her faire coloures,
> And how amonge the grene grasse grewe so many hewes . . .
> Ac that moste moeved me and my mode chaunged,
> That resoun rewarded and reuled alle bestes,
> Save man and his make . . .   (B.XI.336–62)

[Birds I beheld that in bushes made their nests; no man ever had skill enough to make the least of them. I wondered from whom and where the magpie learned to place the twigs in which she lays her eggs, and breeds . . . Much I marvelled who their master was, who taught them to build their nests so high among the trees, so that neither boy nor beast might reach their young. And then I looked out to sea and upwards to the stars . . . I saw the flowers in the forest and their lovely colours, and saw how many shades of colour grew among the grasses . . . but what most moved me, and changed my mood, was that reason rewarded and ruled all animals, except man and his mate.]

Through all those questionings the steady search for a definition of the three good lives continues and gradually their meaning is felt to accumulate into a quite unsystematic yet feeling body of Christian wisdom, in which Conscience takes the lead and the virtues of patience, humility, sincerity and peace of heart have first place, and the acceptance of poverty is commended, for it is the gift of God; and so we move towards the greater virtues of Faith and Hope, presented in the shapes of Abraham and Moses, with whom the Dreamer has a long colloquy, till it is interrupted by their coming upon the man who fell among thieves; and there they meet the Good Samaritan, who is Charity.

Faith and Hope, like the priest and Levite in the parable, draw away ('like duck from falcon'), but the Good Samaritan tends the man, wounded by thieves. This wounded man is no other than the human race itself, that fell among thieves in Paradise, being robbed of Eden by Satan; and nothing can cure him:

> Neither Feith ne fyn Hope, so festred ben his woundis,
> Without the blode of a barn, borne of a mayde.
>
> (B.XVII.92–3)

[Neither Faith nor fine Hope, so festered are his wounds, without the blood of a child born of a virgin.]

So, at least, the Samaritan tells the Dreamer; and when he has further instructed him in the trinity-in-unity of God, by images such as that of a candle, its wick and flame, he sets spurs to his mule and rides off like the wind, towards Jerusalem.

Now the long enquiry is over and the Dreamer is readied for the supreme vision. It is Lent, and he sleeps; and in dream he hears the singing of children in the streets of Jerusalem on the first Palm Sunday of all:

> Of gerlis and of *gloria laus* gretly me dremed,
> And how *asanna* by orgonye olde folke songen.
> One semblable to the Samaritan, and some del to Piers the
>   Plowman,
> Barfote on an asse bakke botelees cam prykye,
> Wythoute spores other spere, spakliche he loked,

As is the kynde of a Knyghte that cometh to be dubbed,
To geten hem gylte spores, or galoches ycouped.
Thanne was Faith in a fenestre, and cryde 'A! *fili david*!'.
Olde Jewes of Jerusalem for joye thei songen
    Benedictus qui venit in nomine domini.
Thanne I frayned at Faith what al that fare bemente,
And who sholde jouste in Jherusalem. 'Jhesus', he seyde,
'And fecche that the fende claymeth, Piers fruit the plowman.'
'Is Piers in this place?' quod I, and he preynte on me,
'This Jhesus of his gentrice wole juste in Piers armes,
In his helme and in his haberioun, *humana natura* ...'

                                                    (B.XVIII.8–23)

[Of children and of glory and praise greatly I dreamed, and how old folk sang Hosanna to the sound of an organ. One similar to the Samaritan, and somewhat to Piers Plowman, came riding, unshod, on the back of an ass, without spur or spear; gallant he looked, as is the nature of a Knight coming to be dubbed, to win his gilt spurs and his slashed shoes. Then Faith was in a window and cried 'Ah, Son of David!' Old Jews of Jerusalem sang for joy 'Blessed is he that comes in the name of the Lord!' Then I asked Faith what all this fuss was about and who should joust in Jerusalem. 'Jesus', he said, 'and he will fetch the fruit of Piers the Plowman which the Fiend claims.' 'Is Piers in this place?' said I, and he gazed at me: 'This Jesus, of his nobility, will joust in Piers' armour, in his helmet and habergeon, human nature ...']

The sublimity of vision and colloquialism of language unite to carry us vividly to the scene described, and onwards to the trial before Pilate and to the crucifixion itself, which has the stamp of a gospel's authority:

'*Consummatum est*', quod Cryst, and comsed forto swowe,
Pitousliche and pale as a prisoun that deyeth;
The lorde of lyf and of lighte tho leyed his eyen togideres.
The daye for drede withdrowe, and derke bicam the sonne,
The wal wagged and clef, and al the worlde quaved ...
Some seyde that he was goddes sone that so faire deyde,
    Vere filius dei erat iste.

                                                    (B.XVIII.57–68)

['It is finished', said Christ, and began to swoon, piteously and pale, like a prisoner dying; the Lord of life and of light laid his eyelids together. Day withdrew in dread and dark became the sun; the wall shook and cleft in two, and the whole world trembled. Some said it was God's son that died so fairly, 'truly this was the son of God'.]

But this triumph of eye-witness poetry, that reaches back

towards *The Dream of the Rood,* five centuries before, and is, in this description, an equal masterpiece, now moves on to an even greater effort of imagination, in picturing the Harrowing of Hell. Thither the Dreamer descends, and sees Christ's approach to Hell's barriers, as a Voice speaking from a light, shining upon that darkness. So it is also seen in the Apocryphal Gospel, known as *The Acts of Pilate,* where Langland undoubtedly found it:

> Efte the Lighte bad unlouke, and Lucifer answered,
> What lorde artow?' quod Lucifer, *'quis est iste?'*
> *'Rex glorie',* the Lighte sone seide,
> 'And lorde of myghte and of mayne, and al manere vertues
>   *dominus virtutum*:
> Dukes of this dym place, anon undo this yates,
> That Cryst may come in, the Kynges Sone of Hevene.'
> And with that breth helle brak, with Beliales barres;
> For any wye or warde, wide opene the yatis.
> Patriarkes and prophetes, *populus in tenebris,*
> Songen Seynt Johanes songe, *Ecce Agnus Dei.*
> Lucyfer loke ne myghte, so lyghte hym ableynte.
> And tho that Owre Lorde loved, into his lighte he laughte,
> And seyde to Sathan, 'Lo, here my soule to amendes
> For alle synneful soules, to save tho that ben worthy;
> Myne thei be and of me, I may the bette hem clayme ...
>
> (B.XVIII.313–27)

[Again the Light bade them unlock, and Lucifer answered: 'What Lord are thou?' said Lucifer, 'what is this one?' 'The King of Glory', the Light soon said, 'and Lord of might and of power, Lord of all virtues. Dukes of this dim place, open the gates at once, that Christ may come in, Son of the King of Heaven.' And with that breath, Hell broke, with Belial's bars; wide open were the gates, in spite of man or guard. Patriarchs and prophets, the people that sat in darkness, sang St John's song, 'Behold the Lamb of God'. Lucifer could not look, the Light so blinded him. And those that Our Lord loved, he caught up into his light, and said to Satan 'See here my soul in amends for all sinful souls, to save those that are worthy; mine they are, and of me, I may claim them the better.']

The Passus ends with jubilation in Heaven; Mercy and Truth meet together, Righteousness and Peace kiss each other, and these four 'wenches', as Langland calls them in his salubrious style when they first appear, are left dancing till Easter dawns, when the poet wakes, and calls to his wife and daughter:

Tyl the daye dawed this damaiseles daunced,
That men rongen to the resurexioun, and right with that
   I waked,
And called Kitte my wyf, and Kalote my daughter –
'Ariseth and reverenceth goddes resurrection,
And crepeth to the crosse on knees, and kisseth it for a juwel!
For goddes blissed body it bar for owre bote,
And it afereth the fende, for such is the myghte,
May no grusly gost glyde ther it shadweth!'

                            (B.XVIII.424–31)

[Till the day dawned these damsels danced, and men rang the bells for
the resurrection, and instantly I awoke and called Kitty my wife and
Calotte my daugther – Rise, and reverence God's resurrection, and
creep to the cross on your knees, and kiss it for a jewel! For it bore God's
blessed body for our good, and it puts fear into the fiend; such is its
power that no grisly spirit may glide where it overshadows!]

The eighteenth Passus of the B Text is the top of
Langland's writing in this vein, our greatest Christian poetry:
yet, when you compare it with Glutton in the ale-house, you
hear the same vigorous voice, uttering things as sharply seen
and heard, in the same simple vigorous speech. The line
'Lucyfer loke ne myghte, so lyghte hym ableynte' is in the
same tone of language as that which describes Glutton in a
somewhat similar condition:

And whan he drowgh to the dore, thanne dymmed his eighen,
He stumbled on the thresshewolde, an threwe to the erthe.

The blinding of Lucifer by the blaze of Christ is as realistic a
detail, in an apocalyptic mood, as that of Glutton, by mere
drunkenness, in a mood of sardonic satire. It is the range of
mind supported by an equal strength of speech that makes
this poet and his poem unlike any other; he has both lion and
lamb in him, and hyena too. To take other examples, here he
is describing the theological sophistries of well-fed dons on
their dais at dinner:

Thus thei dryvele at her deyse the deite to knowe,
And gnawen god with the gorge whan her gutte is fulle.
                                (B.X.56–7)

[Thus they drivel on their dais, discussing the deity, and gnaw God in
their throats when their gut is full.]

and this triumphant poetical rage issues from the same
Christian ferocity as Langland's tenderness, in the same
language of colloquial power:

> The most needy aren oure neighebores, an we nyme good hede,
> As prisones in puttes, and poure folke in cotes,
> Charged with children and chef lordes rente,
> That thei with spynnyge may spare, spenen hit in hous-hyre,
> Bothe in mylk and in mele to make with papelotes,
> To aglotye with here gurles, that greden after fode ...
>
> (C.X.71–6)

[The most needy are our neighbours, if we take careful heed, such as
prisoners in pits, and poor folk in hovels, charged with children and rent
to their landlords, so that what they can spare out of spinning they must
spend on house-hire, and on milk and meal to make a sort of porridge
with, to glut their children, crying out for food.]

With the Harrowing of Hell (as it is called) ends Do-Bet, and
the poem moves on to the Resurrection; once again Christ is
seen in Piers, for the Dreamer, falling asleep, suddenly
dreams that he is in church hearing Mass, and that Piers the
Plowman comes in, painted in blood, with a cross in his hand,
before the common people:

> And righte lyke in alle lymes to owre lorde Jhesu;
> And thanne called I Conscience to kenne me the sothe.
> 'Is this Jhesus the Juster?', quod I, 'that Juwes did to deth?
> Or is it Pieres the Plowman? Who paynted hym so rede?'
> Quod Conscience, and kneled tho, 'this aren Pieres armes,
> His coloures and his cote-armure, ac he that cometh so blody
> Is Cryst with his crosse, conqueroure of crystene'.
>
> (B.XIX.6–14)

[And right like, in all his limbs, to our Lord Jesus; and then I called
Conscience to know the truth. 'Is this Jesus the Jouster?' I said, 'Or is it
Piers the Plowman? Who painted him so red?' Said Conscience then,
and knelt, 'These are Piers' arms, his colours and coat-armour, but he
that comes so bloody is Christ with his cross, conqueror of Christians'.]

And it is by the power of that conquest that the Church is
built; Jesus, fighting in the armour of Piers, has done well,
done better and done best; by his victory the sacrament of
Pardon is established:

And whan this dede was done, *Dobest* he taughte,
And yaf Pieres power and pardoun he graunted,
To alle mannere men, mercy and foryyfnes,
And yaf hym myghte to assoylye men of alle manere synnes*
In convenant that thei come, and knowleche to paye,
To Pieres pardon that plowman, *redde quod debes*.
(B.XIX.177–82. The asterisked line from C.XXII.185, as the B
                                    Text is here corrupt.)

[And when his deed was done he taught Do-Best, and gave Piers power,
and granted pardon to all manner of men, mercy and forgiveness, and
gave power to absolve men of all manner of sins, on condition that they
come, and acknowledge to pay the debt which you owe to the Pardon of
Piers Plowman.]

And so the enigma of the Pardon sent to Piers is solved; Truth
had bought it on Calvary, and had granted it to the race that
fell among thieves, to wipe away their sins, *provided* that they
did their share, and paid their debt of confession, and
whatever else they owed to the sacraments and the Church;
that done, they would be doing well, however many times a
day they, like the just man, had fallen. But they must do their
part too. Grace would be with them.

After the Ascension comes the descent of the Dove 'in the
likeness of lightning', upon Piers and his companions; for
Christ, having put on Piers 'our suit' of human nature, now
puts it off, leaving Piers on earth to build the barn that is to
hold his harvest of souls; the Holy Spirit directs the building
of this barn: it is to be called 'Unity' – Holy Church in
English:

'Ayeines thi greynes', quod Grace, 'begynneth for to ripe,
Ordeigne the an hous, Piers, to herberwe in thi cornes.'
'By God! Grace', quod Piers, 'ye moten yive tymbre,
And ordeyne that hous ar ye hennes wende.'
And Grace gave hym the crosse, with the croune of thornes,
That cryst upon Calvarye for mankynde on pyned,
And of his baptesme and blode that he bledde on Rode
He made a maner morter, and mercy it highte.
And therewith Grace bigan to make a good foundement,
And watteled it and walled it with his peynes and his passioun,
And of al holywrit he made a rofe after,
And called that hous Unité, holicherche on Englisshe.
                                    (B.XIX.313–25)

['Against the time when your grains begin to ripen', said Grace, 'ordain yourself a house, Piers, to garner your corn.' 'By God, Grace', said Piers, 'you must give me timber and ordain that house before you go away.' And Grace gave him the cross with the crown of thorns on which Christ suffered for mankind on Calvary; and of his baptism and of the blood that He bled on the cross, he made a kind of mortar, and it was called Mercy. And with it Grace began to make a good foundation, and wattled and walled it with His pains and passion, and of all holy writ he made a roof afterwards and called that house Unity, Holy Church in English.]

And so the simple Peter Ploughman of the first vision, in virtue of The Incarnation and of Pentecost, has become Peter, the rock on which Christ founded his Church, and is to make of it a barn to store the grain of Christian souls, from fields that are white to harvest.

With such a climax many poets would have felt they had reached the end of their vision and would be ready to lay down their pens. But Langland saw further; he was not celebrating a victory but a desolation. For Antichrist was still to come, with his seven allies, the Seven Sins, and with Old Age and Death and all the terrors of eschatology at his heels, to upturn and destroy the House of Unity and drive out the fools that had taken refuge in it. He is the great enemy of Truth, and the Friars are in his following:

> ... anon ich fel asleope,
> And mette ful merveilousliche that, in a mannes forme,
> Antecrist cam thenne, and al the crop of treuthe
> Turned tyte up-so-doun, and overtilte the rote,
> And made fals to springe and sprede, and spede menne neodes.
> In eche cuntreie ther he cam, he cutte away treuthe,
> And gert gyle growe ther as he a god were.
> Freres folweden that feonde, for he yaf hem copes,
> And religiouse reverencede hym, and rongen here belles ...
>
> (C.XXIII.51–9)

[... presently I fell asleep, and I dreamed most marvellously that, in a man's form, Antichrist then came and at once turned upside down all Truth's crop, and overturned the root, and made False to spring and spread and suffice men's needs. In each country he came to, he cut away Truth, and caused Guile to grow there, as if he were a god. Friars followed that fiend, for he gave them copes and the Religious reverenced him and rung their bells.]

In this destruction and betrayal of the Church the poem ends, and Conscience is left to walk 'as wide as the world lasts' to seek Piers Plowman, who once again has vanished from the poem:

'Bi cryste', quod Conscience tho, 'I wil bicome a pilgryme,
And walken as wyde as al the worlde lasteth,
To seke Piers the Plowman that pryde may destruye,
And that freres hadde a fyndyng that for nede flateren,
And contrepleteth me, Conscience. Now Kynde me avenge,
And sende me happe and hele til I have Piers the Plowman!'
And sitthe he gradde after grace, til I gan wake.

(B.XXA.378–84)

['By Christ', said Conscience then, 'I will become a pilgrim, and walk as wide as the whole world lasts to seek Piers the Plowman who can destroy Pride, and that Friars may have a maintenance who now must flatter to supply their needs and counter-plead me, Conscience. Now, Nature, avenge me, and send me luck and health until I have Piers Plowman!' And then he cried out for Grace, and I awoke.]

It is hard in our days to see Friars as Langland saw them. We need Chaucer's help, and that Chronicler's byword sneer, *Hic est mendicans, ergo mendax* (This is a friar, therefore a liar). But the rest of this vision we can see well enough, a world in moral ruin, seeking some way of good life, and seeking someone who knows how to live and teach it. For Langland, at least, all was to do again; the pilgrimage to Truth had to begin once more from the beginning; and Conscience sets about it, as the Dreamer awakes.

IV. PIERS HIMSELF

It is uniquely fortunate for us that two writers of first genius, but of contrasted natures, almost exactly contemporary with each other, should both have given us a portrait of their age, in the terms of the two high centres of their culture, the Court and the Church, showing us the best things and thoughts of their day in the two languages of English poetry, the old and the new, alliteration and rhyme, at their last and first greatness. Both writers were learned in what most concerned them: Chaucer in all the flowerings of the humane spirit from

Ovid to Boccaccio, Langland in all that touched on Holy Writ: Chaucer intent on the evolving nuances of personality, Langland on the needs and qualities of the soul. Chaucer's art centred itself on romantic love, Langland's utterance on the love of Our Lord; they were both Christians, but Chaucer shows himself as pious rather than religious, with more feeling, let us say, for the Blessed Virgin than for the Holy Ghost; Langland shows little piety or sentiment, but much religious passion. He does not seek comfort but grace. In almost all things each other's opposite, they seem exactly complementary. Together they express a spiritual civilization in being; and they lived the kinds of life they describe. They have passed on the inheritance, enriching it.

They are alike in one rare faculty, though each exercises it in his own manner: the faculty for irony; Chaucer's irony is urbane, sophisticated, *nuancé*, Langland's blazing like a Hebrew prophet's, anger sauced with laughter. The objects of the great ironists are always the same in their satires – affectation and hypocrisy – and we find the same rogues and frauds held up to unfading mockery in both Langland and Chaucer – monks, friars, pardoners, summoners, and other tricksters and double-talkers. Most of these characters have now disappeared from the English scene, or at least into other professions; but the power to see them as they appeared to the searching secular eye of Chaucer and the no less searching, but mystical eye of Langland, gives us a binocular, stereoscopic vision of the body and soul of their Age.

Chaucer, however, has left us no character, among all his many, that embodies the whole duty of man or woman. Rulership may perhaps be seen in his Duke Theseus, wife-manship in his Wife of Bath; a diffused aristocratic principle of *largesse* runs through all he wrote, less as a principle for us to follow than as a noble infection for us to take, if we are capable of it. He has made no myth for us unless, unknowingly, the myth of 'Merry England'. In all other ways he has out-classed Langland easily enough during the six centuries between us and them; everything has gone his way – the language, the verse, the literary conventions, the attitudes and interests, secularisation, humanism, the cult of character, romance, everything. He is an early modern, Langland a late medieval, wrapped up in marvellous but outdated allegories, as if by the mists of Malvern Hills. He seems a poet mainly for medievalists, at first sight.

Yet these are superficial contrasts, and greatness in poetry is not affected by any of them; Langland is a great poet too, and in one respect has a greater hold on our imaginative attention, in that he faces despair. He ends his poem in a desolation as ruinous as that in *The Waste Land*; the Church has tumbled down, the faithful are scattered, bamboozled or seduced, and nothing is left but the individual conscience, by itself, seeking grace 'as wide as the world lasts', crying out for Piers Plowman.

What is this enigmatic figure whose identity so strangely merges with that of Christ and St Peter? To what reality in experience does it correspond? From the character of the poem and from the number of its manuscripts, one would infer some spiritual need that many felt, but which died away or found satisfaction in some other image in the seventeenth century, when *Piers Plowman* sank into oblivion. Milton knew of it, but its language was too difficult and its matter too gothic to suit the taste of that time.

It is tempting to think of Piers as a medieval image comparable to the image of *The Dance of Death*, so popular in the fifteenth century, or like those double-decker family tombs of the same period, where angels support a weight of heraldry in honour of some alabaster lord or lady recumbent on the upper storey, while below there lies the sculpture of a rotting corpse, to show what six months of death will do, even to princes. If these images are parallel to that of Piers, we may think of him as an emblem from an age gone by that can no longer satisfy any more serious need than a wish to understand the art of the later Middle Ages. And I think that if *Piers Plowman* had never undergone revision, that is how we would think of him. He would seem no more than what he is in the A Text, an ideal farmer, a noble peasant, another manifestation of the convention that gave us the virtuous Plowman of Chaucer's *Prologue*, but carried it rather further in its claims for his usefulness to society and for the purity of his vision of God.

But when Langland revised his poem to touch Piers with

divinity, he lifted it out of Time, so that the convention of an Age became a universal and the noble Christian peasant a type of Christ. By this he gave form to an idea often reasserted in his poem, that man is made in God's image of Truth and Love (their fountainhead his heart), and the corollary faith that at one point in history God was made in man's image. The *Imitatio Christi* is a thought to which Western imagination perpetually returns for renewal; it tells us 'what we need to be', and this is especially true of Ages that have a keen sense of spiritual need. The idea of life as a pilgrimage makes good sense with it, for Christians claim of Christ that he is the Way as well as the Truth; these concepts are embodied in Langland's imagery: Do-well, Do-Better and Do-Best, for which Piers stands, are ways of life that Christ himself had lived, so Langland tells us (B.XIX.104–89); the pilgrimage towards them is our quest for Piers, under the guidance of Grace.

Chaucer's use of the imagery of pilgrimage is not so urgent: he makes of it a happy human holiday, something in the manner of Chesterton's poem; he is casual and confident that it is possible

> To shewe yow the wey, in this viage,
> Of thilke parfit glorious pilgrimage
> That highte Jerusalem celestial,

while not neglecting the fact that 'there is good news yet to hear and fine things to be seen, Before we go to Paradise by way of Kensal Green'. Langland's urgency has only once been matched, in *The Pilgrim's Progress*. Langland's pilgrimage is a quest, Bunyan's an escape.

From the furthest extremes of Christian theology, these great poets meet in their knowledge of the world and of the soul's need in the struggle of light with darkness; it is a Light that harrows Hell, and, at the crucifixion 'Lyf and deth in this derknesse, her one fordoth her other' (B.XVIII.65) [Life and death in this darkness, each is destroying the other], and it is 'Life, life, eternal life' that Christian seeks, as he thrusts his fingers in his ears and flees from the City of Destruction. Both Langland and Bunyan see the world as a wilderness and dream of a remedy, a salvation: many are the parallels and the contrasts between their dreams. Bunyan's pilgrim is allowed to reach and enter the Gate of the Celestial City: 'Then I heard in my Dream that all the Bells in the City Rang for Joy.' Langland's pilgrims are dispersed in their desolated world, in which Conscience is left alone, calling after Grace in the search for Piers.

For all the differences between them, Langland and Bunyan are natural Christian poets of an equal urgency and an equal vision of man and his soul in the wilderness of the world, that is also Vanity Fair, the Fair Field of folk; where Langland overgoes Bunyan is that he has shown us Christ in Piers and Piers in Christ, a thing we need to see.

We see a third, and a more modern, picture of the world's wilderness in Samuel Beckett's *Waiting for Godot* (1956), for we are back to that basic vision once again, though the urgency is lost, since the hope is lost. Yet if the old hope is lost, the old criterion remains:

Vladimir: Your boots. What are you doing with your boots?
Estragon: (*turning to look at his boots*) I'm leaving them there. (*Pause*) Another will come, just as ... as ... as me, but with smaller feet, and they'll make him happy.
Vladimir: But you can't go barefoot!
Estragon: Christ did.
Vladimir: Christ! What's Christ got to do with it? You're not going to compare yourself to Christ!
Estragon: All my life I've compared myself to him.

It seems that in our Age there are others that have Estragon's criterion in mind; I quote from a recent short story from America:[3]

'What do people mean when they say somebody is their personal hero?' It comes sooner than I expect. 'Your hero is what you need to be.'
'Then is Jesus your hero?'
'Why do you think that?'
'You say you are scared of dying. Jesus is the one that did not die.' ... 'I think your hero has to be a man. Was Jesus a man?'
'No sir. He was God disguised.'
'Well, that's it you see. You would not stand a chance of being God – need to or not – so you pick somebody you have got half a chance of measuring up to.'

A like and yet a different return to the same image can be seen in David Storey's *Radcliffe* (1963).

> 'But if Christ came to earth as man, why didn't He come as a man we know? Why didn't He use His sex? Isn't it from sex that all our problems and frustrations arise? Yet He refused to acknowledge it by His own example.'

Can eighteenth- or nineteenth-century fiction or drama show parallels for these three passages? I do not think so. No one, outside the pulpit, seems to have felt the need for questionings so extreme. *Piers Plowman* was not republished between 1561 and 1842, and was even then considered as little more than an obscure curiosity of literature; and it remained so until Skeat's great editions began to make it famous once again. It has reawakened in a world more ready for it; in those glossier days before our century began, the need for an image of man raised to the power of Christ may not have been so generally felt. But now the time gives it proof.

NOTES

1. All quotations from the A Text are taken, with slight typographical modification, from the edition by G. Kane (1960). Quotations from the B and C Texts are taken, similarly modified, from the editions by W.W. Skeat (Early English Texts Society, 1869, 1873).
2. Now no longer visible, having been piped to a table-water factory. Bright believed it to be the 'bourne' mentioned in line 8 of the quotation from the opening of the poem, above, beside which the poet lay down to sleep, and beheld his vision.
3. Reynolds Price, 'The Names and Faces of Heroes' (New York and London, 1963).

4

The Character of Piers Plowman Considered from the B Text*

The purpose of this essay is to show reason for believing that the character of Piers Plowman was intended as an emblem or personification of Do-wel, Do-bet and Do-best successively.

It was formerly believed that Langland's poem lacked a preconceived logical form; that the visions merged as it were fortuitously, one into the next, without a plan to determine their sequence or goal; so also the meaning of Piers, the central character, remained imprecise, a puzzle with variations each of which was more deeply mysterious than what went before. But of late the main architectural lines of the poem have been rediscovered,[1] and so it becomes possible to show that Piers himself is functionally related to that architecture, a triple caryatid supporting the whole. This is no very surprising conclusion; for Langland was not an idle allegorist seeking to beautify his verses by the dark introduction of an enigma; he created Piers to clarify his thought, not to obscure it; but because his way of thinking passed out of fashion, Piers, who was designed to embody it, became a mystery. Yet a right understanding of the person of Piers Plowman must be requisite to a right understanding of the poem named after him.

The analysis offered by Skeat showed Piers to have three significances: first 'the type of ideal honest man', secondly the Incarnate Jesus, and lastly ... 'Saint Peter the Apostle ... and this Piers was again succeeded by the Popes of Rome ... the

*Medium Ævum 2 (1933).

ambiguity is surely not very great.'² It is true the ambiguity is not great, but there seems something inconsequential in these epiphanies; the three steps do not belong to the same stairway.

Dr Jusserand maintained what is substantially the same view; he described Piers as 'a variable emblem ... now the honest man of the people, now the Pope, now Christ.'³

Dr Wells does not explicitly repudiate this by now traditional view, but he associates Piers far more significantly with the structure of the poem than did its earlier critics. He writes:

> Here for the first time we meet the *image* of the plow, in this case simply the plow of the farmer. In outward appearance at least Piers himself is no more than an overseer or even a participant in these physical labours. . . . In the *Vita de Do-Best* ... Piers and his plow once more appear, but Piers is now indubitably Christ, his plow the word of God, man the harvest and the barn the heaven of divine rest.⁴

Mr H.W. Troyer, in a still more recent explanation of Piers,⁵ derived from a study of St Thomas Aquinas, advances the interesting theory that Piers is to be understood allegorically, morally and anagogically; his exposition of the critical results that follow from this theory is illuminating; I venture to think that Piers is not so 'multifold' a symbol as he would maintain, but welcome the method of triple interpretation, the application of which is immediately fruitful. The character of Piers can be simplified beyond what Mr Troyer offers without sacrificing the allegorical, moral, and anagogical readings of his character, and yet without omitting anything stated of Piers in the B Text. I have confined my own observations to that Text; for the development of the character of Piers the incompleted A Text is insufficient, and the C Text offers some complications of re-arrangement which might cloud the immediate issue. It is therefore reasonable to adopt the B Text as the surest basis for comment at present.⁶

Mr Troyer's argument, for all its fascination, leads him towards thoughts which I cannot but believe are twentieth-rather than fourteenth-century thoughts; some of his conclusions, indeed, would have been condemned as heretical

in Langland's day and punished at the stake a few years later.
Piers Plowman, as a poem, is almost passionately orthodox,
and is, I think, impossible to reconcile with quasi-heretical
interpretation.

For instance Mr Troyer writes:

> And the plowman tearing his pardon was perhaps to be symbolic of how
> utterly futile the author felt men had made the atonement by their own
> lives, a view certainly not out of harmony with the note of despair on
> which the poem itself ends later on. Whether or not such an extreme
> interpretation is justified, it is apparent that the episode, as those
> preceding it, is one of multifold aspect.

Now such an interpretation is more than extreme; it is
impossible, at least to a Catholic such as Langland was. No
human action, whether that of an individual or of 'man the
race' (to use Mr Troyer's phrase), could possibly make the
Atonement 'utterly futile'. The Atonement was not made by
man and could not be marred by man. Again, in summing up,
Mr Troyer writes:

> Piers is a multifold symbol. He is allegorically man the race. He is
> sometimes an individual man, who is in his integrity a picture of moral
> perfection in the functions of society which the race has developed. And
> he is also the great God-man, the highest achievement of the race in the
> figure of its own redeemer.

Now, setting aside the question whether Humanitarianism
and Perfectibility are rather nineteenth- or twentieth-century
than fourteenth-century ideas, there remains what is in
essence this same heresy. It may be that Mr Troyer did not
intend his words so to be understood; but they suggest once
more the notion that the Incarnation and the Atonement were
somehow man-made (or man-marred); if we excuse the
phrase 'great God-man' for smacking somewhat of
anthropological research, we still have to reckon with the idea
that the Redemption was a *racial achievement*, something only
different *in degree* from the Great Pyramid, that Jesus was a
man upon whose birth the race might congratulate itself. But
in Catholic theology the birth of the Saviour differs not
merely in degree, but *in kind* from all other births; it was the
deliberate and only Incarnation of the Son of God, and was

irrespective of the efforts or deservings of mankind; it was an Act of Grace.

Any account of Piers which involves notions that Langland would have repudiated cannot be wholly acceptable to us; but the triple method of interpretation (allegorical, moral and anagogical), which I take to be Mr Troyer's principal contribution, can be applied without heresy and is of great value in the understanding of Piers.

II.

The allegory of Piers (I have asserted) is simply this, that he successively embodies the ideas of Do-wel, Do-bet and Do-best. These are the three stages recognised by Skeat and Jusserand, but interpreted in accordance with the design of the poem. Piers is therefore *not a man at all*, neither an individual nor an aggregate; he is the allegorical symbol for *three cumulative ways of life*. These three ways of life are exhibited in him, made incarnate; and since it is open to all human beings to live any one of them, it need not surprise us that he appears to be 'a labourer, an overseer, a king, the pope, Adam, St Peter, and Christ, sometimes individually, sometimes compositely' (to quote again from Mr Troyer's article). For to be Piers is to do well or to do better or to do best, as this essay hopes to show; once this is recognised and applied to the visions as a whole, the poem becomes harmonious and consistent, declaring itself logically, as well as psychologically, a unity.

Two lines of argument will be followed in support of this interpretation.

1. To consider, in their order, each personal entry of Piers into the poem, together with the changes that seem to occur in his nature at those entries, and to show not only that the timing of his entries corresponds with the divisions of the poem (*Visio de Petro Plowman, Vita de Do-wel, Vita de Do-bet, Vita de Do-best*), but that the changes in his nature are equally relevant to those divisions.

2. To consider the three groups of abstract virtues which

Langland laid down as appropriate to the three types of life respectively, and to show their exact correspondence to the moral qualities that are stressed in the nature of Piers step by step as it unfolds.

If these arguments can be substantiated they will be seen to lead from different premises to the same conclusion, namely that Langland intended the character of Piers to be the organ of his three abstractions, the Good Life, the Better and the Best; for such a correspondence could not happen accidentally inasmuch as Langland (as Dr Wells has demonstrated) had special genius in the disposing of the larger architectural lines of his work; a man capable of such gigantic and comprehensive planning could not without absurdity be supposed ignorant of the movements of his own hero, of their dovetailing with the main divisions of his poem and of his hero's specific possession of the abstract virtues about which he had chosen to write.

Since the contentions here advanced unite the character of Piers with the structure of the poem as a whole, some account of that structure must first be given; many of the ideas here advanced upon this matter will be recognised as identical with those put forward by Dr Wells in his invaluable article referred to above. I would avoid this recapitulation of what is already known were it possible to conduct my argument without it; but the Piers-idea is so manifestly built into the whole edifice of Langland's thought that I am obliged to repeat some of the conclusions of Dr Wells; and this I shall do without further acknowledgment or restitution by footnote. I can but hope he will not echo the words of Repentance to Covetyse:

> That was no restitucioun,' quod Repentance . 'but a robberers
> thefte;
> Thow haddest be better worthy . be hanged therfore
> Than for al that . that thow hast here shewed.

III.

The poem is divided into four major sections usually designated as the *Visio de Petro Plowman* (Prol. to VII inclusive), *Vita de Do-wel* (VIII to XV inclusive), the *Vita de Do-bet* (XVI to XVIII inclusive) and the *Vita de Do-best* (XIX to the end). Of these sections the least obviously picturesque, and therefore the most generally neglected, is the second, the *Vita de Do-wel*. Yet this *Do-wel* expounds the basic doctrines of all Langland's thought, and for an understanding enjoyment of his poem it is the critical section, as will be presently shown.

The first section (the *Visio de Petro Plowman*) is a study of human life in the Active World as it existed before Langland's eyes; it concerns itself particularly with the following problems (in brief analysis):

1. What, in this business of honest and dishonest money-making that seems to keep the Field of Folk on the move, is to be rendered to Cæsar, and what to God? (Prol., I)
2. How is a corrupt administration to be set to rights? (II, III, IV.)
3. How is society in general to purify itself? (V)
4. The problem of Labour versus Famine and the twin problems of the Shirkers and the Impotent. (VI)
5. Whether the solutions offered to these problems as they arise are pleasing to God, and if so, what is the meaning of Pardon, and what disciplines or virtues underlie these solutions? (VII) *This sub-section may be regarded as the hinge upon which the poem turns towards an abstract consideration of Do-wel, Do-bet and Do-best.*

All these problems are considered *sub specie æternitatis*, and are riders to the principal problem (which is the Grand Subject of the whole poem), namely, how is man to work out his Salvation? Thus far the first major section, which concerns the existing order of the Active Life in the World, as lived by all men, but particularly as lived by the Laity.

The second section, the *Vita de Do-wel*, immediately following, holds the keys to all the others. This section, under the guise of a vague allegorical autobiography of the poet,[7] considers (1) what abstract virtues should underlie the Active Life, and whether they can win Salvation; (and in the answers which this study suggests lie the full understanding of what has gone before in the *Visio*); (2) the virtues that should underlie the Contemplative or Clerkly Life (i.e. the *Vita de Do-bet*); and (3) the virtues that should underlie the Pontifical Life or Life of Spiritual Authority, which is the Life of Do-best.

The whole of his great section (*Do-wel*), and all these disquisitions are seasoned as well with Langland's mental autobiography as with a running commentary on the existing state of affairs (with particular reference to the clergy and their shortcomings), and on problems germane to the central argument, such as the possibility of Salvation for pre-Christian 'clerks' (like Aristotle), or 'worthies' (like Trajan), and the general unreasonableness of man in the indulging of his instincts, contrasted with the notorious decency and sweet moderation of the lower creatures.

This section, then, expounds the true principles upon which to base human conduct if Salvation is to be attained, whether by living the 'lewed' life of Do-wel, the 'clerkly' life of Do-bet, or the 'episcopal' life of Do-best; thus it supplies the *moral argument* upon which the whole fabric of vision and allegory is based. Unless that argument be grasped it is almost impossible to understand what the poem as a whole is driving at; and because it has been neglected, Langland has no general fame other than as the author of discontented and disconnected satires, somewhat lively in their presentation, but defaced by a dreary intermingling of prolonged theologisings; matter enough for social historians and philologists, but no great matter for those who ask of a poem some largely imagined and harmonious unit of vision. And yet, in this precise respect, *Troilus and Criseyde* itself is not greater than *Piers Plowman*.

The third section (*Do-bet*) is simply the embodiment of Langland's foregoing theories of the Clerkly Virtues, shown allegorically in a narrative; and the fourth section (*Do-best*) allegorically embodies the Life of Authority, and the need for it in a world beset by corruption from within the human heart, and menaced by the assault of Antichrist from without.

Of these four sections, as has been said, the second is a kind of abstract of the other three, or, if that is too inaccurate an expression, it has a more-than-narrative relationship to them;

it is their exposition. Of the other three, the first is concerned with, or as if dedicated to, God the Father; the next (*Do-bet*) with God the Son, and the last with God the Holy Ghost, proceeding from Them just as *Do-best* proceeds from *Do-wel* and *Do-bet*: as if God in creating the world was Active, in redeeming the world was Contemplative, and in sustaining the spiritual life of Christendom was Authoritative. This last is the anagogical aspect of the poem.

IV.

Into this structure, at certain premeditated points, irrupts the figure of Piers Plowman. Perhaps in no other word of equal scope does the Hero appear so seldom in person; but every appearance in this poem has a calculated significance.

Piers first 'put forth his hed' (V. 544) when the secular world of Action had confessed its sins and was attempting satisfaction for them (the third part of a valid penance) by seeking St Truth. This would seem a late entry for the hero; but if he be accepted as an emblem of Do-wel, of the Active Unlettered Life as it should be, there is no earlier point at which he could have made his appearance; for a glance at the analysis of the first section (above) shows that the first three sub-sections are quite general, and deal with all the world, not omitting the governing class, and as such are not amenable to the simple solution of 'Do-wel', but ask the higher wisdom of Holy Church who offers advanced reflections on the purposes of human life under the hand of God; her teaching is quite beyond the province of Piers as Do-wel, just as is the advice later given to the King. Up to this point, therefore, there is no mention of either Do-wel or Piers. The Confession of the Seven Sins is again quite general; it is not even confined to the laity (Wrath was a Regular), and it is prompted by the sermon of Reason, who proves that the pestilences were in consequence of sin (V. 15) and for no other reason. Here again it would not have been becoming to the trend of the allegory for simple unlettered Do-wel to usurp the position and authority of Reason in preaching repentance to the world. And therefore the figure of Piers is still withheld. Indeed, he

remains hidden until the more exalted and theoretic advice
has failed. In their efforts to seek the Shrine of Truth the
worldlings 'blustreden forth as bestes' (V. 521), not knowing
which way to turn. They had had *spiritual* advice from their
Confessor, and were trying to follow it; what they lacked was
practical advice; and this, as might be expected, the finical
Palmer, all decked out and arrayed with the trophies of his
pilgrimages, could not supply. For practical advice a practical
man is needed and therefore, modestly, but with the
assurance of one who speaks from fifty years' experience,
Piers emerges as a leader, 'the type of ideal honest man', in
short *Do-wel*.

At first he offers them spiritual advice in practical form, a
sort of map of the common road to Truth (i.e. to Honesty,
Even-handedness), a Mosaic *Carte du Tendre* (V. 568
onwards); and in this there is nothing which the ordinary
unlettered Christian was not supposed to know ... the Ten
Commandments, the obligations of Penance and
Amendment and Charity, etcetera. But even this is too
abstruse for the for-wandered world:

> 'This were a wikked way . but who-so hadde a gyde'
>
> (VI.1)

So with a still more practical insight Piers sets them all to
work. That had been his own solution to the problem of
seeking Truth; that had been his own life;

> I dyke and I delue . I do that Treuthe hoteth.
>
> (V. 552)

that, in fact, was as much as, in his simplicity, he knew, or
needed to know, in the Active Life of Do-wel.

It should be noted that the problems of Famine and
Unemployment, which in essence are no less general than
those of Public Administration or Social Purification, were
shelved by Langland until after the emergence of Piers. This
is because Langland believed that Famine and
Unemployment could be avoided if only the secular world
would lead the simple, honest, hard-working Life of Do-wel,
each according to his station; whereas those other problems of

the purposes of human endeavour in general, and the right
practice of statecraft, were above the powers and pretensions
of a simple farmer. They therefore come under the
arbitration, not of Piers, but of Conscience or Reason or Holy
Church.

The last and most vexed matter in this first epiphany of Do-
wel under the form of Piers is that of the Pardon sent by
Truth to his servant.

> Treuthe herde telle her-of . and to Peres he sent,
> To taken his teme . and tulyen the erthe,
> And purchaced hym a pardoun . *a pena et a culpa*
> For hym, and for his heires . for euermore after.
>
> (VII.1–4)

The 'purchace' is of course the purchase of Calvary when
'god bouȝte vs alle' (VI.210), and is our Redemption. Now,
that Redemption is believed, and has always been believed,
conditional; it is for the Christian to avail himself of it by Faith
and Works. It will be seen presently that the essence of Do-
wel, theoretically speaking, includes Faith and Works with no
little emphasis. And this should be borne in mind in
considering the enigmatic text of the Pardon sent by Truth.
(This pardon, it may be noted, links up with that other
pardon that is conditional upon *redde quod debes* in XIX.388;
virtually they are the same in promise and condition.)

The condition in the pardon of VII is thus expressed:

> Al in two lynes it lay . and nouȝt a leef more,
> And was writen riȝt thus . in witnesse of treuthe;
> *Et qui bona egerunt, ibunt in vitam eternam;*
> *Qui vero mala, in ignem eternum.*
>
> (VII.110–13)

This pardon lay in the hand of Piers the unlettered
ploughman, simplest embodiment of Do-wel, or *Bonum
Agere*; there is an irony in that he could not even read it, did
not know that it referred precisely and exclusively to himself.
He had accepted it without examination upon pure Faith; he
had not so much as unfolded it.

> 'Pieres,' quod a prest tho . 'thi pardoun most I rede,

> For I wil construe eche a clause . and kenne it the on Engliche.'
> And Pieres at his preyere . the pardoun vnfoldeth.
>
> (VII.106–8)

This trustful illiteracy of Piers, because it is entirely in character with the Life of Do-wel, is the first of two important points that emerge from this episode of Truth's pardon. The second is the 'pure teen' (VII.116) for which Piers tore up the pardon when the priest (who could not recognise *Bonum Agere* in Piers any more than Piers did himself) explained to him that it was no pardon at all but the simple statement of an exactly proportionate requital; such a pardon as might be conceded by Mrs Be-done-by-as-you-did.

Perhaps all readers have found this 'teen' obscure. Vexation or petulance seem scarcely appropriate impulses in a character such as that of Piers, whatever that character embodies; yet the action of pardon-tearing is somehow satisfactory to the reader psychologically; it is almost as if Piers had torn the priest up, and revenged us upon his sophistries. But I think a better explanation would be to think of 'teen' as disappointed mortification. *Piers believed the priest* (Do-wel is humble and obedient to the Church); their later jangle does not concern the pardon but arises from his resentment of the gratuitous and insulting mockery flung at him by the priest. Piers believed that the pardon (like so many others in the fourteenth century) was worthless, and so, in his disappointment, committed himself to the pure assurance of his Faith rather than to a piece of parchment; for as he tears it he repeats:

Si ambulavero in medio umbre mortis, non timebo mala; quoniam tu mecum es.

But there is mortification as well as disappointment; as if he thought that perhaps after all the simple Life of Action was of insufficient merit, in spite of his fifty years of following Truth. More could be demanded of him.

> 'I shal cessen of my sowyng,' quod Pieres . 'and swynk nouȝt so harde,
> Ne about my bely-ioye . so bisi be namore!

Of preyers and of penaunce . my plow shal ben herafter,
And wepen whan I shulde slepe . though whete-bred me faille.'
(VII.117–20)

These are the words immediately following in which Piers announces his conversion to the clerkly Life of Do-bet; and for this reason *he does not return in person into the narrative* until Passus XVI, '*primus de Do-bet*'.

It may well be asked: 'If Piers embodies Do-wel, why does he drop out of the poem through all those long Passus that purport to deal with Do-wel?' (VIII–XV). I suggest in answer that in the first place the *Visio de Petro Plowman* (Prol.-VII) exhibit Do-wel allegorically, whereas the *Vita de Do-wel* exhibits it morally; in the case of Do-wel alone the practice is discussed before the moral theory; (whereas in the case of Do-bet and Do-best the theory is fully discussed in the preceding *Vita de Do-wel*, and the practice of those Higher Lives is not shown until the sections that bear their name). Thus, since Piers has demonstrated how to handle the Active World, there is no need for him to reappear until he is wanted to demonstrate the handling of the Contemplative World. He makes three Grand Appearances, one for each kind of Life, and it would have confused the symmetry of the allegory to have brought him in redundantly as Do-wel. Secondly the *Vita de Do-wel*, as has been said, is really far wider in scope than the mere good Active Life, inasmuch as it includes disquisitions on the other Lives, and on other matters. It is, in so far as it concerns the Lives of Piers, purely theoretic or moral, whereas the Hero is *always* flesh and blood, a figure of the actual world, whether Active, Contemplative, or Authoritarian. Compare with the robustness of Piers those shadowy phantoms, Thought, Clergye, Imaginatyf, or even Haukyn; Piers is not a theory but a Life, and for so long as he represents Do-wel, the perfection of Unletteredness, it would be inappropriate to introduce him into a realm of disputation such as is the section called the *Vita de Do-wel*.

Piers, then, bursts into the poem at precisely the point where the practice and example of a simple honest man (Do-wel) can benefit the Active World, and disappears, uttering a prophecy of his transformation into Do-bet (VII.117–20), just at the moment when Langland retires into a realm of speculation, whither Piers as Do-wel cannot follow him, and where the path of Do-bet has not yet sufficiently been marked out for Piers as Do-bet to be intelligible. Without that long hiatus in the narrative allegory of the poem, where Do-wel, Do-bet and Do-best are theoretically evaluated, the changes in the meaning of Piers would indeed have been confusing; for imagine Passus VIII–XV omitted; what key would then remain to the triple gates of Langland's thought?

The correspondence that has been traced between Piers and the structural disposition of Do-wel, exists also, and more obviously, in Do-bet. No sooner does *Passus xvj et primus de Do-bet* begin than Piers returns into the poem in person; and he returns a changed being; here is no more the simple, unlettered and incorruptible farmer, but a teacher who can expound the allegory of the Tree of Charity, with its Triune props (XVI.21–72), and, later, the Holy Trinity Itself (XVII.138–256); a healer and tender of the sick and afflicted (in the person of the Good Samaritan, XVII.48 onwards; identified with Piers in XVIII.10); and a Jouster in whose armour Christ is to ride to His Passion (XVIII.21–5). The full importance of these roles will be seen when the theoretical essences of Do-wel, Do-bet and Do-best have been considered; what is here emphasised is that a strong change takes place in the character of Piers, and that *this change coincides with the Do-bet division of the poem*; this correspondence, too, cannot be accidental.

From VIII.25, there is no more mention of Piers until XIX.6. In these 412 lines are described the Passion of Christ and the Harrowing of Hell. Let us for the moment be cautious of any hasty identification of Christ with Piers; that they are in an important sense identified cannot be denied; but it would be truer to say of them that Jesus *lives* Piers (for Piers is a way of Life), than that Jesus *is* Piers or that Piers *is* Jesus. Indeed the plain truth is best stated by Langland himself when he says:

> This Iesus of his gentrice . wole iuste in Piers armes,
> In his helme and in his haberioun . *humana natura*;
> That Cryst be nouȝt biknowe here . for *consummatus deus*,
> In Piers paltok the Plowman . this priker shal ryde;

(XVIII.22–5)

The reason for our caution is that Piers is primarily of *this* world (as, humanly speaking, are the Active, Contemplative and Pontifical Lives). This explains why there is no mention of Piers in the long and splendid Harrowing of Hell; Christ had for a while borrowed the human garments of Piers, but yielded them up again (it may be understood) at death, at the line:

> 'Consummatum est,' quod Cryst . and comsed forto swowe.
> (XVIII.57)

Thereafter Christ clearly is recognised as Divine (though some still deny and scoff); Lucifer and Goblin know with Whom they have to deal.

> Some seyde that he was goddes sone . that so faire deyde,
> *Vere filius dei erat iste, etc.*
> And somme saide he was a wicche ...
> (XVIII.68–9)

Piers does not return to the poem until after Hell has been harrowed: he returns in the opening lines of XIX, which is headed *Passus xix^{us}; et explicit Do-bet; et incipit Do-best.*

I do not know what importance to attach to this heading; it contains the suggestion that we are to expect a little Do-bet (which will be concluded), and that the rest will begin Do-best. If this suggestion be accepted, it will be found to support the theory here advanced. What is most noticeable about this re-entry of Piers is its likeness to his re-entry at the beginning of the previous Passus. *No apparent change has taken place in the character of Piers.* If the passage already quoted (XVIII.22–5) be compared with the lines

> thise aren Pieres armes,
> His coloures and his cote-armure . ac he that cometh so blody
> Is Cryst with his crosse . conqueroure of Crystene
> (XIX.12–14)

the similarity is obvious.

If this similarly be taken in conjunction with the hint given by the Passus-heading, it is not difficult to believe that we still

have here to do with Piers as *Do-bet*; and this interpretation of
the allegory fits with the return of Christ to Galilee after His
descent into Hell and *before* the sending-forth of the Disciples
with loosing and binding power, which, for Langland, is one
of the turning-points in Christian history. For Christ was still
humanly embodied, as the episode of Doubting Thomas
proves (XIX.161–76), and it was in the body of Piers, who
had not yet become Do-best. '*Explicit Do-bet*' might then
properly be written after line 176 of XIX (the story of
Doubting Thomas), which is immediately succeeded by these
lines:

> And whan this dede was done . Do-best he tauȝte,
> And ȝaf Pieres power . and pardoun he graunted
> To alle manere men . mercy and forȝyfnes,
> Hym myȝte men to assoille . of alle manere synnes,
> In couenant that thei come . and knowleche to paye,
> To Pieres pardon the Plowman . *redde quod debes.*
>
> (XIX.177–82)

Whether or not this explanation puts too much weight on
the mere heading of a Passus, the final change in the
significance of Piers does not come until this point. He is no
longer identifiable in any sense with Christ, but is one to
whom Christ *delegates power*. The power was won by Christ
(as Langland explains in the mouth of Conscience,
XIX.26–55) when he descended into and harrowed Hell, an
action in which Piers, as we have seen, had no part. Christ,
therefore, *as God*, has won a Victory, the fruits of which are
entrusted to the New Piers. And in this way the New Piers
becomes Do-best, the embodiment of the Life of Authority.
This Authority is confirmed and upheld by the Holy Ghost at
Pentecost (XIX.196), and is the sanction by which Piers is to
build the House of *Unitas*, 'holicherche on Englisshe'
(XIX.325).

The argument here offered has so far shown a
correspondence between each change in the significance of
Piers and the several transitions from Do-wel to Do-bet and
Do-bet to Do-best. It may be objected as follows: 'Why, if
Piers is Do-best, the Life of Authority that should sustain the
Church, does he appear to desert his trust, or at least to leave
it in the hands of Conscience?' It is true that after XIX.331

Piers ceases to dominate the poem and Conscience assumes the role of Hero. Indeed Piers once more is lost . . . we are not told when or how he vanishes from the Barn of Holy Church which he has been at such pains to build; when he is most needed (at the onslaughts of the Deadly Sins under Pride, XIX.331, and of the Host of Antichrist, XX.52), he is nowhere to be found, and the poem ends with the quest for its Hero:

> 'Bi Cryste,' quod Conscience tho . 'I will bicome a pilgryme, . . .
> . . . To seke Piers the Plowman . that Pryde may destruye . . .
> . . . now Kynde me auenge,
> And sende me happe and hele . til I haue Piers the Plowman!'
> And sitthe he gradde after grace . til I gan awake.
>
> (XX.378 to end)

I think this was intended as a melancholy comment on the world; an intimation that in Langland's opinion the proper exercise of Authority had vanished from the earth; and it is in keeping with his expressed estimate of Bishops and Cardinals (cf. XIX.411–15, Prol. 78, 79, VII.13, XI.303–10, etc.). It may be noted that the difficulty of Piers' vanishing at this point is not overcome by supposing him to be the pope or Man the Race. Neither of these had disappeared; indeed there were shortly to be two popes at once; on the other hand, the Babylonish Captivity at Avignon had been in full swing, at the time of the writing of the B Text, for nearly seventy years. Possibly Langland had this declension of the Life of Authority in mind. There are other possibilities also that suggest themselves glibly enough; such as that perhaps Langland had in mind a more general collapse of the Order of Christendom than that figured forth in the Papal Captivity, which he might have regarded as a symptom of his declining era rather than as its disease: or possibly Langland wished to stress the necessity of a renewed personal effort in all men, and therefore chose to portray them as fighting through the Dark Night of the Soul under Conscience only; or, like earlier prophets he may have had no wish to speak smooth things to an unruly people. Conjectures of this kind are always easy and often worthless; readers of Langland are more likely to experience surprise at the absence of topical allusion that can now be understood than the reverse. The matter of dating the texts illustrates this paucity of topical comment, this reserve of allusion that should caution us against rash assignment of historical interpretations, and inner readings of Langland's unexpressed sentiments about contemporary personages and events.[8]

A correspondence between the personal entries of Piers and the architectural divisions, Do-wel, Do-bet and Do-best, has been indicated, and a second line of argument remains, namely the discovery and tabulation of the Virtues assigned by Langland to those ways of life, and the fitting of them to Piers in the three stages of his growth.

Before this new phase in the argument is attempted, a consideration of the supposed identity of Piers and Christ may be offered. What is here contended is that Piers and Christ are parallel exemplars of the same sets of ideas. That Christ lived Do-wel, Do-bet, and Do-best successively, Langland explicitly tells us (XIX.104–89); that Piers is a parallel embodiment of those lives is the thesis of this paper. I use the word parallel designedly, for by a curious but not unlawful play of ideas, the metaphor from Geometry fits the thesis with a pleasing exactness; for we are told of parallel straight lines that they meet at Infinity; and that is precisely where the characters of Piers and Jesus meet, and are one. They meet in the Infinity of Christ's Nature and in that of Do-wel and Do-bet:

> '... Do-wel and Do-bet . aren two infinites,
> Whiche infinites, with a feith . fynden oute Do-best,
> Which shal saue mannes soule . thus seith Piers the Ploughman.'
>
> (XIII.127–9)

These three ways of life, lived allegorically by Piers and historically by Christ, are inexhaustible. An infinite goodness in simplicity and even-handed Action; an infinite goodness in compassionate care for the ignorant and the sick and a readiness to suffer for others, learnt in Contemplation; and an infinite goodness in Command; each road leads to Salvation. Each way of life is to be understood *allegorically*, as bodied in Piers and as touching the proper relations between man and man; and each is in the same way to be understood *morally*, as having in the abstract certain basic essential or characteristic virtues; and each way is to be understood as touching everlasting things, analogically that is, namely the fulfilling of God's purposes in creating, redeeming and giving Grace to man.

I do not say that Langland was meticulously precise in his use of the Piers symbol; it would, for instance, be impossible, perhaps, to go through the poem substituting for every mention of Piers the words Do-wel, Do-bet or Do-best; in the last-cited passage, for instance, it is not very clear in which capacity Piers is being quoted. We are told immediately before that 'one Pieres the Ploughman' has 'sette alle sciences at a soppe saue loue one', and this suggests Do-wel, the first Piers. But to overwork the interpretation of an allegory that has so large and general a scope is the treason of pedantry. There is, however, one passage in the poem which seems to undo much of the argument so far advanced by this paper. It occurs in Passus XV, in the allocution of that strangely tongueless and toothless being *Anima*. Anima is defining Charity to the Dreamer in a passage of extraordinary poetic force. The passus in question is headed *Passus xv^us : finit Do-wel; et incipit Do-bet*, and if this can be accepted as evidence, we are justified in supposing that somewhere within this passus is the turning-point away from the matter of Do-wel and towards the matter of Do-bet. I suggest that the turning-point comes at XV.144; for it is at this line that the nature of Charity comes up for discussion; now Faith, Hope and Charity, under the forms of Abraham, Moses and the Good Samaritan, are the subjects of Passus XVI and XVII, so that this turning-point passage can be considered as a *moral* explanation of or introduction to the Good Samaritan, who is an *allegorical* emblem of Charity; and this figure turns out later (XVII.10 onwards) to be indistinguishable from Piers and Jesus, so that it is raised, and with it the whole discussion, to the *anagogical* plane of heavenly Truth.

If these three shadowings of meaning be allowed to drift like veils over the discourse of Anima, an understanding of it will arise that is not inconsistent with the interpretation of Piers as Do-wel, Do-bet, and Do-best; the passage in question is as follows: Langland is moved to exclaim at the lyrical account of the person of Charity given by Anima:

> 'By Cryst, I wolde that I knewe hym,' quod I . 'no creature
>   leuere!'
> 'With-outen helpe of Piers Plowman,' quod he . his persone
>   seestow neuere.'
> 'Where clerkes knowen hym,' quod I . that kepen holykirke?'
> 'Clerkes haue no knowyng,' quod he . but by werkes and bi
>   wordes.
> Ac Piers the Plowman . parceyueth more depper
> What is the wille and wherfore . that many wyȝte suffreth,
>   *Et vidit deus cogitaciones eorum.*
> ... For there are beggeres and bidderes . bedemen as it were,
> Loketh as lambren . and semen lyf-holy,
> Ac it is more to haue her mete . with such an esy manere,
> Than for penaunce and partifnesse . the pouerte that such taketh.
> There-fore by coloure ne by clergy . knowe shaltow hym neuere,
> Noyther thorw wordes ne werkes . but thorw wille one.
> And that knoweth no clerke . ne creature in erthe,
> But Piers the Plowman . *Petrus, id est, Christus.*
>
> (XV.189–206)

It would seem clear from Langland's instant association of the names Piers the Plowman with Clerkes (for the force of the question in the third line of the above seems to be 'Then do the Clergy recognise true Charity in the hearts of men?'), that Piers as Do-bet, allegory of the Clerkly Life, was intended (this would corroborate the *incipit Do-bet* suggestion made above); and indeed I think it is for Do-bet that Piers is here standing. But it is a Piers–Do-bet on the anagogical plane; for *Anima* associates Piers not with 'clerkes' as the Dreamer does, but with God and Christ. What then is to be understood by this passage? The virtues of Do-bet (as will presently be shown) are to teach, to heal and to suffer; these, on the heavenly or anagogical plane, as attributes of God would be just such as Christ manifested on earth in his contemplative character, when he 'did bet'; but the contemplations of God penetrate into the human heart, and can see if Charity exists there or not. Since, however, Christ was God uniquely incarnate, that knowledge of the inner human motive was also, for the first and last time, known upon earth, by Jesus during his ministry of Do-bet when he was living the second life of Piers. No Piers-life, *of itself*, can teach men to see into the true motives of their fellows; but the Piers-life raised to the Heavenly plane, as it was by Jesus, could bring that knowledge to earth in virtue of the Incarnation. This gives a new and and I believe a true value to the phrase *Petrus, id est Christus* and saves the allegory from obscurity and even from wreck. Another analogy from Euclid may clarify my contention; a chord cuts a circle at two points; if the chord be moved to a tangential position, there are still two points at which it cuts; but they are coincident. The chord of Do-bet cuts the circle of life in Heaven and on Earth; and in Christ Heaven and Earth were united; the symbol Piers is filled by the reality Christ: symbol and reality coincide.

V.

As has been said, the theoretic explanation of Do-wel, Do-bet and Do-best is largely contained in the second section of the poem, that which is called Do-wel. This explanation is of snowball growth, but I have gathered together the principal pronouncements offered during the course of Passus VII to XIX. All but one occur within the *Vita de Do-wel*, as will be seen.

DO-WEL	DO-BET	DO-BEST
VIII.78 ff. Thought speaking:		
Three fair virtues that are not far to find.		
True of tongue and hand; wins livelihood by labour or land; trusty of his tally; takes but his own; is not drunken or disdainful.	Is the same, but does right more; low as a lamb; loving of speech; helps all according to their needs; has broken the purses of the avaricious; 'And is ronne into Religioun, and hath rendred the bible,' preaching 'Suffer fools gladly' and doing them good with glad will.	Is above both; a Bishop's Cross he bears to hale men from Hell and bash down the wicked. Must protect Do-wel. If Do-wel or Do-bet go contrary to Do-best, the King they have set up above them (i.e. God) will cast them in irons unless Do-best pleads for them.

DO-WEL	DO-BET	DO-BEST

IX.1 ff. Witte speaking:

Lives in the Castle of the four Elements, is set there to guard Anima for Kynde. Do-wel is Lord of the Marches against 'a proud pricker of France, Princeps hujus mundi.'	Do-bet is handmaid to Anima and daughter to Do-wel.	Do-best is above both, a Bishop's peer. What he bids must be done. Anima is led by his teaching.

IX.107 ff. (Still Witte)

Do-wel is true wedded life, works and wins to sustain the world. To beget bastards is to do ill. (Piers is married at his first entry: see VI.80.) But of course no more is heard of his wife when he becomes Do-bet.

IX.199 Witte still speaking:

To do as the law teaches. To dread God. Wicked will drives away Do-wel.	To love friend and foe. To suffer.	To give and guard both young and old, to heal and help. Do-best comes of Do-wel and Do-bet. He brings down the proud for the protection of Do-wel.

X.129 Dame Studye speaking:

May he grow deaf who blinds men's wits with fine distinctions between Do-wel and Do-bet. Unless a man lives the life Do-wel he need not hope for Do-bet, though Do-best 'drawe on hym' day after day.

X.187 Dame Studye still speaking:

See that you love loyally if you have a fancy to Do-wel.	Do-bet and Do-best are of Love's kin (also, by implication, pray for enemies, return good for evil).	

X.230 ff. Clergye speaking:

A common life; to believe in the Church, and all the articles of the Faith that are necessary to know, i.e.	Do-bet is to suffer for the good of your soul all that the Book, by the Church's teaching, bids, viz. Practise what	Do-best is bold to blame the Guilty, being clean within himself.

DO-WEL	DO-BET	DO-BEST
in One God without beginning. His true Son who saved Man from Death and the Devil, through the Holy Ghost that is of Both, but all Three are One. The Lewed that wish to Do-well must so believe.	you preach. Be what you seem.	

X.330 Langland speaking:
Do-wel and Do-bet are Dominus and Knighthood? (cf. A Text: Knighthood, Kingship and Caesardom are Do-wel, Do-bet and Do-best?) Scripture replies that neither Kinghood nor Knighthood help to Heaven.

XI.402 Langland suggests that Do-wel is to see much and suffer more, but is rebuked by Imagynatyf, who retorts *Philosophus esse, si tacuisses.*

XII.30 Imagynatyf speaking:
Faith, Hope and Charity are Do-wel, as St Paul says. Do-wel does as loyalty teaches; if married, love your mate. If you are Religious (i.e. Do-bet?), keep your rule and do not run to Rome.

XII.103 The Drunken Doctor speaking:

Do no evil to fellow Christians. And (later, line 115), Do-wel is to do what Clergy teach.	Do-bet is he that labours to teach others.	Do-best practises what he preaches.

XII.127, Clergye speaking, quoting Piers Plowman:
Clergye denies all knowledge of his own, for Piers Plowman has set all science at a sop, save Love only (i.e. Piers Plowman, in the role of Do-wel, has asserted that Salvation is gained by Love, not learning). Piers says (Clergye continues) that Do-wel and Do-bet are two infinites, which, with a faith, find out Do-best. And that shall save man's soul.

Ibid., 136, Patience speaking:
'Disce, doce et dilige inimicos.'

Disce is Do-wel.	Doce is Do-bet.	Dilige is Do-best.

(Patience claims she learnt this from Love (line 139), but cf. the remarks of the Drunken Doctor.)

DO-WEL	DO-BET	DO-BEST

XIV.16–21, Conscience speaking to Haukyn:

Do-wel, Do-bet, and Do-best are the three parts of Valid Penance, i.e.
          Contrition.   Confession.   Satisfaction.
(This doctrine is expanded in XIV.87–96. It is not so much a doctrine as an analogy.)

XIX.104 ff., Conscience speaking:

Christ, turning the water to wine began Do-wel, as Wine is like Law and the Holy Life and thus Christ taught us to love our enemies. He was then known as the Son of Mary.

Later in His Ministry He made the lame to leap and comforted the sad, was crucified, rose again, and earned the title of Son of David. The He was Do-bet.

He taught Do-best when He gave Piers Authority to bind and unbind sin on condition of '*redde quod debes.*'

Langland was a poet who liked to be seen feeling for his ideas; he tries out successive notions, and noses his way among opinions before the reader's eyes. Never, perhaps, a learned man, as Chaucer was, he gives the effect of one who listened gladly to disputation, contributing now and then his native opinion to a discussion that was, philosophically, somewhat above his head; much as an undergraduate, reading for Honours in History, and having friends reading Greats, might pick up from conversation as much of philosophy as he could clumsily understand and despise the rest as quibbling subtlety.[9]

Langland's definitions, then, unlike the successive definitions of Justice in the *Republic* (where every successive definition is allowed to cancel its forerunner), are *cumulative*; he has not the dialectic technique so much as the ruminative technique; he has a set of ideas at the back of his head, and, being a better poet than logician, he *feels* for them, rather than *thinks* them. With this ruminant poet, then, each restatement may be taken as a new slant of thought upon the same idea, a succession of facets cut upon the same stone.

It is therefore justifiable to gather together into three lots all that is offered to us as Do-wel, Do-bet and Do-best respectively, and to presume that each lot, as a whole, and taken with the general context of the poem, sums up all that

Langland ever thought about the Lives. It will be quickly noticed that the virtues of Do-wel encroach upon those of Do-bet and Do-best, as though at first Langland had not completely disentangled the virtues proper to it from those proper to the other two. Nor is this apparent confusion surprising, for he is emphatic that whoever would Do-bet, must first Do-wel; so also with Do-best. Thus, much of what belongs to Do-bet and Do-best also belongs to Do-wel, and all that belongs to Do-wel, belongs also to Do-bet and Do-best. For the Lives are Infinites, can be lived inexhaustibly without contradiction among themselves.

First to collect the material into three lots:

Do-wel is a manual life lived in honesty of word and deed; reliable, sober, humble-hearted; protects the Soul against Satan; exists in matrimony (i.e. celibacy is not a condition to Salvation); it does the world's work, is obedient to Law, and fears God; is the prerequisite of Do-bet; is loyal in love (i.e. charitable and trusty); is a common life to be lived in the Articles of the Faith, as taught by the Church, and particularly in the Holy Trinity; is to live in Faith, Hope and Charity; to hurt no fellow-Christian; to obey the clergy; is an 'infinite', that, by Faith, finds out Do-best; is '*Disce*' (book-learning cannot be meant here; I take '*disce*' to mean willing attention to the teaching of the Church); is (analogous to) Contrition (the first part of a valid penance); is obedience to the Great Commandments of Christ, the wine-like Law of Love, even of your enemies.

Do-bet is all this, and in addition: *low as a lamb*,[10] *loving of speach*; *helps all according to their needs*; has broken the purses of the avaricious; has entered Holy Orders and expounded the Bible; is handmaid to the Soul; *loves friend and foe*; suffers; is based upon Do-wel; *is of Love's kin*; is to suffer what the Bible, by the Church's teaching, enjoins. Is to practise what you preach and be what you seem; is to keep your rule and not to run to Rome (?); is to labour to teach others; is an 'infinite'; is '*Doce*'; is (analogous to) Confession (second part of a valid Penance); is to heal the sick, comfort the afflicted and suffer (martyrdom, if necessary).

Do-best is above Do-wel and Do-bet; bears a Bishop's crook to hale men from Hell and bash down the wicked;

protects Do-wel; intercedes with God for those who have
offended against Do-best; has authority over Anima; *succours
and guards young and old, heals and helps*; issues from Do-wel
and Do-bet; draws on *Do-wel to Do-bet* (i.e. encourages and
ordains candidates for Holy Orders?); *is of Love's kin; must
practise what he preaches*; is found out by Do-wel and Do-bet
'with a feith'; and saves man's soul (so also do the other lives,
of course; but here, I think, is meant that it has the authority
to ordain the other two lives in such a way as to make them
worthy of Salvation); is *Dilige*; is (analogous to) Satisfaction
(third part of valid Penance); has Authority to bind and
unbind on condition of *Redde quod Debes*. (It would seem at
first that this was a virtue of Dobet, the priestly life, inasmuch
as Priests have power of communicating Absolution; but they
do not have this power in virtue of their Contemplative lives,
but in virtue of the *Episcopal Authority* that ordained them.)

To condense these scattered sayings about the three lives:
The life of Do-wel is inexhaustible in itself and is sufficient
for Salvation; it is a life of Faith and Work, the life of the
manual worker and layman, to live which he must be humble,
temperate, obedient to the Church, honest, compassionate,
fearing God and loving men with a warm neighbourly love.
He must know and believe in the simple elements of the
Christian Faith. In the character of this life it is not difficult to
recognize the spiritual lineaments of Piers Plowman as they
are portrayed in the *Visio*; the following quotations will
authenticate this recognition:

> I haue ben his folwar . al this fifty wyntre;
> ... I dyke and I delue . I do that treuthe hoteth;
> Some tyme I sowe . and some tyme I thresche,
> In tailoures crafte and tynkares crafte . what Treuthe can deuyse,
> I weue an I wynde . and do what Treuthe hoteth ...
>
> (V.549–55)

> ... ȝe mote go thourgh Mekenesse . both men and wyues,
> Tyl ȝe come in-to Conscience . that Cryst wite the sothe,
> That ȝe louen owre lorde god . leuest of alle thinges,
> And thanne ȝowre neighbores nexte.
>
> (V.570–73)

I parfourned the penaunce . the preest me enioyned,
And am ful sori for my synnes . and so I shal euere....

(V.607–8)

late Mercy be taxoure,
And Mekenesse thi mayster . maugre Medes chekes....

(VI.40, 41)

And that thow be trewe of thi tonge . and tales that thow hatie.

(Ibid., 52)

In dei nomine, amen . I make it my-seluen.
He shal haue my soule . that best hath yserued it,
And fro the fende it defende . for so I bileue,
Til I come to his acountes . as my *credo* me telleth,
To haue a relees and a remissioun . on that rental I leue.
The kirke shal haue my caroigne . and kepe my bones;
For of my corne and catel . he craued the tythe.
I payed it hym prestly . for peril of my soule,
For-thy is he holden, I hope . to haue me in his masse,
And mengen in his memorye . amonge alle Crystene.
    My wyf shal haue of that I wan . with treuthe, and nomore,
And dele amonge my douȝtres . and my dere children.
For thowghe I deye to-daye . my dettes ar quitte,
I bare home that I borwed . ar I to bedde ȝede.
And with the residue and the remenaunte . bi the rode of Lukes!
I wil worschip ther-with . Treuthe bi my lyue,
And ben his pilgryme atte plow . for pore mennes sake.

(VI.88–104)

In exclaiming at the beauty and depth of these lines, it is easy to forget that perhaps those very qualities of beauty and depth arise from the disregarded meditation of the *Vita de Do-wel*, and that in this love-attracting character of Piers are no more than the simple virtues of Do-wel, exactly as they have been discovered by our analysis, but rounded forth with a consummate allegorical imagination.

It would be tedious to particularize every instance in which Piers at his first entry fulfils emblematically the moral obligations of the Active Life. So simple is the allegory, and so well-framed to illustrate Do-wel in practice, that further comment is perhaps superflous; but there is one episode of special poignancy to show the implications of that true neighbourly Love, which is to include even the enemies of Do-wel; it is the Episode of the Britoner who

> ... a-bosted Pieres als,
> And bad hym go pissen with his plow . for-pyned schrewe!
>
> (VI.156–7)

When the too-courteous Knight failed to bring the wretch to reason Piers felt obliged to send for Hunger, who took the offender, buffeted him about the cheeks so that he looked like a lantern all his life after, and beat him so as almost to burst his guts. But the sight of the Britoner's misery touched Piers' heart.

> Thanne hadde Peres pite . and preyed Hunger to wende Home ...
> 'Ac I preye the, ar thow passe' . quod Pieres to Hunger,
> 'Of beggeres and bidderes . what best be to done?
> For I wote wel, be thow went . thei wil worche ful ille;
> For myschief it maketh . thei beth so meke nouthe,
> And for defaute of her fode . this folke is at my wille.
> They are my blody bretheren,' quod Pieres . for god bouȝte vs alle;
> Treuthe tauȝte me ones . to louye hem vchone,
> And to helpen hem of alle thinge . ay as hem nedeth.'
>
> (VI.202–12)

Material evils, for Langland, could best be combatted by spiritual good; at the same time even God used violence to 'bring folke to his wille' – as may be seen from the sermon of Reason (V.13), and the behaviour of Kynde (XX.79), who is *assisting* Conscience by sending fevers, fluxes, coughs, cardiacles, cramps and toothaches; for sickness reminds men of death, and therefore of Judgment, and therefore brings repentance – so it is not out of character in Piers to 'houp after Hunger' (VI.174); Treuthe would have done the same. And yet the loving-kindness of Piers, which is so pre-eminently a quality of Do-wel, moves him to ask Hunger if there is not a kindlier way of handling wasters justly.

To condense the sayings that concern Do-bet, it is easier to omit those which are included in Do-wel, for they are included *ex hypothesi*, and need not be repeated. Do-bet, then, adds nothing to Do-wel except the following: he is a

Contemplative or Clerk who teaches, heals and suffers, and lives in accordance with what he professes.

It is true that in his entry in XVI Piers is not described as a Priest, but all the other conditions of Do-bet are fulfilled in him; he teaches Langland at great length the nature of the Tree of Charity and how it is supported by the Holy Trinity (XVI.25–89). The particular praise accorded to Virginity by Piers (Ibid., 67–72) is what might be expected of a Contemplative, or Cleric, and is therefore in character with Piers as Do-bet. Further there are the twin disquisitions on the Trinity (XVII.138–249), in both of which Piers fulfils the role of teacher. As healer and succourer of the afflicted he becomes the Good Samaritan (XVII.48–79), though the actual identification of Piers with him is kept back by Langland for the more affecting surprise of the later line:

> One semblable to the Samaritan . and some-del to Piers the
> Plowman.
>
> (XVIII.10)

And as Sufferer, Piers is united to the sufferings of Christ between Palm Sunday and Good Friday:

> 'Is Piers in this place?' quod I . and he preynte on me,
> 'This Jesus of his gentrice . wole iuste in Piers armes
> 'In his helme and in his haberioun . *humana natura* ...'
>
> (XVIII.21–3)

Two things equal to the same thing are equal to one another; and this maxim is of clearer service in the matter of Piers and Do-bet than it is in the matters of Do-wel and Do-best. But even in Do-best the correspondence between that Life and Piers is evident enough, although, as has been admitted, the disappearance of the Plowman from his barn *Unitas* when it is in its last jeopardy, is strange; one looks for him to hold his ground. But this difficulty is inherent in the fable, and not in the interpretation that is put upon the character of Piers.

The virtues of Do-best over and above those of Do-wel and Do-bet are simply these; to exercise episcopal authority, for the protection of the simple, the abashing of the wicked, and the maintaining of the sacramental life of the Church (particularly are mentioned the Sacraments of Penance and of the Altar; cf. XIX.178–82, and Ibid., 384–6). The Life of Do-best is in fact that which cares for the salvation of men through the right administration of the instituted Christian Church.

It is to Piers, therefore, in his final significance, that Grace gives the four oxen of the Evangelists, the grain of the four Cardinal Virtues, the Cross of Christ and the Crown of Thorns for the timbering of the Church (XIX.257–321); for it is in receiving these gifts and in putting them to the use of Christendom together with the Sacraments committed to his charge, that Piers Does-best. Piers is the embodiment of God's Authority on earth; and Do-best is a way of Life in which that Authority is embodied.

The sowing of the four seeds of Prudence, Fortitude, Temperance and Justice (XIX.271–308), and the ploughing and harrowing with the Four Evangelists and the Four Fathers of the Church (XIX.257–69), is reminiscent of the Life of Do-bet, in that these are allegorical Acts of Teaching; and the Mortar of Mercy, made of the Blood and Baptism of Christ (XIX.320–1), recalls, at a distance, the loving-kindness of Do-wel in handling his blood-brother, the Britoner, on whose misery he had pity (VI.210). But, as can be seen from the table of Abstract Qualities of the Three Lives, which I offered above, this inclusion of Do-wel- and Do-bet-elements in Do-best is essential to Langland's thought. Nothing is more certain in his mind than that you cannot Do-better unless you have first Done-well, and still Do-well; nor can you Do-best unless you continue to Do-well and to Do-better also.

How could this central idea be better expressed than by embodying it in a single man, in a Piers? We cannot forget the first Piers, though we pass on to the second or to the third; the cumulative quality in the Lives is thus not only stated as a theorem, but demonstrated in a growing and inclusive personal symbol in Piers. The progress of Piers is not as that of caterpillar to chrysalis to butterfly, but as that of blade–ear–grain, where one identity becomes successively more and more fruitful while remaining visibly the same; it is this *organic* quality in Piers which, for me at least, is the master-stroke of Langland's myth-creating power; without this understanding of its hero the reader loses sight of the fine contours and frontiers, and the poem becomes a mapless jungle of visions and discourses.

Allegory, once believed to be the life of poetry, is now commonly thought the death of it; this may have come about from the general changes in English ways of thinking; but I suggest it comes more particularly from the contempt in which the allegorical aspects of later works such as *The Faerie Queene* are commonly held. Hazlitt has voiced this contempt once and for all; the difference between the allegory of Spenser and that of Langland is the difference between a pleasing formal artifice and a natural growth; there is a topiary effect in *The Faerie Queene*; the allegory is the carpentered work of an unmatched artist-craftsman; but in Piers Plowman the allegory is organic, the bone in the body. His allegory we now have to understand by an intellectual process not unlike deliberate translation, for we are unaccustomed to reading in allegory. Just as the reader of a French book is not *reading French* as long as he mentally translates it into his own tongue while reading, so in Langland we are not reading allegory as long as we are analysing and making an argued interpretation. The real reader of a foreign tongue thinks immediately in that tongue; the language of allegory asks the same unselfconscious comprehension.

It remains to be noticed that the allegorical scheme here deduced from the B Text is strongly hinted in the A Text, where Piers is clearly the simple embodiment of the Active Life of Do-wel, and where the rough suggestions of the moral natures proper to Do-bet and Do-best respectively are in complete harmony with their later elaboration in the B Text. The extension of the embodiment of Piers as Do-wel to his embodiment (in the B Text) as Do-bet and Do-best is the very signature of the Author of A. It seems to me impossible that A mind could have caught on to and developed this allegory and also the moral natures of the Higher Lives from the A fragment, and have done so exactly in the manner of A, unless the B Mind *was* the A mind: in other words, I believe that Langland wrote both A and B.

NOTES

1. H.W. Wells 'The Construction of Piers Plowman', *P.M.L.A.* XLIV, No. 1.
2. *The Vision of William concerning Piers the Plowman, in three parallel texts, etc., by William Langland*, ed. W.W. Skeat (Oxford, 1896) II, pp. XXVI-VII.
3. J.J. Jusserand, in *Piers Plowman, a contribution to the history of English mysticism* (London, 1894), pp. 29, 155.
4. *P.M.L.A.* XLIV, No. 1, p. 128 and *passim*.
5. Howard William Troyer, 'Who is Piers Plowman?', *P.M.L.A.* XLVII, No. 2.
6. All references throughout are to the B Text.
7. See Mensendieck 'The Authorship of Piers Plowman', *Journal of English & Germanic Philology* IX (1910), No. 3.
8. Notwithstanding the position sketched by Mr Cargill in *P.M.L.A.* XLVII, No. 2, which appears to me untenable and inaccurate.
9. Cf. G.R. Owst, *Literature and Pulpit in Medieval England*.
10. I have put in italics those virtues in Do-bet and Do-best upon which Do-wel seems to encroach, or to have included before.

5

The Pardon of Piers Plowman★

I.

It may seem simple to ask again what the visions of *Piers Plowman* are about, yet it is a question that has been a little over-borne by its younger sister 'who wrote them?' By putting the elder question twice, first to the A Text and then to the B, the natural assumption that they are both about the same thing begins to dwindle and vanishes as our reading proceeds; for not only does it become gradually clear that the main theme of the B Text is very different from that of the A, but, which is more important, one perceives that the two poems belong to separate species of poetry, to different orders of the imagination (in consequence of their different themes), and therefore call for different kinds of response from their readers, as they called for different kinds of treatment by their poet.

These differences in purpose and quality are the subject of this paper and I shall try to show the nature of the transformation of A into B, and how it was dictated in the poet's mind by a long musing over that enigmatic but crucial Pardon granted to Piers in the eighth Passus of the A Text, the Pardon that is Pier's reward for setting the world to work. The meditation of the intervening years led the revising poet towards another and more mystical world, so that his poem, touched by some metaphysical philosopher's stone, found

★Sir Israel Gollancz Memorial Lecture (1945); *Proceedings of British Academy*, Vol. XXXI.

itself wholly transmuted, 'as it is wont to chance that a man goeth in search of silver and beyond his purpose findeth gold'.[1]

This paper is not offered as a contribution to the long-drawn controversy over the authorship of *Piers Plowman*. It is offered as an investigation of poetry. The metamorphosis from A to B is striking, beautiful and unique, and will here be studied for its own sake. It may be that some readers, interested in controversy, will find or draw an argument for one theory or the other from this investigation, but no such corollary is intended here. It is, however, my opinion that the present state of this battle authorises me still to believe that both texts were written by the same man, William Langland, and I shall use his name freely throughout on this assumption; this will not invalidate the inquiry into the nature of these poems as poetry, and those who adhere to the theory of multiple authorship can mentally substitute A 1, A 2, Johan But, B 1, B 2, and C for the name Langland whenever they wish to do so, without losing anything of the argument.

I was led to think about these poems in the way proposed by a passage in the preface to Sir Israel Gollancz's edition of *Wynnere and Wastoure* and I cannot do better than begin by quoting it, for it is not only a true critical starting-point for my subject, but also a fair foundation for a paper given, as this is, in honour and memory of his scholarship.

> When *Wynnere and Wastoure* was a new poem, it seems to have stirred the heart of a young Western man, and perhaps to have kindled in him the latent fire of a prophet-poet, destined to deliver a weightier message to his fellow-countrymen. Ten years later than *Wynnere and Wastoure* the first version of *The Vision of Piers Plowman* set before all classes of the realm the evil conditions of the time, pointed to the corruptions in Church and State, and denounced even greater evils than those dealt with dramatically and dispassionately by our poet. The old man of *Wynnere and Wastoure* inspired Langland, the prophet-poet of England.[2]

WYNNERE AND WASTOURE AND THE A TEXT OF PIERS PLOWMAN

No reader of *Wynnere and Wastoure* and of the A Text of *Piers*

Plowman can fail to be struck by their general resemblances to each other, and any who follows Gollancz's suggestion far enough to make a close comparison will be led to support his view that these resemblances are too many and too exact to be attributable to an ambient literary tradition that the poets happened to share. Langland must have known the old man's poem itself; in his early twenties it must somehow have fallen upon his ears, or even into his hands, as the poem travelled those hilly Western regions, that were the last home of our more ancient style of poetry; in that style it set him dreaming. A great tradition is common property and there was no theft in his appropriation of images and phrases from the older poem; the summery brilliance of the sun, the drowsy gaze of a man lying beside a stream on a May morning among the Malvern Hills, lay to his hand:

> Als I went in the weste, wandrynge myn one,
> Bi a bonke of a bourne, bryghte was the sone,
> Vndir a worthiliche wodde, by a wale medewe;
> Fele floures gan folde ther my fote steppede. . . .
> Bot as I laye at the laste, than lowked myn eghne,
> And I was swythe in a sweuen sweped be-lyue.
> Me thoghte I was in the werlde, I ne wiste in what ende,
> One a loueliche lande that was ylike grene,
> That laye loken by a lawe the lengthe of a myle. . . .[3]

Or again there was another flavour to be borrowed, a foretaste of Glutton in the Ale-house:

> And thou wolle to the tauerne, by-fore the toune-hede,
> Iche beryne redy withe a bolle to blerren thyn eghne,
> Hete the whatte thou haue schalte, and whatt thyn hert lykes,
> Wyfe, wedowe, or wenche, that wonnes ther aboute.
> Then es there bott 'fille in' & 'fecche forthe', Florence to schewe,
>   'Wee-hee', and 'worthe vp', wordes ynewe.[4]

Fainter and more fragmentary are other phrases, parts perhaps of a common idiom rather than a personal influence; *hope I no other; witt and wylle; while my life dures; wiete wittirly*, and so forth. Here and there opinions chime together, as in their contempt for japers and janglers. In the description of gorgeous apparel they have a similar technique, though the earlier poet has the advantage in opulence over Langland, as his opportunities are more heraldic. In their use of the alliterative cadence it would be a fine critical ear that could draw with certainty a distinction between them; each fashions his narrative allegory in what seems, at first sight, a similar manner, namely by advancing two meanings to be apprehended simultaneously (the literal and the transferred), of which the first is to be accepted as a fantasy and the second as the actual state of affairs in contemporary England; their world is this world and their time the present. A chief theme, common to both (indeed the only theme of *Wynnere and Wastoure*), is the proper use of wealth, argued in the manner of a poetical debate (also a part of long tradition), accented with invective and satire. The A Text of *Piers Plowman* ends with a longish moral *significacio*, and such an ending Gollancz believes also to have concluded *Wynnere and Wastoure*, more briefly, however.

> Probably very little of the poem is lost. The dreamer no doubt was roused from his vision by the sound of trumpets, and found himself resting by the bank of the burn, the tale ending with some pious reflection, by way of conclusion.[5]

These are indeed great resemblances; what are the differences? There is a formal difference and a difference in the degree of genius shown. With regard to the formal difference, the A Text outsoars *Wynnere and Wastoure* by the addition of a further level of meaning of which every reader must become presently aware: it adds a continuous moral counterpoint to the other two levels already mentioned, the literal and the transferred. This is not simply to be explained as a chance difference in visionary power between the two authors; it is a technical difference in poetical construction, a difference in allegorical convention. The two-meaning poem that varies from an Aesopian type, such as the political fable of the Lion, the Wolf, the Fox, and the Ass,[6] to the more visionary kind of State-allegory –

> Sum tyme an Englisch Schip we had
> Nobel hit was and heigh of tour;
> Thorw al cristendam hit was drad,
> And stif wolde stande In vch a stour[7] &c.,

was a well-known form of thought and presentation that worked its way to immortality in such poems as Chaucer's *Parliament of Fowls* and Dunbar's *The Thrissil and the Rois*. *Wynnere and Wastoure* is of this kind but lacks their competence and beauty. Two meanings are all it has. But there existed a richer kind of allegory, much used in preaching and biblical exegesis, by which a moral is continuously implied and drawn from the story; in Langland, indeed, it is for ever bursting forth, as when Lady Meed promises a Church window in which her name is to be engraved in return for absolution from a Friar, and the indignant author intrudes upon the incident with:

> But god to all good folk . such graving defendeth
> And saith, *Nesciat sinistra quid faciat dextera.*[8]
>
> (A.III. 54–5)

There may, as Gollancz suggests, have been 'some pious reflection' at the end of *Wynnere and Wastoure*, but it is not a poem morally imbued all through. Thus, although it was a source and in some senses a model for the A Text of *Piers Plowman*, it was not so in this, the moral sense. Langland's poem seems to add to it this richer kind of allegorical interpretation which is the basis of a poem like *Cleanness* or *Patience*; but these in turn differ from *Piers Plowman* and *Wynnere and Wastoure* in that they lack the topical English content and are no more than ethical retellings of the stories of the Deluge, Sodom, Jonah, and so forth.

From this point of view, then, the A Text of *Piers Plowman* seems to be a poem *sui generis*; we may find a sort of analogue in the *Roman de la Rose*; the literal story of the garden lover has the transferred meaning that applies itself to the experiences of actual love-affairs, it tells their characteristic story, so to speak; but it is also packed with moral advice springing from a whole system of erotics, the morality of Cupid; and in these three senses we are expected to understand the fantasy. But the secondary meaning is typical rather than topical, and the morality of super-sensuous aristocratical paganism (with borrowings from Christianity) but neither fully Christian nor wholly serious. It is a play-time poem. I do not suppose Langland ever heard of it.[9]

Apart from the greater merit of his poem in its formal construction in three voices, the degree of Langland's personal genius was incomparably greater than that shown by the poet of *Wynnere and Wastoure*, though the latter shows himself a glittering performer in the coining of alliterative phrase; Langland's superiority is, however, always to be seen in his grasp of affairs, even on the most secular level. The other poet has nothing real to tell us about wealth and its uses. Winner abuses Waster for idleness, roistering and improvidence; Waster retorts that extravagance keeps money in circulation, that thrift is a kill-joy; better than hoarding is to give to the poor.

> Let be thy cramynge of thi kystes, for Cristis lufe of heuen!
> Late the peple and the pore hafe parte of thi siluere;[10]

The disputants seem perfectly satisfied that the whole problem of wealth turns on the question of spending or saving it, and Waster's interest in the poor is momentary, a debating-point. In Langland the problem is more deeply seen in the antitheses of wealth and want, means and ends. Nothing is concluded in the argument of the older poem, though the debate is wound up by the King with summary but frivolous advice. Winner is to go to the Pope of Rome where he is best liked until such time as the King shall send for him to finance a war with France, when he may expect promotion. Waster is to go to Cheapside and keep a tavern the better to swindle rich travellers; all very trivial advice compared to Langland's, hardly to be taken as serious; the 'old man' writes as a comedian, a flyter, but Langland as a man with a message.

In contrast to the colourful incoherence of *Wynnere and Wastoure*, the A Text is a masterpiece of intellectual organisation. When those vivid things in Langland that give him rank as an artist with Pieter Brueghel the Elder have been listed, such as are rough laughter, a gift in proverbs, peasant sympathy, Christian faith, irony, skill in visualising (crowds especially and tumultuous landscapes), a rich colour sense, a deep pity, and so forth – it still remains to praise his best power (and Brueghel had it too); namely, a strong architectural instinct for planning and carrying out a great composition, a design enormous in itself and wild with detail.

It is not he who loses himself in a tangle of digressions, or if he does it is seldom; the unaccustomed modern reader, missing some association of idea, may cry out that he is lost, that the poet has no control; but however many and however long his digressions, he seems like a man giving himself more room, rather than like one who has lost his way. There are, however, some exceptions to this impression in both texts, which will be touched upon later.

The A Text is the anatomy of England; he has a surgeon's eye and his scalpel is Christianity. He carves his subject cleanly, with an unfaltering poetical authority and an instinct for the essential shape of things. Never was a professed dreamer more practical; shrewdness and charity of heart, good sense and good theology and an extraordinary gift for parable organise the wide survey of his country, and raise his poem above the level of an elaborate political squib like *Wynnere and Wastoure*; there the design is trivial and less well carried out, presenting a battle of words, rather than an argument brought to a victorious end by thought and sympathy.

II. THE STRUCTURE OF THE A TEXT

Langland's narrative has a strategy; it is presented not in disorderly 'Fitts', but by Passus, each a real step that carries the reader logically onwards to the next. The main problems he propounds are four, each with its subdivisions. They are the purpose of wealth, the abuses of government, the sins of society and the fear of famine; the narrative leads logically through these themes to that Pardon which, it is here contended, was the root-cause of the rewriting of the poem. It moves in a single onrush or trajectory, the changes of scenes within it notwithstanding. Although this part of the poem is familiar to many readers, a brief analysis may have place to show the essential shapes within it, and how they are organised into the allegory.

(i) The purpose of wealth (A. Prologue and Passus I)
The whole world of English life is gathered into a field which

almost all are using as a Tom Tiddler's Ground with varying degrees of honesty and success. The main body is of beggars, businessmen, several sorts of ecclesiastical swindler, lawyers, trades-people, barons and bondmen; their whole activity is the amassing of wealth. Noble exceptions are a poor plowman or two and a few hermits who live 'for loue of vr lord'. On either side of the field are set the Tower of Truth and the Deep Dale, to one or other of which all must eventually come; but the folk he pictures in the field seem unaware of them just as Bunyan's man with the muck-rake is unable to look any way but downwards.

When the question 'What is the purpose of wealth?' is set in this context of Heaven and Hell, it leads beyond itself to further questions which only the Church can answer and it is logical that she, clothed in awe and beauty, should be the first visitant and instructress of the questioning Dreamer. Her replies go to the roots of human need and purpose. God has given man five senses *to worship Him with*.[11] As He has given these senses, so He has given their simple worldly satisfactions, namely food, drink, and clothing; these may be worked for, they are the constituents of wealth; but this kind of wealth is a means and not an end.

> All is not good to the ghost . that the body liketh.
>
> (A.I. 34)

The just debts of the body, like Caesar's penny, may be paid, but the soul has an overriding debt to God; real wealth is wealth of the spirit.

> When all treasure is tried . truth is the best;
> I do it on *Deus Caritas* . to deem the sooth.
>
> (A.I. 83)

That God is love and truth our treasure is too difficult a saying for the Dreamer, so he asks another question, Pilate's question, about truth and how it can be known.

> 'Yet have I no kind knowing',[12] quoth I . 'thou must teach me better,
> By what craft in my corpse . it commenceth and where.'
>
> (A.I. 127)

To which the Church answers roundly that truth and love are known by simple intuition, by a natural recognition in the human heart.

> 'Thou dotest, daft,' quoth she . 'dull are thy wits
> It is a kind knowing . that kenneth thee in heart
> For to love thy lord . liefer than thyself;
> No deadly sin to do . die though thou shouldest.
> This, I trow, be truth.'
>
> (A.I. 129)

An answer that Blake would have understood. Thus ends the catechism of the first Passus which has dealt with the general ends of life and how we know them. Now, by a verbal ingenuity in which he is seldom deficient, the poet turns to his next problem, and the narrative steps forward into another field of inquiry (still, however, related to the abuses of wealth), namely the corruptions of government as seen in Lady Meed and Wrong.

(ii) The abuses of government (A Text. Passus II, III, IV)
These brilliant Passus are so well known as to need little analysis. With a rollicking irony the poet indicts English officialdom of simony and bribery from bishops and civil lawyers down to Randolph the Reve of Rutland; all are guests at the wicked wedding of Lady Meed and False, an alliance of reward and dishonesty egged on by flattery and guile. Her wedding present, by a fine stroke of allegorical vision, is a charter, establishing the bridal couple as lords of the seven deadly sins. Langland reserves comment on their effect upon society at large for a later Passus. Meanwhile he has to speak of graft and outrage. The former has a Passus to itself, pictured in the trial of Lady Meed before the King; first she is taken to Westminster, where she makes easy friends with judges, lordings and friars and gets herself shriven at the cost of putting up a church window. Brought before the King she is charged by Conscience with the perversion of justice and the corruption of religion and we see a picture of England given over to the fraudulent official, the rascal summoner, the simoniac parson, the gaoler and the hangman, and every other functionary that money can buy.

The solution propounded for this state of affairs is that
Meed should marry Conscience, and Conscience is to bring
Reason to his aid; but while the debate is still in progress, a
new character appears; it is Peace with her complaint against
Wrong, that is, against a particular form of outrage or
aristocratic oppression exercised through 'Purveyors', who
made arrangements for the commissariat of feudal retinues in
their periodical cross-country journeys from one estate to
another; they are accused of billeting themselves without
mercy or honesty on innocent and helpless villages, raping
the women, robbing the stable and the fowlyard, breaking
into barns and commandeering wheat. Goneril utters a like
complaint against the hundred knights of Lear. The petition
of Peace was no dream of Langland's, nor even a piece of
conventional invective (as the charges of corruption, for their
generality, might be considered); it was a matter of recent
history and the rolls of Parliament for 1362 bear the poet out,
at least in respect of non-payment for exactions.[13]

Langland's King listens to Peace with a just attention and
Reason prompts his judgement and verdict.

> 'By him that stretched on the Rood' . quoth Reason to the King
> 'But I rule thus thy realm, . rend out my ribs!'
> 'I assent,' quoth the King . 'by St. Mary, my lady....'
> ... 'I am ready,' quoth Reason . 'To rest with thee ever;
> So that Conscience be our counsellor . Keep I no better.'
> 'I grant gladly' quoth the King . 'God forbid he fail
> And as long as I live . live we together.'
>
> (A.IV. 148)

As always with Langland the answer to a practical problem is
a practising change of heart.

(iii) The sins of society (A. Passus V)

Langland now takes us back to have a look at Lady Meed's
wedding present. The scene is once again the field of folk,
where Conscience with a cross preaches to the throng;
Repentance runs to rehearse his theme and William the poet
weeps water at his eyes. The deadly sins make their
confession; the link between them and Lady Meed is not
restated but implied; such linkages are common in this poet;
for instance the last words in the sermon of Conscience are,

Seek Saint Truth . for he may save you all,

a penance manifestly linked to the advice previously given by Holy Church, as the writer expects you to understand. We shall see many examples of this, for all his poetry is shot through with such foretastes and echoes which are there for the reader to discern as he may; they resemble the tentative statement of a theme by one group of instruments in an orchestra, taken up and developed later in the symphony by another. This is, however, not a perfect analogy, for the musical composer effects it by a conscious technique of musical artifice, by utter skill; there is no reason for thinking that these echoes and foretastes in Langland are placed where they are to suit an exact theory of composition; but it is an element so frequent in his writing as to call for notice; to explain it one is driven to say 'that is how his mind worked'; it is as though, on the way to one idea, he would pause or even turn aside a little to see how he could use another, recognise it as a true part of his thought, and pass on with an intention to revisit it when the right moment came. There is something whole and strong in his thought; he does not waste any part of it, for every part of it was also a part of him and of what he believed, and therefore in some way connected with every other of his thoughts, consistent with them. At moments it may seem that 'his speech was like a tangled chain; nothing impaired, but all disordered'; if we remember that he was playing with a plait of three threads it may sometimes help us to see that the disorder is often less his than ours. Allegorical thinking needs practice.

The confession of the deadly sins which occupies the bulk of this Passus needs little analysis for the present purpose of showing the architecture of the poem; it must be understood that these seven Hogarthian phantoms that make confession are intended as the transgressions of the field full of folk embodied or taken as it were in bulk, and divided into the normal medieval categories of self-examination. Thus the seven sins are not new characters in the poem, they are the sins of the crowd he had pictured in the Prologue, and have been with them all the time (thanks to Lady Meed). They make their crude and blundering acts of contrition as best they may, each a little masterpiece of presentation and a source-book for the social historian; to Langland, however, what mattered was that the hearts of his sinful folk were changed, for a moment at least; they must press on to their penance.

> A thousand of men then . thronged together
> Weeping and wailing . for their wicked deeds
> Crying upward to Christ . and to his clean mother
> To have grace to seek saint truth . God lend they so might!
>
> (A.V. 260)

(iv) The fear of famine (A. Passus VI, VII)

The next Passus as last introduces the hero of the poem, the man whose name is given to these visions taken as a whole, Piers Plowman. Langland has kept him back until now for a clear reason. Of the problems he has so far raised, only the Church could satisfy the first, only Conscience and Reason the second, and only Repentance the third. But his fourth question was a question in economics, which meant, for Langland, in things agrarian; so he chose a simple Christian plowman to solve it; the same perhaps of whom there is a 'foretaste' in the opening lines of the poem:

> Some put them to the plough . and played full seldom
> In harrowing and in sowing . swonken full hard.

Now, in Passus VI, he is at last ready to develop this touch, and the almost forgotten plowman, the strength of Langland's economy, steps forward into the poem to take control. Silent hitherto and unperceived, he knows what the farmers of Devonshire call 'the Three Ups of Life', when to stand up, when to speak up, and when to shut up. He also knows St Truth and works for him.

> I have been his fellow . these fifteen winters;
> Both sowed his seed . and seen to his beasts,
> And eke kept his corn . carried it to house,
> Dyking and delving . I do what he bade me,
> There is no labourer in this land . that he loveth more,
> For though I say it myself . I serve him for pay.
> He is the most punctual paymaster . that poor men have.
>
> (A.VI. 33–41)

For Piers and his Master, Truth and Love are practical things, concerned with digging and delving and garnering corn, but there are also moral guides to practise that he knows by heart, namely the two Great Commandments and the laws of Moses; to him who works by them Piers promises:

> Then shalt thou come to a court . clear as the sun,
> The moat is of mercy . The manor all about,
> And all the walls are of wit . to hold will there out;
> The battlements are of Christendom . to save the human race,
> Buttressed with the Belief . where through we may be saved.
> The Tower there Truth is in . is set above the sun,
> He may do with the day-star . what dearly pleases him;
> Death dare not do . thing that he defendeth.
>
> (A.VI. 75–84)

But the crabbed pilgrim's progress to the Tower of Truth described by Piers is not suited to all tastes:

> 'By Christ', quoth a Cut-purse . 'I have no kin there!'
>
> (A.VI. 118)

and others more reasonably say:

> 'This were a wicked way . but whoso had a guide.'
>
> (A.VII. 1)

So Piers promises to lead them, but first they must help to plough his half-acre; this is of course another symbol for the working world. In the early 1360s there had been a new outbreak of plague, killing men rather than women and thus aggravating a shortage of labour already acute; corn was fetching famine-prices.[14] Langland's solution was that all must work, each in his degree, to avert starvation. It is in exact pursuance of what Holy Church had told the Dreamer in Passus I. Work is honesty and that is practical Truth. Harvest will bring food for all and that is practical Love.

There is no reason to suppose that Peirs stands here (in the A Text) for anything more than an ideal type of English country christian whose work pleases God and succours man. He is a character in the sense that Wynnere is a character, but incomparably better drawn; like the heroes of Shakespeare, Piers is himself a natural poet to judge by his imagery, but that is accidental in his nature; the essentials are that he is a farmer and a christian. He knows how to handle men and get his field ploughed; he has a wife and children; he is a good son of the Church.

Work will avert famine, but what of those who cannot or will not work? Shortage of labour does not solve all the problems of unemployment; there are always the cripples and the wasters. They have their say; the former

> ... complained them to Piers . with such piteous words
> 'We have no limbs to labour with . we thank our lord for it.
> But we pray for you, Piers . and for our plough too
> That God for his grace . our grain multiply
> And yield you a return . for the alms you give us here!'
> (A.VII. 116–20)

The latter, more brazenly,

> 'I was not wont to work', quoth a Waster . 'Yet will I not begin!'
> (A.VII. 153)

Piers has no answer for both. The blind or broken-shanked or bed-ridden,

> They shall have as good as I . So me God help.
> (A.VII. 132)

but for the wasters his first impulse is to hand them over to hunger.

> Hunger in haste . hent Waster by the maw
> And wrung him so by the womb . that both his eyes watered.
> (A.VII. 161)

This is a kind of solution to the problem, but not a Christian kind and Piers repents it:

> ... 'They be my blood-brethren . for God bought us all,
> Truth taught me once . to love them each one,
> And help them in all things . according to their need.'
> (A.VII. 196)

And so a better solution is propounded; for the love of God even wasters are to be supported; if not with plenty, at least with a dole sufficient for life:

Bold bidders and beggars . that may swink for their meat,
With hound's bread and horse bread . hold up their hearts
... And if the boys grumble . bid them to swink,
And they shall sup the sweeter . when they have it deserved.

(A.VII. 202–6)

With these solutions and with this seventh Passus ends Langland's survey or vision of his England in triple allegory; he had mapped her evils and shown their remedy in true life; it would be hard to imagine a more clear-sighted survey in so short a space, in language better suited, or in imagery more memorable. The masterly grasp of essentials and the clarity of their poetical organisation, together with the moral voice that speaks through it, are what distinguish it from *Wynnere and Wastoure*, which for all its slightness and superficiality resembles it in this fundamental respect that it is a topical narrative allegory about fourteenth-century England, sauced with satire, in the popular style.

(v) The Pardon (A. Passus VIII)

We are now led to the crucial Passus of the Pardon sent to Piers. It is represented in the poem as a puzzle as well to him as to the Dreamer. It has been a puzzle to all his commentators and, I suppose, a surprise, at the least, to every reader. I do not think it can be fully understood except in the light shed upon it by the B Text, and for this I offer the good reason that it was the Pardon and his ponderings upon it that in the end forced the revising poet to recast the whole work, not merely by augmentation and the rewriting of individual lines, but by adding a mode of meaning that was to transmute it into a new species of poetry, the greatest imaginable to a medieval mind, of which Holy Scripture itself was the exemplar.

All our understanding, then, depends upon a study of this Pardon and how the reader is to take it. Unfortunately there are variant readings in the manuscripts of the very lines upon which the weight of interpretation must fall, and therefore the larger architectural survey of the poem which is attempted in this paper must here give way for a moment to a closer scrutiny.

The new critical edition, eagerly awaited, of the A Text, upon which the late Professor Chambers and Professor Grattan were so long at work, has not yet appeared and the present conjectures must therefore of necessity be based on the information given in Skeat's edition, which may be deemed standard until the new one is available.

By any text, the gist of the eighth Passus is as follows: Truth hears tell of the work done by Piers and his fellow helpers from the Field of Folk, and as a reward a Pardon is granted to him and to them and to their heirs for ever. Piers takes the Pardon trustfully but when it is unrolled at the request of a priest among his followers, it is contained in two lines of Latin:

Et qui bona egerunt, Ibunt in vitam eternam;
Qui vero mala, in ignem eternum.

A dispute arises as to its meaning; the priest denies that it is a pardon at all and Piers tears it up in mortification. The noise of the disputes wakes the Dreamer, who is left meditating the meaning of his vision. All readers of the poem are left to do the same.

The question is, *Was it a valid pardon?* and the variants in the text force us to inquire into this more deeply than the Dreamer himself, whose chief concern was *What did the Pardon mean?* Our first question, however, must be *Where did it come from?* Did Langland mean us to think it came from Truth Himself? For if so it must be considered as in some way valid, whatever logical trap the priest set for Piers about it. This question leads us to the variant readings.

Passus VIII of the A Text in Skeat's edition opens thus:

Treuthe herde telle her-of . And to Pers sende,
To taken his teeme . and tilyen the eorthe;
And purchasede him a pardoun . *A pena et a culpa*
For him, and for his heires . euer more aftur.
And bad holden hem at hom . and heren heore ley3es,
And al that euere hulpen him . to heren or to sowen,
Or eny maner mester . that mihte Pers helpen,
Part in that pardoun . the Pope hath I-graunted.

(A.VIII. 1–8)

There seems to be some confusion here, even in the author's mind. First we are told that it is Truth who purchases and sends the Pardon; then that it is the Pope who has granted it. Which of these is meant? The whole question of its validity depends upon our being sure. That it was purchased by Piers from the Pope, and not by Truth, is supported by the readings in three manuscripts where the third line (above) reads:

> And purchace him a pardoun.
> (Trin. Col. Cambridge R.3. 14, and Harl. 875.)
>
> And purchasen him a pardoun.
> (Univ. Coll. Oxford.)

If we accept either of these alternatives the meaning becomes:

> 'Truth heard tell hereof and sent [a message] to Piers to take his team and till the earth and purchase himself a pardon [from the Pope].'

A reading of this kind seems to be preferred by Chambers, for he writes of this passage:

> The poet goes on to tell how Truth heard of Piers setting folk to work, and bade him purchase a pardon from the Pope; all Piers' helpers are to have a share in it.[15]

If this is indeed the true intention of the passage, then we can but note that this all-important Pardon, whether papal or not, is at least backed by the authority of Truth who told Piers to buy it; to that extent it is warranted genuine, whatever it means.

If on the other hand the true reading is as Skeat printed it in his text ('And purchasede him a pardoun'), then it was Truth who bought it and there can be no dispute as to its efficacy as an instrument of grace, even if its application is enigmatic. But a different question arises, namely, *Where and when did Truth purchase this pardon*? I believe we must look to the preceding Passus for the explanation, to a line already quoted in another context:

> And heo beoth my blodi bretheren . for god bou3te vs alle.
> (A.VII. 196)

'God bought us all' at the Redemption and our pardon was 'purchased' not in Rome but on Calvary, a pardon held to be valid for all generations of christians,

> For him, and fo rhis heires . euer more aftur

an hereditary force that no merely papal pardon can have.

This is the meaning that I think the poet intended us to take and it remains for us to consider how the Pope came into the business at all. I can only suggest that it was the momentary aberration of a poet who, seeking to alliterate his line, overlooked the fact that he was blurring his thought. It is noticeable that the line is revised in the B Text; the Pope is removed, but the alliteration wrecked:

> Pardoun with pieres plowman . treuthe hath ygraunted.
>
> (B.VII. 8)

In the C Text all difficulties are evaded:

> Pardon with peers plouhman . perpetual he graunteth.
>
> (C.X. 8)

If it be thought that these arguments establish that it was indeed Truth who bought and sent the Pardon for Piers and his fellows, then its efficacy cannot be questioned; truth lies in it somewhere and the priest who impugned it, causing Piers to destroy it 'for puire teone' is the villain of the piece,[16] a sophist who understands the letter but not the spirit; more than that, he is an ignoramus (though he should be a man of learning), for he gives no sign of recognition that the Pardon is nothing but a quotation from the Athanasian Creed.[17] For all that, it may seem a grim joke to offer as a piece of Heaven's forgiveness the most threatening sentence from the *Quicunque vult*. Sheep are to enter bliss and goats to burn. Where is the pardon for a goat?

Piers, perhaps because he could not read, had not unrolled the Pardon; he had taken it on faith. But now that he had had it explained to him (in its bleakest sense) by the meddling priest whose office and learning he should be able to trust, he tears it up, exclaiming:

'*Si Ambulauero in medio umbre mortis, non timebo mala, quoniam tu
    mecum es.*
I shall cease of my sowing', quoth Piers . 'and swink not so hard
Nor about my livelihood . so busy be no more!
Of prayer and of penance . my plough shall be hereafter....'

(A.VIII. 102–4)

Of this passage Chambers writes:

Piers' pardon had been a reward promised in exchange for righteous
deeds done. But the priest has denied that the document is a pardon at
all, and the voice of authority seems to be on the side of the priest. So
Piers abandons his charter. It is disputed; so be it; he will trust no longer
to parchment, to bulls with seals, but to the Psalmist's assurance that
death can have no terrors for the just man.[18]

Just so; but who is just? A point instantly taken by Langland.

'*Contra*', quoth I as a Clerk . and commenced to dispute,
    '*Septies in die cadit iustus*:
Seven times a day, saith the Book . sinneth the righteous man.'

(A.IX. 16–17)

If none can do well, if all are goats, what is the force of a
Pardon for sheep? Thus the story of Piers, at its first telling,
came to an abrupt end in paradox, leaving the poet to supply
what explanation he could.

All this maketh me . to muse on dreams
Many a time at midnight . when men should sleep,
And on Piers the Plowman . and what a pardon he had.

(A.VIII. 152–4)

And he roamed about, looking for an explanation,

All a Summer season . For to seek Do-well.

(A.IX. 2)

(vi) The Significacio (A. Passus IX, X, XI)

What do the stumbling meditations of the concluding Passus
add to the swift narrative we have so far traversed? It can
hardly be denied that they show a confusion of thoughts if not
of thought; the bewilderment felt by a modern reader, his
suspicion that the poet has lost his way, that perhaps, even, it
is another poet, may be noted, but, at the last, not wholly

shared; meanwhile it may be partly and naturally explained. These Passus have something of the inconsequence that we sometimes see from verse to verse in the Psalms, where the connection of ideas is often hidden, almost inexplicable, but is accepted with an uncritical and yet intelligent pleasure, a leap of familiar understanding, by reason of many more or less unthinking repetitions. Langland was never far from his Psalter; it would seem to have influenced not only his thoughts but his habit of mind. Some of his ideas may seem to us jerkily connected and by strange associations of idea, but the connections are there and grow easier by familiarity with them. There are two other considerations that may be urged in the defence of his apparently diminishing grasp on the conduct of his poem. First, the narrative impetus, the vision and story of the Field of Folk was spent; the tale had told itself to the tearing of the Pardon, an act that has some relish of poetical finality. *Explicit hic visio willelmi de Petro de Plou3mon.* The poet then began to write a commentary and found himself forced into something more like a sequel for which a fresh wind of the imagination was needed. His commentary was leading beyond itself, as will presently be seen; by some grammarian's trick of thinking in him, the positive Do-well suddenly sprang a comparative and a superlative upon him, Do-better, and Do-best, matters for which, in 1362–63 he was perhaps not fully prepared. Secondly, the nature of this huge new triple subject is of itself more difficult than the state of England to describe poetically, and cannot but have been less familiar to him; tangible England he had seen and lived in some thirty years, but a world of abstract thought is a latecomer to the mind and is in any case less manageable, does not so easily divide itself into subjects (as wealth, government, society, economics), does not yield images so freely, is less obviously a poet's world. All these considerations may help to mitigate any bewilderment that may come upon us in reading the closing Passus of the A Text.

When we ask ourselves what these Passus of *Significacio* are about, we are forced to say that they touch on many topics not very obviously related to each other or to the story of Piers. At first the going is easy; the Dreamer meets a couple of Friars and puts his question, much as the Field of Folk had questioned the ignorant Palmer about St Truth. The two Friars give a sort of answer; in the parable of the Man in the Wagging Boat, they seem to say that although a just man may sin seven times a day, he does no *deadly* sin,

> for Do-well him helpeth
> That is charity the Champion.
>
> (A.IX. 40–1)

If a man's will is not turned against Charity (Do-well), his soul is safe though he stumble; they seem satisfied with this, but not so the Dreamer; the equation of Do-well with charity is too simple; he takes leave of them, turned in upon his own thought. Thought instantly shows him that he is entering upon three fields of inquiry, not one.

> 'Art thou Thought'? quoth I then . 'canst thou me tell
> Where that Do-well dwelleth . do me to know?'
> 'Do-well', quoth he, 'and Do-better . and Do-best the thrid
> Be three fair virtues . and be not far to find....'
>
> (A.IX. 67–70)

Not far to find! It was to take him perhaps fifteen years to find them in their fullness.[19] Meanwhile his task of commentary had tripled itself in a sentence. By that grammarian's trick, Thought had added to the *qui bona* of the Athanasian Creed a *qui meliora*, a *qui optima*, of which nothing had been said in the Pardon to Piers. Yet this new trinity, that seems in the poem to take its origin in a verbal whim, corresponded to a reality defined in the *Meditationes Vitae Christi* and in St Thomas Aquinas, whose work was certainly known, at least by hearsay, to Langland. St Thomas had already distinguished three types of human life, that of Martha who did well and that of Mary who did better; and that third life which combined the virtues of both, a Mary–Martha life that did best of all, the Active, the Contemplative, and the Contemplative-returned-to-Action.[20]

How long Langland had foreseen this branching of his thought it is impossible to say; I do not think it can have been a part of his original design, even though the Dreamer seems to accept it without surprise. It was a development, however, that once perceived could neither be disregarded nor suppressed; yet how difficult to include it in the compass of a *significacio*! Setting out to show what pardon the Active life of the laity in England might hope for, he found himself involved with the clergy and the episcopate, for these, as Thought also told him, were Do-better and Do-best. But there was more than that. In the wake of the Three Lives there followed other necessary but intractable topics, as old and as vast ... Faith and Works ... Learning and Simplicity ... Wealth and Poverty ... Free Will and Predestination ... the Righteous Heathen ... the nature of Charity ... somehow they were all involved, they branched out intertwiningly from the three great limbs of his thought.

It must be said that Langland never deals with any question like an expert; he feels his way towards it often luckily, by images, allegories, and examples; where one fails, he abandons it and tries another with no better guides for his intuition than his christian religion and his common sense. Of all great poets he is the most unprofessional, the only great poet, perhaps, wo is openly contemptuous of poetry-writing as such.[21] Very far from his mind and nature is any such rigid, such careful systematisation as gives a formal charm to the disciplined imaginations of Dante. Contemptuous of the art of poetry, we find him at this stage of his search just as contemptuous of theology,[22] yet here he found himself engaged upon an adventure in thought that involved both, and his mind filling with gigantic intellectual presences; as if some small craft, placidly making port, found itself suddenly in an unknown sea with a school of whales breaking surface round it.

How was all this new material to be organised? He knew at least how his own mind worked: by rumination. Rumination could be given a poetical cast by making an allegory of the growth of his mind, of the stages in his thinking; so he imagined a series of ghostly advisers each figuring one such stage ... Thought – Wit – Study – Learning – Scripture. It was a way of organizing his inquiry. Perhaps, for us, these shadowy figures are not easy to identify with precision,[23] but however tenuous they seem to us, for him they were a help in forming and unifying his work; they gave it a sort of shape.

He struggled to find other images for what he had to say; after rejecting the parable of The Man in the Wagging Boat offered by the two Friars, he tried again in the parable of the Castle of *Caro*. It starts brilliantly. In the Castle lives *Anima* the beloved of God, and Sir Do-well is Lord of the Marches to protect her against Sir *Princeps huius mundi*; Do-bet is her lady-in-waiting, daughter to Do-well; these with Do-best are Masters of the Manor. There is also a Constable of the Castle to keep them all, Sir Inwit, and he has five sons called See-well, Say-well, Hear-well, Work-well, and Go-well. These are promising *dramatis personae* and lure the reader into a hope for some adventure in the manner of *The Bludy Serk*. That poem, however, was still unwritten. The *Pilgrim's Progress*, too, was still in the future.

No adventure befalls the Lady *Anima*; her story falters and dissolves before an untimely interruption into what is perhaps the least well managed passus in the poem. Untimely it may be to the reader hoping for a romantic parable, but to Langland it seemed more important to tell of Kuynde who made this Castle,

> That is the great God . that beginning had never
>
> (A.X. 29)

the creating Father who made man in His own image – gave him ghost of his Godhead – and gave him Conscience, Constable in Chief:

> After the grace of God . the greatest is Inwit
>
> (A.X. 48)

and this moves him to think of those who lack this leadership within, the sots who have drowned it in drink; children and half-wits, over whom the fiend has no power, for they are not, or not yet, responsible. From this he is led to think of education and the wisdom that is begun in the fear of God; learning and teaching recall Do-better to his mind, the clerkly life, and some of the dangers of knowing too much; yet it is by knowledge that Do-better springs from Do-well, and Do-best from both.

> Right as the rose, . that red is and sweet,
> Out of a ragged root . and of rough briars
> Springeth and spreadeth ...
> So Do-best out of Do-well . And Do-better doth spring.
>
> (A.X. 119–23)

Do-better is the child of Do-well not only in this sense, however, but also in the literal sense; priests are the children of layfolk.

It is by this roundabout of meditation that Langland has returned to the theme proposed, namely, 'What is Do-well?' and has marked out its first essential character, namely, that it is a family life of Christian marriage; a sermon upon this ends the Passus with that kind of practical advice we always find in this poem, where common sense flows from spiritual vision.

In this eleventh Passus a second essential character of Do-well is also marked out with equal positiveness; Do-well is defined in terms of active manual labour:

> 'It is a well fair life' quoth she . 'among these simple folk
> *Active* it is called . husbandmen use it.
>
> (A.XI. 179, *et seq.*)

Now, in the twelfth Passus, he passes to a third, namely, the unlearnedness of Do-well. As the purpose of his *significacio* was to explain and justify the Pardon granted to those *qui bona egerunt*, he did not, at that first writing of his poem, see why he should not fulfil this purpose at the expense of those grammatical intruders, Do-better and Do-best; so in defence of Do-well for his unlettered simplicity, Langland adopted a strategy of denying the efficacy of Learning as a means of salvation. He argued this partly from his own observation of the clergy of England who (he thought) used their learning to such ill purposes that they endangered their own souls and those of other people, and partly from what happened to Solomon and Aristotle, who, for all their learning, were said to be in Hell. Happier are the ignorant, the 'lewd jots' whose simple *Paternosters* pierce Heaven; it is the argument used also by Andrew Marvell:

> None thither mounts by the degree
> Of Knowledge, but Humility.[24]

Thus was victory for Do-well gained at the cost of slighting the attainments of clergy. It was a truth halved by prejudice.

A lesser man than Langland might have rested in his anticlericalism all his life; he believed himself to have grounds enough for it, and it had been the burden of his song from the Prologue, where the Parish Priest is described as asking leave to live in London,

> To sing there for Simony . for silver is sweet

to the Pardon, which an officious priest had impugned. Yet there was something in Learning that the poet felt bound to honour, as he shows in the very drift of his allegory. Thought, Wit, Study, Clergy and Scripture, however abstractly personified, are an abstract of instruction; wisdom, says Dame Study, is one of the precious pearls that wax in Paradise.[25]

But this question of the place of Learning in the scheme of salvation brought other questions into Langland's mind; it would be truer perhaps to put it thus, that at the time of writing the A Text he had in mind a number of notions, as yet not very distinct to him, but all in some way fundamental to his christianity; and as he pondered on Learning, these other notions began to move in his mind by a sort of sympathy as if every thought that came to him in the matter of Learning disturbed, touched, and mingled with all his other thoughts, much as one aching tooth will set others on to ache. The resulting complex of his thoughts may be shown in brief tabular analysis:

I. Learning is nowadays pursued for the sake of its rewards in wealth:

> Wisdom and wit now . is not worth a rush
> But it be carded with Covetousness.
>
> (A.XI. 17)

(The same complaint as that of the Prologue:

> I saw there Bishops bold . and Bachelors of Divinity
> Become Clerks of Account . the King for to serve.)

Therefore Learning in alliance with worldly gain is somehow mixed up with and introduces the contrary notion of true christian poverty, a subject treated at length in the revised poem.

II. Learning leads to an intellectualism which allows men to chatter about God, though they have Him not in heart:

> Clerks and acute men . carp often about God
> And have Him much in their mouth . but mean men in heart.
>
> (A.XI. 56)

Learning is thus linked with the question of practising what you preach, of which the reviser has also much to say.

III. But the test of entry into Heaven is neither one of Wealth nor of Poverty, but of Belief and Baptism:

> Paul proveth it is impossible . rich men in Heaven
> But poor men in patience . and penance together
> Have heritage in Heaven . and rich men none.
> 'Contra!' quoth I, 'by Christ! that I can tell you,
> And prove it by the Epistle . that is named Peter;
>   *Qui crediderit et baptizatus fuerit, salvus erit.*'
> 'That is *in extremis*', quoth Scripture . as Sarasens and Jews
> May be saved so . and so is our Belief.
>
> (A.XI. 225)

Thus Faith becomes important in the argument, and the Righteous Heathen. This also is much developed in B.

IV. But Do-well is defined as the Active Life of Work,

> True tillers on earth . tailors and cobblers
>
> (A.XI. 181)

and thus is introduced the antithesis of *Faith and Works*.

V. But however well a man works,

> For how so I work in this world . wrongly or otherwise
> I was marked without mercy . and my name entered
> In the legend of life . long ere I was
>
> (A.XI. 252)

which glances at the topic of *Predestination* (one on which, for a wonder, Langland had less to say than Chaucer).

VI. Solomon was a man of learning; he did well 'in work and word':

> Aristotle and he . who wrought better?
> And all Holy Church . holds them to be in Hell!
>
> (A.XI. 262)

whereas St Mary Magdalen, Dismas the Penitent Thief, and

> Paul the Apostle . that no pity had
> Christian kind . to kill to death?
> And none (to say sooth) . are sovereigns in Heaven
> As are these, who wrought wickedly . in the world, when they
>   were.
>
> (A.XI. 281)

All these were saved by their *Faith*. (David has also somehow got into this category, though more properly he belongs with Solomon his son.) Thus *Learning*, previously opposed to *Unlearned Works*, is now opposed to *Unlearned Faith*, and linked with the problem of *Heathen salvation* too. All these topics, paradoxes and contradictions were in solution in Langland's mind and began to crystallise as he pondered the place of brains in the scheme of Salvation; for the moment he was only able to mention his difficulties and pass them by on his way to the climax he was seeking, namely, corroboration for the Pardon and justification for Do-well. He passed them by. Perhaps he was impatient to finish his poem, and indeed, to some extent, 'the latter end of his commonwealth forgets the beginning'; beautiful as it is, it suggests haste, for whereas the Pardon had been sent as a reward (apparently) for the work done on Piers' half-acre by the Field of Folk, yet if we consider the last lines of the twelfth Passus, it would seem that they were finally saved, not by their works but by their simple faith.

> Are none rather ravished . from the right belief
> Than are these great clerks . that con many books;
> Nor none sooner saved . nor sadder of conscience
> Than poor people as plowmen . and pastors of beasts.

> Cobblers and tailors . and such lewd jots
> Pierce with a *paternoster* . the palace of Heaven
> Without penance at their parting . into high bliss!
>   *Brevis oracio penetrat celum*

Whatever doubts had been raised as to the meaning of Do-well, and whether the followers of Piers were saved by their Faith or by their Works, a high visionary assurance overrules argument in an outburst of poetry and sees poor people saved by sincerity in prayer.

Visionary assurance is not intellectual proof. Langland had not so much finished as finished off his poem. If we feel that his *significacio* is not of equal force with that which it was to explain, we shall be feeling no more than he felt himself; not because he had explained too little, but because Thought had driven him to see how much more there was that needed explanation; he had tripled his problem and this would force him to triple his poem. He had matter for a meditation that was to change his cherished opinions and alter the poetical centre of gravity of his work, not merely by addition in length but by addition in depth also; it would need a new kind of poetry.

The twelfth, last, and hastiest Passus of the A Text is of slight importance, at least to our present study. Preserved in only one manuscript it is remarkable also for its concluding lines in which one Johan But puts forth his head.

> And so bad Iohan but . busily wel ofte,
> When he saw thes sawes . busyly a-legged
> By Iames and by Ierom . by Iop and by othere,
> And for he medleth of makyng . he made this ende.
>   (A.XII. 101–4)

How many lines were added by this interloper is still in dispute; that they were added at some time later than 1377 seems certain from the line

> Furst to rekne Richard . kyng of this rewme.
>   (A.XII. 108)

The Passus, as a whole, has two purposes; first, another mild rebuke to the Dreamer for his presumption in seeking to know Do-better, coupled with the advice to hold fast to that which is good; *quod bonum est tenete*, almost as if *quod melius* were no business of his, and secondly to bring the poem to an end by the simple literary device of killing off the author, who, meeting with hunger and fever, perishes abruptly:

> Deth delt him a dent . and drof him to the erthe
> And is closed vnder clom . crist haue his soule!
>
> (A.XII. 99–100)

The Passus adds nothing to any of the problems raised previously and is no more than a trick-ending of immeasurable inferiority to the close of Passus XI, whoever wrote it or had part in writing it.

III. ADDITIONS AND ALTERATIONS WHERE THE TEXTS RUN PARALLEL

> Now the B-Text runs parallel to the A-Text (apart from additions and alterations made by B) to the point where this vision appears, telling how the search for Do-wel was abandoned. This 'Vision of how the abandoned search was resumed' is the beginning of the B-continuation. (R.W. Chambers and J.H.G. Grattan, *Modern Language Review*, vo. xxvi, No. 1, p. 9.)

When a poet alters his own work, we cannot always see, or even feel, the reason for the change. Why, for instance, did Chaucer find it necessary to rewrite the Prologue to the *Legend of Cupid's Saints*? A question as easy to trip on as a text in the Galatians (to take a phrase from Browning). In the case of *Piers Plowman* we can at least be sure that the B version was written after the A, which is more than we know of the versions of the Prologue to the *Legend*. If we assemble and consider the changes made by Langland in the earlier part of his poem, we should therefore be able to assess in some degree the new directions in which his mind was working; but since the manuscripts are so full of variations from each other, only the larger changes (that cannot be due to scribal interference) will help us in attempting such an assessment.

But no such charge will here be considered on aesthetic grounds, whether it gives a more or a less 'poetical' experience to the reader, for not only would this lead to judgements too subjective, but also it would be foreign to the author's genius; I do not believe he troubled himself greatly about the aesthetic effect of what he was seeking to deliver. A lucky natural gift made poetry of his use of language, but I cannot think he studied particularly to touch that kind of perfection.

The major additions seem to be of the following kinds.[26] First, those which fill out the picture of English society; secondly, those which enforce or elaborate some point in christian morality; thirdly, what I can only call *Foretastes*; insertions, that is, into the early part of the poem, of ideas which are only developed in their fullness at the very end of the B-continuation; and lastly those additions that show something of 'The supernal things of eternal glory', to use a technical term from medieval criticism of allegorical poetry.[27] These classes of addition are worth a detailed consideration.

THE PICTURE OF ENGLISH SOCIETY   In comparing the A Text with *Wynnere and Wastoure* it became clear that both were topical narrative allegories, the former enriched by a moral meaning, about the state of England. The B Text additions of our first category most emphatically bear this out; this part of the poem is more in England than ever, and it may be here useful to point out the time–place scheme of the B Text as a whole which is exactly parallel to the scheme by which the character of Piers seems to change; for just as he seems at first to be a simple christian farmer, then Christ, and finally St Peter and the Popes who succeeded him, so the time and place in the first part of the poem (in both versions, but more emphatically in B) is fourteenth-century England; in the second part (not in A) it is Jerusalem in the First Passion Week; and in the third part it is unspecified Christendom at any time between the Coming of the Holy Ghost and the Coming of Antichrist. This increasing shadowiness in person, time and place gives the poem an extraordinary sense of growing dimension; and this is made possible by the fact that we start so firmly in England; for as we see the reign and Kingdom of Richard II caught gradually up into the 'universal world' so we also see common humanity caught up into the life of God and of His Church.

The first major interpolation is in the Prologue (B, Prol. 87–209) and its function is obvious; it completes the original picture of contemporary England by the inclusion of the King, the Knighthood that 'led' him and the might of the Commons 'that made him to reign'. Rebuke veiled in advice is offered by 'a lunatic' (clearly the poet himself), and an Angel, the voice of Heaven, who reminds the King that he is no more than the Deputy of Christ,

O qui iura regis . Christi specialia regis

(a touch which binds England to those supernal things, which it was also a part of the revising poet's intention to enforce). There follows immediately the highly topical (and terrestrial) fable of the Cat and the Ratons, which puts the political situation of 1376–77 in a brief sardonic fancy.[28]

Another series of large additions that adds rich English colour to the allegory is found in the additions to the confessions of the Seven Deadly Sins which are much enlarged; the missing penitence of *Wrath* is added for completeness; it is mainly devoted to a description of the jangles in Convents and Monasteries (of which the former are the more spiteful); there is a touch of London life added to *Envy*, and of the common practices of business morality to *Avarice*; in like manner, *Sloth* is greatly expanded by many dark details of contemporary abuse. The reviser has thrust in fifteen years' worth of social observation.

The second class of large additions, that reinforce the moral teaching of the poem, is obvious and frequent and need scarcely be illustrated by examples.

The third, which I have ventured to call 'foretastes', is less easily perceived, but when once it is so, is strange and striking.

FORETASTES   We have seen already that it is a character of Langland's writing to throw out hints and images to be developed later in the poem, and some of the larger insertions in the B Text strongly suggest that this was, or became, a conscious device. It should here be said that we cannot be sure whether he started his revision from the Prologue, having in mind some plan for how the visions were to continue after the point at which the A Text comes to an end, or whether he started on the continuation itself, and, having written or roughed it out, returned to the early part of the poem and revised it in the light of what he had added. Some inserted passages seem to point faintly towards the latter procedure; but if that was how he worked, it is strange that he has missed some important opportunities for clarifying his meaning at an early stage; examples of this will presently be offered, but first some of these strange 'foretastes' may be shown.

There are two interpolated passages in the B Prologue which run thus:

> I perceived of the power . that Peter had to keep,
> To bind and to unbind . as the book telleth,
> How he left it with love . as our Lord commanded,
> Among four virtues . the best of all virtues,
> That cardinal are called. . . .
>
> (B, Prol. 100–4)

Then, after a brief fling in pun-fashion at those other Cardinals of the court (whose Pope-making he declines to impugn), he goes on to describe the spiritual basis of society thus:

> And then came Kind-Wit . and clerks he made
> For to counsel the King . and the Commons save. . . .
> The commons contrived . by kind-wit crafts
> And for profit of all the people . plowmen ordained
> To till and labour . as true life asketh.
> The King and the commons . and kind-wit the third
> Shaped law and loyalty . each man to know his own.
>
> (B, Prol. 114–22)

Thus within 22 lines we have the following association of somewhat unusual ideas into one connected argument: the binding-and-loosing power of the Church, the cardinal virtues, the natural gifts of the spirit, which give counsel to the King, Clergy and Commons, shape the law, till the earth and bind society.

Exactly the same association of ideas, expanded, not to say expounded, at much greater length, comes at the very end of

the poem, where its treatment clears some of the mystery
from the meaning of Piers' Pardon, to solve which was the
grand motive of the B Text.

> And when this deed was done . Do-Best he taught
> And gave Piers power . and pardon he granted
> To all manner of men . mercy and forgiveness, . . .
> . . . In covenant that they come . and acknowledge to pay
> To the Pardon of Piers Plowman . *redde quod debes*.
> Thus hath Piers power, . be his pardon paid,
> To bind and to unbind. . . .
>
> (B.XIX. 177–84)

Almost immediately there follows the Coming of the Holy
Ghost and the gifts of the spirit and how they are to be used
(exactly as the Prologue insertion suggests):

> And then began Grace . to go with Piers Plowman
> And counselled him and Conscience . the Commons to
> summon. . . .
> To some he gave wit . to show things in words,
> Wit to win their livelihood with . as the world asks,
> Such as preachers and priests . and apprentices of law,
> They loyally to live . by labour of tongue. . . .
> And some he learnt to labour . a loyal life and a true
> And some he taught to till . to ditch and to thatch. . . .
> And some to ride and recover . what unrightfully was won
> And fetch it from false men . and the laws of Folville.
>
> (B.XIX. 208–41)

And then, after again insisting on *redde quod debes*, and
equipping Piers and his Farm of Holy Church with four oxen
(the Evangelists), four stotts (the Fathers) and the two
harrows of the Old and New Testaments, the author brings
the similarity of these two passages full circle with:

> And Grace gave grains . the cardinal virtues
> And sow them in man's soul. . . .
>
> (B.XIX. 269)

Were these later passages written to expand the interpolation
in the Prologue, or was that interpolation thrust in as a
foretaste of his grand conclusion? Which is the voice and
which the echo? There are other examples. There is, for
instance, a large interpolation in Passus V, continuing for 30

lines. They are among the words of Repentance at the end of the confession of the Seven Sins. Within them occur so many 'foretastes' or 'echoes' of what is to come later, that it is impossible to conceive of either passage having been written without the other in mind, and both are central to the whole argument of pardon and redemption. The earlier passage is as follows:

> And then had Repentance ruth . and counselled them all to kneel,
> For I shall beseech, for all sinful, . our Saviour for Grace....
> 'Now God', said he, 'that of thy goodness . began the world to make
> And of nought madest all . and man most like to thyself,
> And after suffered him to sin . a sickness to us all,
> And all for the best, I believe . whatever the book telleth,
>   *O felix culpa! O necessarium peccatum Adae!*
> For through that sin thy son . sent was to this earth
> And became man of a maid . mankind to save....
> And afterwards with thine own son . in our suit didst die
> On Good Friday for man's sake . at full time of the day....
> The sun for sorrow thereof . lost sight for a time....
> Feddest with thy fresh blood . our fore-fathers in darkness,
>   *Populus qui ambulavit in tenebris, vidit lucem magnam*
> And through the light that leapt out of thee . Lucifer was blinded
> And blew all thy Blessed . into the bliss of Paradise.
> The third day after . thou wentest in our suit,
> A sinful Mary saw thee . ere St. Mary thy dame....
>   *Non veni vocare iustos, sed peccatores ad penitenciam*
> And all that Mark hath made, . Matthew, John and Luke
> Of thy doughtiest deeds . were done in our arms....'
>
> Then Hope hent a horn . of *deus, tu conversus vivificabis nos*
> And blew it with *beati quorum . remisse sunt iniquitates.*
>
>   (B.V. 485–515)

Can anybody doubt that this was written in direct relation to Passus XVIII and XIX, to Langland's account of the Harrowing of Hell and its consequences? Phrase recalls phrase and image recalls image; for instance 'our suit' (human flesh), the armour in which Christ is to do 'doughty deeds', rings forward to

> This Jesus of his gentle birth . will joust in Piers' arms
> In his helm and his habergeon . *humana natura*
>
>   (B.XVIII. 22–3)

or again the blinding of Lucifer by the Light shining in darkness recalls the earlier passage thus:

> Dukes of this dim place, . anon undo the gates
> That Christ may come in . the King's son of Heaven
> And with that breath, Hell brake . with Belial's bars
> In spite of guard and guardian . wide open the gates,
> Patriarks and prophets . *populus in tenebris*
> Sang St John's song . *ecce agnus dei*
> Lucifer might not look . for light so blinded him.
>
> (B.XVIII. 317)

One or two such similarities might be dismissed as accidental, since the Harrowing of Hell was a well-known story, but such a clenching together of images that were to be used again at greater length at the peak of the poem can hardly be other than a deliberate anticipation, a piece of purposeful revision; and the purpose is clear enough. It is to link the Confession of the Field of Folk, that is, of Do-well, with the pardon purchased on Calvary, and with that binding and unbinding power which Langland says was won by Christ's conquest over falseness and death and Hell.

This technique of anticipation, the casting of a seed into the poem that it may flower again later, may be seen in many places; for instance, the first hint we are given in anticipation of the jousting of Jesus at Jerusalem (fully described in B. XVIII.10–30), comes far earlier, in these lines:

> And then spake Spiritus Sanctus . in Gabriel's mouth
> To a maid that was called Mary . a meek thing withal,
> That one Jesus, the son of a judge . should rest in her chamber
> Till *plenitudo temporis* . were fully come,
> That Piers' fruit flowered . and fell to be ripe.
> And then should Jesus joust therefore . by judgment of arms
> Whether of them should take the fruit . the fiend or himself.
>
> (B.XVI. 90)

Another example may be seen in the lines:

> Such arguments they move, . these masters in their glory
> And make men misbelievers . that muse much on their words
> *Imaginative* here-afterward . shall answer to your purpose.
>
> (B.X. 113)

which not only foreshadows the coming of Imaginative some seven hundred and fifty lines later, but also the Doctor on the Dais, God's Glutton of Passus XIII.

Against this notion of revisionary foresight it may be urged and must be admitted that if the poet knew what was coming he missed some important opportunities very strangely. For instance, in the third Passus of the B Text there is a large addition celebrating the rule of love that is to come on earth, when there shall be 'peace among the people and perfect truth'; it is difficult to know when this Golden Age is to be. I am unable to believe with Skeat that it has something to do with the jubilee of Edward III, and incline to think it eschatological; for before this happy time is to come about, 'men shall find the worst' (B.III. 323) and if this refers to the Coming of Antichrist, as perhaps it may, it is so feeble a foretaste of that event as pictured in B.XX. 51, that one would suppose the poet ignorant at the time of revision how the poem was to end. So, too, when he came to revise the line

> Actyf lyf or contemplatyf . Crist wolde hit alse
> (A.VII. 236)

he was content to rewrite it thus

> Contemplatfy lyf or actyf lyf . Cryst wolde men wrouȝte
> (B.VI. 251)

which does nothing to prepare the reader for the fact that these Lives are the basis of Do-well, Do-better and Do-best, of which he presently has so much to say, for they are the backbone of the whole B Revision from the eighth Passus onwards.

THE SUPERNAL THINGS OF ETERNAL GLORY   Into the morning daylight of his English scene the reviser has flung a shaft here and there from that further world to which Do-well, Do-better and Do-best are the roads. Even in the A Text, as has been said, that world had been adduced as the type, end, and sanction of Christian life, and particularly in its moral aspect, that is, the solving of contemporary problems by Christian principles; but now this moral note is

softened and exalted by touches, rare as they are, which add a
quality lyrical and contemplative to what before was mainly
admonitory. One such passage, the foretaste of the
Harrowing of Hell, has already been considered, of which the
key-note is redemptive love; another interpolation on the
same subject is put into the mouth of Holy Church:

> For truth telleth that love . is treacle of Heaven
> May no sin be on him seen . that useth that spice....
> For Heaven might not hold it . it was so heavy of itself
> Till it had of the earth . eaten its fill.
>   And when it had of this fold . flesh and blood taken
> Was never leaf upon linden-tree . lighter thereafter
> Light to bear and piercing . as the point of a needle
> That no armour can keep out . nor no high wall;
> Therefore is love leader . of the lord's folk in Heaven....
> And, to know it in its nature, . it begins in a power
> And in the heart is its head . and the high well.
>
> (B.I. 146)

This is, perhaps, the finest passage in the revised Prologue;
another such glimpse may be caught in a passage where the
Church, traditionally the Bride of Christ, is seen in Heaven as
the Bride of Man also:

> My Father the Great God is . and ground of all graces,
> One God without beginning . and I his good daughter,
> And hath given me mercy . to marry as I will
> And whatsoever man is merciful . and loyally loves me
> Shall be my lord and I his love . in the high Heaven
>
> (B.II. 29)

Gathering together what has been said of all these classes of
addition we may discern the following trends and qualities in
the revising poet so far; an insistence on the Englishness of his
scene, as it is and as it ought to be; a great emphasis upon the
need, fullness, and efficacy of confession, a hinting
consciousness of the great vision of Redemption to come
later, and a more touching sense of the enfolding and creative
love of God the Father. These things are made into a poetry
that has moments of lyrical contemplation, suggestive of a
mystical rather than a moral vision, in so far as these can be
distinguished.

IV. THE POINT AT WHICH THE TEXTS BEGIN TO DIVERGE

The A-Text is not a brief first draft of the B-Text. It is a fragment of a poem which, had it been continued, would presumably have been continued in much the same way as the completed B-Text. For the accounts of Do-wel and Do-bet and Do-best in the A-Text forecast a continuation on the same lines as we ultimately get.

The A-Text breaks off so suddenly in the middle of Do-wel, because the poet feels unable to solve the problems he has raised. (R. W. Chambers and J. H. G. Grattan, *M.L.R.*, vol. xxvi, No. 1, p. 10)

It is my present purpose to suggest that the A Text is indeed 'not a brief first draft of the B-Text', but was undertaken by the author, under the stimulus of *Wynnere and Wastoure*, as a topical narrative allegory about the moral condition of England; his narrative went vigorously forward to its climax, which was a Pardon for that moral condition, granted to the Field of Folk. This Pardon, however, was enigmatic, even to Langland, so he set himself to ponder and explain it; but as he did so, other immense and unexpected problems arose before him; he grappled with them as well as he then knew how, without swerving more than he could help from what seemed to be his poetical task, namely the justification of the followers of Piers and the assertion of the truth of their pardon. As we have seen, this high assurance was reached at the end of his eleventh Passus, but only by denigrating the clergy and by evading the issue whether the simple were pardoned for their works or their faith.

Langland's honesty did not allow him to rest for ever in such a conclusion; as the years went by he continued to ponder and, as he did so, his thought insensibly changed its objective; he found himself committed to a poem not about England but about Salvation and the Three Ways that led to it, of which up till then he had explored but one. To make this new theme effectual in poetry, he found himself driven to reshape his poem by a known technical expedient of adding a fourth plane of meaning, the anagogical as it was called, the meaning in *aeterna gloria*. More will be said of this later; for the moment let us consider his effort to achieve the difficult grafting of the new vision on to the old at their point of divergence. We have seen that some at least of his alterations forecast the distant shape of his final solution, but between that and his retouchings of the story of the Field of Folk lay a perplexing middle that was to be the intellectual core of the poem, in that its chief business was to expound the moral nature of the Three Lives (with fairness to each), and to give hearing to some of those other problems, (Faith, Works, Learning, Wealth, Poverty, and the rest) that had already forced their way into the A Text. This would involve much theological speculation; neither nature, nor perhaps education had fitted Langland to be an exact theologian, yet theology had to be faced; the poet had already confessed his difficulties through the mouth of Dame Study, who had frankly admitted:

> Theology hath troubled me . ten score times
> For the more I muse thereon . the mistier it seemeth
>
> (A.XI. 136)

and this must be accepted as an apology for that bewilderment which makes him 'break off so suddenly in the middle of Do-wel, because the poet feels unable to solve the problems he has raised'.

The divergence between the two poems begins to be very marked where A.X is being converted into B.IX, that is, exactly where the theologising starts; and it is not until B.XI, where the author leaves the older poem behind and launches into new work that his firmness of grasp seems increasingly to return to him; it is as if he were encumbered rather than helped by what lay before him in A.X and XI. To deal with A.XII was simple enough; it could be scrapped altogether; and except for a few touches – the scornful character of Scripture (A.XII. 12 to B.XI. 1), the hint of on-coming age in the Dreamer (A.XII. 60 to B.XI. 59), a tag from 2 Corinthians and another from Thessalonians, both used in other contexts in B (A.XII. 22 to B.XVIII. 393, and A.XII. 56 to B.III. 335) – it was scrapped.

But how to deal with A.X and XI was another matter; they both contained much that he still wanted to say, and yet they had somehow led him to a conclusion that was in a sense false, or incomplete; to detect exactly at what point a ramified argument is going astray is always one of the most difficult problems in revision, and I am bound to think the revising poet's second thoughts, particularly in B. XI, have strayed even farther from his distant objective than did the A Text before him. Indeed the impression is sometimes given that he had no text before him, that he was revising this part from memory; as he seems to have been unhappy in the new conduct of his argument, so also his power as a poet seems temporarily occluded. Interpolations such as those at B. IX.35–44, 61–72, 96–129 and 143–59 are like the movements of a pedestrian who in leaving a track that seemed to be leading him astray, strays even farther, with uncertain foot. In B. X, however, he returns to his path, his interpolations are better managed and his poetical vision returns in some degree. I would instance two such interpolations, one for its change in emphasis and the other for its imaginative sympathy, deeply related to the new turn of his argument.

The former is a redefinition of the Three Lives that begins at B. X.230. If this is compared with the far briefer sketch of them given in the corresponding passage in A.XI. 179–200, it will be seen that Do-wel is now seen as a life based on elementary faith (particularly what the Church teaches of the Trinity and other articles of the faith as warranted by the Gospels and St Augustine) as opposed to the mere activities of 'trewe tilieries on erthe . taillours and souteris, and alle kyne crafty men' recommended as Do-wel in the A Text (A.XI. 181–2). The purpose of this seems to be an insistence that simple plowmanship is not enough and that some instruction to the lewd is absolutely necessary to salvation; and this prepares the reader for the wisdom of Imaginative later on who points out that Do-wel is lost without Do-better to instruct him in the articles of the Church 'that falleth to be knowe'.

> Take two stronge men . and in Themese caste hem,
> And bothe naked as a nedle . her none sykerer than other,
> That one hath connynge . and can swymmen and dyuen,
> That other is lewed of that laboure . lerned neuere swymme;
> Which trowestow of the two . in Themese is in most drede?
>
> (B.XII. 161–5)

Without Do-better, Do-well would drown, for ignorance. So too Do-bet is redefined in terms of suffering and practising what you preach, pointing thus more surely to the life of Christ as Do-bet, which is to come, rather than simply saying (as A does) that it consists in feeding the hungry, healing the sick, and obeying the rules of conventual life. The alterations in Do-best insist on the moral qualities that underlie his episcopal authority rather than on the fact stressed in A that he controls benefices. All these changes are well wrought to make a better coherence with the later developments of the revised poem.

The second interpolation, that is so poetically striking and shows the returning vision that seemed to be failing in B.XI, takes up the story of Noah from A.X. 159 again and gives it a marvellous new twist in the direction of the great argument he is now conducting, whether their learning, which had helped to build the wisdom of mankind, had saved Solomon and Aristotle.

> But I ween it happened with many . that were in Noah's time
> When he shaped that ship . of shingles and of boards
> Was never wright saved that wrought thereon . nor other workman else
> But birds and beasts . and the blessed Noah,
> And his wife with his sons . and also their wives;
> Of wrights that wrought it . none of them was saved.
> God leave it fare not so by folk . that teach the Faith
> Of Holy Church, that is our harbour....
>
> (B.X. 399–406)

> At Doomsday will the deluge be . of death and fire at once;
> Therefore I counsel you Clerks . the wrights of Holy Church
> Work ye the works that you see written . lest you be worth naught therein....
> What Solomon says I trow is truth . and certain of us all
> There are wise men, and well-living . but their works are hid
> In the hands of Almighty God . and He knows the truth
> Whether for love a man will be allowed there . and for his loyal works....
>
> (B.X. 411–33)

This anticipates the *et vidit deus cogitationes eorum* of B.XV. 194–5. An imagination that touches home so closely as to think with compassion on the labourers of Noah who were lost for all their labour, and to see in them an analogy for such as Solomon and Aristotle, whose wisdom supports a faith that can save others but not them, unless indeed their love, known only to God, has lifted them into his hand, such an imagination shows the returning powers of the poet.

After the Divergence of the Texts

So far in following the process of revision we have only considered some interpolations made in the B version before it finally parts company with the A. When it does so, although some arguments are new and some opinions reversed, the life of the poem is nevertheless not interrupted, for the revising poet has continued the allegory of his own maturing mind (so far pictured in Thought, Wit, Study, Clergy, Scripture) by the introduction of a further figure, *Imaginative*, which claims to have followed the poet for five and forty winters; it is to be associated with the concept of Memory, the memory of an adult man reviewing his opinions in the light of his experiences.[29] It is through this figure that the author retracts and redresses the injustices done in A.XI by the denigration of clergy, retaining the course of his allegory while changing the course of his argument, an ingenious and poetical way of saving his work from self-contradiction.

The study of the author's revisionary method that has been offered has been suggestive rather than exhaustive, and its purpose to show such changes as seem to bear on the transformation of the poem from one about England into one about the search for eternal life; in the course of this transformation, Langland found himself faced with many new problems, as we have seen; two of the most important of which are an understanding of Do-wel, Do-bet and Do-best, and an understanding of the part in them played by Faith, Works and Learning. The great additions of the B Text are too many and too complex to be treated fully here, but something may be said of his handling of each of these two problems, to show how he has lifted them into the fourth plane of allegory already mentioned, that is, into the supernal things of eternal glory.

Do-wel, Do-bet, and Do-best

There is a particularly strange passage in the A Text that so far as I know has received little attention; it runs:

> And as Do-wel and Do-bet . duden hem to vnderstonde,
> Thei han I-Corouned A kyng . to kepen hem Alle,
> That ȝif Do-wel or Do-bet . dude aȝeyn Do-best,
> And were vnbuxum at his biddinge . and bold to don ille,
> Then schulde the kyng comen . and casten hem in prison,
> And puiten hem ther In penaunce . with-outen pite or grace,
> Bote ȝif Do-best beede for hem . a-byde ther for euere!
>   Thus Do-wel and Do-bet . and Do-best the thridde
> Crounede on to beo kyng . and bi heor counseil worche,
> And Rule the Reame . bi Red of hem Alle,
> And otherwyse elles not . bute as thei threo assenten.
>
> (A.IX. 90–100)

This seems a very dark saying; but that it was clear in meaning to the reviser seems certain, for he repeated it almost verbatim in the corresponding passage of the B Text. The sense seems to be:

> And as Do-wel and Do-bet gave them [the wicked] to understand, they have crowned a King to control them all, so that if Do-wel or Do-bet rebelled against Do-best, and were disobedient to his bidding and bold to do evil, then the King should come and cast them into prison, and put them to their penance without pity or grace, where they should stay for ever, unless Do-best prayed on their behalf. Thus Do-wel, Do-bet and Do-best, all three, crowned one to be King and to work by their counsel, and rule the Kingdom by the advice of them all, and otherwise not, except by their assent.

On the face of it, it seems an obscure statement of some form of social contract, and we are incited to ask who is this King? When was he crowned by these three lives? What is this pitiless prison that only the prayers of Do-best can save the disobedient from? And if he is King why should he be controlled by those who have crowned him?

There is another passage, if anything darker still, that seems to give a partly similar message; it is one of the interpolations at the point of divergence of the two Texts:

> Ac there shal come a kyng . and confesse ȝow religiouses,
> And bete ȝow as the bible telleth . for brekynge of ȝowre reule,

> And amende monyales . monkes and chanouns,
> And putten hem to her penaunce . *ad pristinum statum ire*,
> And Barounes with Erles beten hem . through *beatus-virres*
>   techynge,
> That here barnes claymen . and blame ȝow foule.
>
> (B.X. 317–22)

and then, after a brief and excessively difficult passage about the donation of Constantine and the Abbot of Abingdon, irrelevant to our present purpose, the passage ends:

> Ac ar that kynge come . cayme shal awake.
> Ac dowel shal dyngen hym adoune . and destryen his myȝte.
>
> (B.X. 329–30)

I confess that the lines here quoted seem to me very hard to translate and it may be that some textual corruption has made them untranslatable. I offer, nevertheless, what may be accepted as a rendering:

> But there shall come a King and bring you Religious people [i.e. Do-bet] to confession, and make you better [possibly 'beat', but I think the sense is against it] for breaking the Rule of your Order, and amend nuns, monks and canons, and put them to their penance [namely to] return to their former state [? obedience to their Rule], and make barons and earls better themselves [?] through the teaching of the First Psalm [in respect of] what their children claim, blaming you [Religious people] foully [? for having defrauded them of their inheritance].... But ere that King shall come, Cain will awake; but Do-well shall ding him down and destroy his power.

The similarity of thought in these two prophecies, vague though they be, suggests that the second is some sort of recollection or development of the first; a King is to come and bring to penance those who are disobedient, especially the Religious Orders, though a part of the Laity also will come under reproof. The second passage adds that before this is to happen, Cain shall awake; but Do-well will deal with him.

Conjecture as to what these things meant to Langland must be insecure,[30] but by reference to the end of the poem an interpretation can be found which gives a good sense. In Passus XX there is a vision of the coming of Antichrist

And the Religious reverenced him . and rung their bells
And all the convent came forth . to welcome that tyrant
And all his followers as well as himself . save only fools.

(B.XX. 58)

It is true that in the event, the fools, though called upon by Conscience to come into Unity, make no attempt to 'ding him adown', and he passes like a tornado through the poem leaving all in havoc save Conscience. There is, however, some whiff of similarity to the passage quoted about Cain, and if that hint be accepted, we may conjecture that all these three passages are linked in meaning, and that their meaning is eschatological. From this we may infer that the King who is to come and 'confess the Religiouses' is Christ at His Second Coming. This would answer our questions who is this King and what his prison? The question whether Do-best can pray them out of prison is more difficult; it is raised again in the case of Trajan, who

... had been a true knight . [and] took witness at a Pope
How he was dead and damned . to dwell in torment....
Gregory knew this well . and willed to my soul
Salvation for the Truth . that he saw in my works.

(B.XI. 136)

However in Trajan's case, Langland seems to think the prayers of Do-best were not enough, for he adds:

Not through prayer of a Pope . but for his pure Truth
Was that Saracen saved . as St Gregory beareth witness.

(B.XI. 150)

Perhaps we are safe in suggesting that the 'prison' in A.IX. 94, is Purgatory and not Hell, in which case the prayers of the Church are held to have efficacy. This leaves only one question to be answered, namely, when was Christ 'crowned' and controlled by Do-wel, Do-bet and Do-best, and in what sense? Again the answer seems to be given at the end of the poem. After the vision of the Harrowing of Hell, the poet goes to hear Mass, and there has a dream of Jesus as Christ Conqueror which is expounded to him by Conscience. 'In His youth', says Conscience

> this Jesus . at a Jew's feast
> Water into wine turned . as Holy Writ telleth,
> And there began God . of His grace to do well.
>
> (B.XIX. 104)

Later, says Conscience,

> He made lame to leap . and gave light to the blind,
> And fed with two fishes . and with five loaves
> More than five thousand . sorely hungred folk.
> Thus he comforted the care-stricken . and caught a greater name
> Which was Do-bet....
>
> (B.XIX. 121)

and at last, having been crowned on Calvary[31] and having won His triumphs over Hell, He returned in resurrection to Galilee and to the Disciples,

> And when this deed was done . Do-best He taught
> And gave Piers power . and pardon he granted
> To all manner men . mercy and forgiveness
> (And gave[32] him might, men to assoil . of all manner sins
> In covenant that they come . and acknowledge to pay
> To the Pardon of Piers Plowman . *redde quod debes*
>
> (B.XIX. 177)

Thus, by taking all these scattered passages together, the full meaning of the first becomes clear. Christ, by living Do-well, Do-bet and Do-best in His own person, is crowned by them on Calvary, having been obedient to those ways of life and having appointed them as the advisers by which His Kingdom is to be ruled.

Faith, Works, and Learning

These are matters powerfully entangled in both A and B Texts. As has already been noticed, the Field of Folk seem to receive their Pardon for their Work under Piers; Piers had begun their instruction by telling them that the way to Truth is by obedience to the Commandments (and this, as we shall see, counts as 'Works');[33] on the other hand he adds that when they come at last to 'the Court, clear as the sun, where Truth is in' they will find it

Buttressed with the Belief . wherethrough we may be saved
                                          A.VI. 79

which clearly gives importance to Faith. So too, when Piers
turns from his work of labour in the fields, quoting the psalm
of trust '*si ambulavero in medio umbre mortis, non timebo mala*',
he glances also at a text from St Matthew:

Ne soliciti sitis . he saith in his gospel
                                        (A.VIII. 112)

which is a pointer to the verse that ends 'Shall he not much
more clothe you, O ye of little faith?'
    Faith and Works are thus alternately stressed, and it is far
from clear, as we have seen already, whether it is the 'true
tilling' of Do-Well or his simple *paternoster* that has the
greater power of his justification in the eleventh Passus of the
A version. But these two conceptions, from the very start, are
complicated by a third, namely that of Learning. For when
Piers quotes the psalm about the valley of the shadow, the
derisive priest retorts upon him for his show of Latin and
suggests in mockery that Piers should turn priest himself and
preach on the theme *Quoniam literaturam non cognovi*.
    When Langland comes to consider the effects of Learning
on the learned, he finds that their skill in the subtleties of the
Faith does not issue in those Works to which it commits them:

Thus they drivel on their diais . the Deity to know
And deem God into the gorge . when their guts are full.
But care-full man may cry . and call at the gate,
Both of hunger and of thurst . and for chill quaking
And no man comes nigh him . to amend his need....
                                          (A.XI. 42)

God is much in the gorge . of these great masters,
But among mean men . His mercy and His works.
                                          (A.XI. 53)

But their lack of inward charity is not the only count against
the learned nor even their failure to practise what they preach.
Their Learning itself is a danger to Christendom. It is the old
business of the *Song of Nego*,

Now o clerk seiith *nego*;
And that other *dubito*;
Seiith another *concedo*;
And another *obligo*,
Verum falsum sette therto;
Than is al the lore i-do.
Thus the fals clerkes of har hevid,
Makith men trewth of ham be revid.[34]

Subtleties in discussion, as whether Two Members of the Trinity could be held to have conspired to slay the Third,[35] or why God allowed the Serpent to seduce Eve[36] (says Langland), must shake the Faith of simple folk.

Such motions they move . these masters in their glory
And make men misbelieve . that muse on their words.

(A.XI. 70)

Better not to know such things; *Non plus sapere quam oportet sapere*. Christ Himself had spoken against learning when He said 'Take no thought beforehand what ye shall speak'[37] and St Augustine had confessed *Ecce, ipsi ydiote rapiunt celum, ubi nos sapientes in infernum mergemur*.[38]

And thus, through a tangle of thoughts on the effect of Learning on Faith and Works, the Author had passed to his first conclusion, the justification of Do-wel by his simplicity, and the damning of the Doctors.

In this conclusion, however, he was unable to rest; he came in middle age to see that without Learning there could be no Faith, not even the simple Faith that reposes on a *paternoster*; for who is to teach a tinker how to say his prayers except a learned priest?

And as a blind man in battle . beareth weapon to fight
And hath no hap with his axe . his enemy to hit,
No more can a man of natural wit . unless clerics teach him
Come for all his wit . to Christendom and be saved
Which is the coffer of Christ's treasure . and clerics keep the keys.

(B.XII. 107)

This is the advice of *Imaginative*, the power of a man in middle age, to see the images of memory in their true perspective. The Dreamer stands self-rebuked for his earlier contempt of Learning.

We have seen in outline the complex of ideas centring round Faith, Works, and Learning in the A Text; we have seen that in the A Text, aiming at the justification of the Pardon of Piers, Langland made what might be called a false landing and finished off his poem as best he might, justifying Do-wel at the expense of Do-bet; and we have seen that the reviser has not suppressed any of these things, although he was obviously of a different opinion; true to the existing organisation of the poem on the lines of a spiritual autobiography, he leaves on record the prejudices of his youth in all their insolence and passes on to his maturity and the change of his views. That is why the next Passus in the B Text (B.XI) deals with his wayward worldly life, giving the passage of time,

> Till I forgot Youth . and hastened into Eld
>
> (B.XI. 59)

and met with *Imaginative*.

But even *Imaginative* cannot fully resolve the whole problem, for all his arguments about the Penitent Thief, Trajan and Aristotle, classic examples of Faith, Works and Learning, respectively. The trouble was that poetically speaking these three historical figures, though they made an argument, did not make a picture; without a picture, without a story, the argument hung fire, for Langland's thinking was always clearer to him when it came under an allegory, a narrative; we have seen this not only in his organisation of the English scene, but also in his effort to dress his later arguments in a sort of autobiography. He was never really at home with *nego*, *dubito* and *concedo*. He was, however, given to thinking in terms of trinities; Do-wel, Do-bet and Do-best; Faith, Works, Learning. It was in puzzling over these and how to match them with each other that he suddenly hit upon a new trinity and a new story that could embrace his whole thought; the trinity was that of the three virtues, Faith, Hope and Charity, and the story was the story of the Good Samaritan.

> (I do it on *Deus Caritas* . to deem the sooth).

Most delicately, most gradually, the allegory is introduced; the unsuspecting reader can hardly see it happening until it has happened. First, as if in continuation of the series of his ghostly companions (Wit, Study, Imaginative, Conscience, Patience, and the rest), Piers Plowman returns into the poem

> and all for pure joy
> That I heard name his name . anon I swooned after
> And lay long in a lone dream . and at last methought
> That Piers the Plowman . all that place showed me.
>
> (B.XVI. 18)

He teaches the ravished dreamer how to understand the tree of Charity and its Triune support and the first notes of the theme of the Incarnation are sounded:

> Then spake *Spiritus Sanctus* . in Gabriel's mouth
> To a maid called Mary....
>
> (B.XVI. 90)

the life of Christ is then swiftly told up to the Crucifixion; very naturally this is followed by the coming of Faith, in the form of Abraham its great exemplar, and he too teaches the dreamer the nature of the Trinity and speaks of the Incarnation and the Sacrament of the Altar; in his bosom lie many, Lazarus, the Patriarchs and Prophets, in safe keeping against the day when Christ descending into Hell shall release them from the power of the Fiend. And, as that is matter for hope, it is Hope who immediately appears, in the form of Moses.

Why should Moses stand for Hope? He bears the tables of the Law, *Dilige Deum et proximum*, which link exactly with those words spoken by Piers when he first set the world to *work*.

> You must go through meekness . both man and wife,
> Till you come into conscience . that Christ knows the Truth
> That you love Him more dearly . than the life in your hearts,
> And then our neighbours next....
>
> (A.VI. 51)

Abraham is to Faith as Moses is to Works; each justifies his claim to have saved many souls; and so it is argued:

> And as we went thus in the way . wording together
> Then saw we a Samaritan . sitting on a mule
>
> (B.XVII. 47)

who brings a parable within a parable to tell the story of Faith, Hope and Charity. Of all the subtle foretastes in which this poem abounds, the phrase *sitting on a mule* is the most pregnant; it is the first hinting that the Samaritan, Charity, is Christ Himself. But the story is not yet far enough told for a full identification; so great a vision must open with extreme gradualness, and except for this hint, the true identity of the Good Samaritan is held in reserve. Meanwhile we see him tend the man who fell among thieves while Faith and Hope play the parts of the Priest and the Levite:

> Faith flew away . and Spes his fellow too
> Forsight of the sorrowful man . that had been robbed by thieves
>
> (B.XVII. 88)

Who is this sorrowful man but the human race, fallen among thieves in their first garden?

> For in my palace, Paradise, . in person of an adder....
> Thievishly thou didst rob me....
>
> (B.XVIII. 333)

And neither Faith nor Hope is sufficient for the wound:

> 'Have them excused', said the Samaritan . their help my little avail
> No medicine upon earth . can bring the man to health,
> Neither *Faith* nor fine *Hope*, . so festered are his wounds,
> Without the blood of a boy . born of a maid.
>
> (B.XVII. 90)

So the Samaritan begins his teachings, and in image upon image tells of the death of Death (*O Mors, ero mors tua*), and of the mystery of the Trinity (like a Hand: fist, finger and palm; like a Torch: wax, wick and flame), and of repentance and pardon. In this story and in this teaching that crowns it, Faith, Works and Learning are made one with Faith, Hope and Charity; Allegory has resolved argument.

But there is a climax still to come, the hinted identifications have still to be made manifest; it is kept back for the next Passus, the next dream, for the Good Samaritan has spurred his mule

> And went away as wind . and there-with I awaked.
>
> (B.XVII. 350)

Weary and wet-shod, Langland 'went forth after, all my life-time' until again he slept:

> And of Christ's passion and penance . reaching to the people
> (Resting myself and deep asleep . till *ramis palmarum*),
> Of children chanting *gloria laus* . I greatly dreamed....
> One semblable to the Samaritan . and something to Piers the
>   Plowman
> Barefoot upon an ass's back . unbooted came riding....
> Then was *Faith* in a window . and cried '*A! fili David!*'
> As doth an herald of arms . when the adventurous come to joust
> Old Jews of Jerusalem . for joy they sang
>   *Benedictus qui venit in nomine domini*
> Then I asked of *Faith* . what all this affair meant....
> 'Is Piers in this place'? said I . and he peered upon me,
> 'This Jesus of His gentle birth . will joust in Piers' arms,
> In his helm and in his habergeon . *humana natura*.
>
> (B.XVIII. 1–23)

At last Charity and Learning, the Good Samaritan and Piers, are made one with Christ, and He one with humanity. This is (I suppose) the top of all English allegorical writing, the greatest gathering of the greatest meanings in the simplest symbols.

Thus in the B Text, the seeds set so unregardingly in the A have grown to their flower and fruit. It would indeed be true in a certain sense to say that there is no material in the revised poem which is not present or implicit in the earlier one. Yet it might not have been given to the revising poet to see it all so clearly, to let it grow to its natural organic shape. The *Canterbury Tales* are unfinished; a hundred more stories are implicit in its plan; but of all those untold tales we could not name one that is implied by the structures of the poem in the sense that the story of the life and passion of Christ is implicit in the A Text of Piers Plowman, as are also the stories of the

Harrowing of Hell, the building of Piers' Barn of Holy Church, and the Coming of Antichrist, given the allegorical genius to see them there. From the moment when Thought first told the Dreamer of Do-well, Do-better, and Do-best, the stories of the Incarnation and the founding of Christendom were inevitable *exempla* for who could perceive and tell them. In the course of the years they were perceived and told.

It need hardly be said that they are the most striking additions made in the revision; if one were to imagine the A Text published with the B Prologue, the resulting poem would still be near in kind to *Wynnere and Wastoure*. Both these other additions have outsoared what is topical and temporal, albeit the Prologue is more securely anchored to fourteenth-century England than ever; the author has found the ways to Paradise 'by way of Kensal Green'.

Allegory is a way of thinking, parallel thinking; thought directed to a subject on several levels of reality at once. It seems to have arisen out of Christianity and spread to science and poetry; but in Holy Scripture was its home. Origen distinguished three meanings, the historic, the moral, and the spiritual;[39] that is the verbal, the moral, and the mystical.

In the dedication to Leander of Seville of his lectures on the Book of Job Gregory the Great puts forward a similar view:[40]

You must know that there are some parts which we explain historically, others we search out by allegory, investigating symbolical meaning, in others we open out only moral lessons, allegorically conveyed, while there are some few which we discuss in all these ways together, exploring them by a three-fold method.

A fourth way of interpretation was also discovered, especially for biblical exegesis, popularly expressed in the tag:

Littera gesta docet, quid credas allgoria
Moralis quid agas, quo tendas analogia[41]

and this is elaborated in the *Summa* of St Thomas, Question 1, Article 10, and quoted in Mr. H. W. Troyer's extremely suggestive article 'Who is Piers Plowman?'[42] An even clearer account of the fourfold method of interpretation appears in the *Convivio* of Dante.

Writings may be taken and should be expounded chiefly in four senses. The first is called the literal, and it is the one that extends no further than the letter as it stands; the second is called the allegorical, and is the one that hides itself under the mantle of these tales, and is a truth hidden under a beauteous fiction.... It is true that the theologians take this sense otherwise than the poets do, but since it is my purpose here to follow the method of the poets I shall take the allegorical sense after the use of the poets.

The third sense is called the moral, and this is the one that lecturers should go intently noting throughout the scriptures for their own behoof and that of their disciples. Thus we may note in the Gospel, when Christ ascended the mountain for the transfiguration, that of the twelve apostles he took with him but three; wherein the moral may be understood that in the most secret things we should have but a few companions.

The fourth sense is called the anagogical, that is to say 'above the sense'; and this is when a scripture is spiritually expounded which even in the literal sense, by the very things it signifies, signifies again some portion of the supernal things of eternal glory....[43]

I have assembled these few accounts of the nature of allegory not because I imagine, or think I can prove, that Langland had access to any of them, but to show that it was so current a commonplace of medieval exegesis that it would be no wonder if our author knew of it; he may indeed have known it more intimately than we can, who, by reading, can apprehend it intellectually but cannot easily let it live in us as a way or habit of thinking and feeling. Langland was, perhaps, no great reader, but he gives the effect of a great listener.

His knowledge must have been largely derived from what he heard in sermons or got from conversations with other men.[44]

The allegorical method was then a regular method of presentation and analysis for the makers of sermons and the renderers of the Bible; but to reverse the process, to use it as a method not of criticism but of creation in this its most complex, fourfold manner, seems to belong to Langland alone in the field of English poetry. To know that Holy Writ may have four meanings and to discern them is one thing, but to create a great work on this biblical scale is a feat of poetry almost above ambition.

If this method of interpretation is difficult for the twentieth century, an analogy from music may be useful. A fugue must have at least two voices, and commonly has three or four, as a glance at the fugues of Bach will show. Each voice enters in a key different by an appointed musical interval from that of the preceding voice; episodes and counter-themes are allowed and are used to bridge intervals between the reintroductions of the main theme, which may disappear for many bars at a time; in the development the voices pursue and overtake each other and lie as it were parallel in their appointed musical planes, and the whole sweeps to a conclusion that is mathematically pre-ordained and yet leaves that freedom to genius which distinguishes a great fugue from one which any qualified musician might compose in meek obedience to the rules. So it is with this kind of poetry; if we listen, in the poems we have discussed, for these serial and simultaneous voices, we hear but two in *Wynnere and Wastoure*, three in the first version of *Piers Plowman*, and four in the second,

> but match'd in mouth like bells,
> Each under each.

It remains to link the analysis here attempted with ideas already advanced elsewhere as to the structure of the poem. The existence of a fourth voice within it (so much more important than a fourth author) was first discerned by Mr Wells, albeit he did not fasten upon it the official name, the *sensus anagogicus* of medieval theory; that was the work of Mr Troyer.[45] Both of these scholars see the same truth, but in different ways; for whereas Mr Troyer sees Christ as God in the image of Man, for whom he believes Piers to be 'a multifold symbol', Mr Wells stresses that man is made in the image of God; either of these approaches is valuable, but that of Mr Wells the more fundamental, for if we follow its implications under the guidance of Mr Wells, the poem as a whole takes anagogical shape, into which the character and meaning of the symbol Piers easily fits; whereas if we follow the line suggested by Mr Troyer, we reach an answer only in respect of the symbol Piers, which it must be said in fairness to Mr Troyer is the special point of his inquiry. The doctrine that man is made in the image of God is fully stated in both A and B versions of the poem:

'Kind' quoth he, 'is Creator . of all kinds of beasts,
Father and Former . and first of all things;
The Lord of Life and of Light . of joy and of pain.
Angels and all things . are at his will,
But man is most like to Him . of mark and of shape;
For a word that he flung . waxed forth the beasts
And all things at his will . were wrought with speech
   Dixit et facta sunt
Save man that He made . image to Himself
Gave him ghost of his Godhead . and granted him bliss,
Life that ever shall last . and all his lineage after.

(A.X. 27–37)

Wells expounds the importance of this idea to the reviser of the poem thus:

> He evidently considered that, since God is a Trinity, man must in some sense also be a Trinity. Each of the three parts of the *Vita* begins with allusions to the interrelation of the three parts of the Trinity and each is clearly dedicated to a special Person of the Trinity. At the conclusion of the *Vita de Do-wel* we are told that even the Saracens believe in God the Father. It is this Person of the Trinity who clearly presides over the Life of Do-wel. Christ as Piers the Plowman is the central theme of the *Vita de Do-bet*. In this part of the poem the life of Christ, his crucifixion and the harrowing of hell supply the chief narrative elements. The *Vita de Do-best* is no less clearly dedicated to the Holy Spirit.... Such is the spiritual trinity of man according to *Piers Plowman*, a thought of no inconsiderable importance in the organization of the work.[46]

It would seem that although the writer of the A Text knew well enough that God is a Trinity and that Man is made in His Image, the notion that Do-well, Do-better and Do-best were in some sense parallel to the functions of the Three Persons of the Trinity did not dawn upon him, or at least become a part of his poem, until the process of revision began. But once he had apprehended it, it became the thought upon which the whole revision was moulded; once more there was an equation of Trinities. We may even make a simple table of the organisation of the new poem:

Sensus literalis:	Piers the Farmer	Piers the Teacher	Piers the Builder of the Barn
Sensus allegoricus:	Laity	Clergy	Episcopate
Sensus moralis:	Do-wel	Do-bet	Do-best
Sensus anagogicus:	God the Father	God the Son	God the Holy Ghost

If to this tabular presentation we add that it is indeed only a table, that all the meanings harmonise and interplay their counterpoint, mingle, vanish, reappear and combine in every variety, and that every combination is graced with images of intense poetical force and told in language equal to the design, it becomes possible to view the whole poem in one complex imaginative act, to see it as a great and single vision made of many visions, held and harmonised in the mind of the revising poet, and written down so that we can hold it in the same way.

The uniting symbol is Piers;[47] choosing him for hero was the masterstroke of the revising hand. The simple farmer about whom the A Text poem on England had centred, became the changeable but constant centre of the three ways of Christian salvation.

It has been seen in this inquiry that the revision of the poem was dictated by the enigmatic character of the Pardon sent by Truth to the Field of Folk; in what light do we now see this Pardon, after studying the revision? Are we any nearer to knowing whether it was a pardon or not? If our analysis has been correct, in the Vision of Pentecost and the Building of the Barn of Unity ('Holy Church in English'), Piers was the *exemplum* for Do-best, as in the Vision of the Incarnation and especially of the Passion, Piers was the *exemplum* for Do-bet. But Piers had also been the symbol of the first vision, the vision of England, and in this, as we can now see, he stands for Do-wel, or in Latin *qui bona egerunt*; it is his very name, and the Pardon is truly his. But there is more in it than this: his followers have to be considered.

If we turn to the first advice given to them by Piers we find him use this allegory of entry into Heaven:

> Grace is the guard on the gate . a good man in truth;
> His man is called Amend-you . for many men know him;
> Tell him this token . for Truth knows the sooth:
> 'I performed the penance . that the priest enjoined;
> I am sorry for my sins . and so shall I ever
> When I think thereon. . . .'
>
> (A.VI. 85)

Penance includes one more of those trinities in which Langland so often thought; it has three parts, *contritio cordis, confessio oris* and *satisfactio operis*; at one time in his revision he began to play with this thought, seeking in it an analogy for Do-wel, Do-bet and Do-best.

> 'And I shall ken thee', quoth Conscience . 'of contrition to make,
> That shall clean thy cloak . of all kinds of filth,
> > *Cordis contricio etc.*
> Do-wel shall wash it and wring it . through a wise confessor,
> > *Oris confessio*
> Do-bet shall beat it and cleanse it . as bright as any scarlet,
> And dye the grain with a good will . and God's grace to amend
> > thee
> And afterward send thee to satisfaction . to sew it up,
> > *Satisfaccio Dobest*'
>
> (B.XIV. 16)

But he leaves this fancy, and comes back to a simpler statement:

> *Ergo*, Contrition, Faith and Conscience . is the nature of Do-wel,
> And are surgeons for deadly sin . when shrift of mouth faileth.
> But shrift of mouth more worthy is . if man be inly contrite;
> For shrift of mouth slayeth sin . be it never so deadly....
> But Satisfaction seeketh out the root . and both slayeth and
> > voideth it
> And, as if it had never been . bringeth deadly sin to nought.
>
> (B.XIV. 87)

Now when the Pardon was sent to Piers, his followers had already shown Contrition and made Confession through the figures of the Seven Deadly Sins, and were even then engaged on the search for St Truth, which seems their act of Satisfaction. The revising poet therefore has made clear that such men are also written in the Pardon by the name of Do-wel, *qui bona egerunt*, even though they had sinned; for they were 'inly contrite', they had made their shrift of mouth, and they were 'seeking out the root' in satisfaction. They were 'kyndelich Do-wel', The Pardon Truth had sent them was their Pardon; He had bought it and they had earned it.

In this new light upon their repentance, let us look at their Pardon once again. All in two lines it lay:

> *Et qui bona egerunt, Ibunt in vitam eternam*
> *Qui vero mala, in ignem eternum.*

Understood on the human planes of the A Text, here is justice, but no mercy, for on any human plane justice and mercy are at variance; one must yield to the other. But on that further plane of *aeterna gloria*, in the life of God, where justice and mercy are one, Langland saw them manifested with equal power in the Incarnation, the Atonement, and in Pentecost; by these the simple followers of Piers, 'blustering forth as beasts' on their pathless penance, are to find mercy as well as justice in the Pardon of Truth. To show the richness of its meaning and the strength of its foundation, Langland had to write not only a new poem, but a new kind of poem, one that can awaken in the reader a new kind of attention to some portion of those supernal things of which Dante wrote.

NOTES

1. Dante, *Convivio*, Second Treatise, ch. xii, tr. P. H. Wicksteed.
2. *Winner and Waster*, ed. Sir I. Gollancz (Oxford, 1931).
3. *Wynnere and Wastoure*, Fitt I, 32–5, 45–9.
      As I went in the west, wand'ring alone,
      Along the bank of a brook, – bright was the sun, –
      'Neath a wondrous wood, by a winsome mead;
      Many flowers enfolded where my foot stepped....
      But at last, as I lay, lock'd were mine eyes;
      And swiftly in a dream swept was I thence.
      Methought I was in the world, wist I not where,
      On a lovely lawn, all alike green,
      Immurèd with mountains a mile round about.
4. Ibid., Fitt II, 277–82.
    But thou betakest thee to the tavern before the town-head,
    Each one ready with a bowl to blear both thine eyes,
    To proffer what thou shalt have, and what thy heart pleases,
    Wife, widow, or wench, that is wont there to dwell.
    Then is it but 'Fill in!' and 'Fetch forth!' and Florrie appears;
    'We-he!' and 'whoa-up!', words that suffice.
                                           (tr. Gollancz)
5. *Wynnere and Wastoure*, Preface.
6. *The Political Songs of England*, ed. Thomas Wright, Camden Society (1839), p. 195, 'A Song of the Times.'
7. *The Minor Poems of the Vernon MS.*, ed. F. J. Furnivall, Part II, E.E.T.S. (1901), p. 715, No. 19, 'Seldom seen is soon forgot.'
8. Quotations from *Piers Plowman* have, for convenience, been

modernised throughout, except where the established text of Skeat is necessary to the argument.

9. For an interesting contrary opinion, which nevertheless leaves me unconvinced, see Doroth Owen, *Piers Plowman, a Comparison with Some Earlier and Contemporary French Allegories* (1912).

10. *Winner and Waster*, Fitt II, 255–6:

Let be the cramming of thy coffers, for Christ's love of Heaven!
Let the people and the poor have part in thy silver;

(tr. Gollancz)

11. A.I. 16.

12. 'Yet I have no natural knowledge.'

13. *Rotuli Parliamentorum*, vol. ii, p. 267, items 10–17. Attempts to curb the abuse of Purveyance go back to *Magna Carta* at least; see McKechnie, *Magna Carta*, p. 386. Item 10 of the *Rotuli Parliamentorum* for 1362 contains the petition 'q̄ le heignous noun de Purveiour soit change & nome Achatour'. The petition of Peace against Wrong seems to be a reminiscence of these transactions in Parliament, and may be held to support the traditional dating of the A Text to shortly after 1362.

14. Hoc etiam anno (1361) fuit grandis pestilentia, quae viros potius consumpsit quam foeminas.... Hoc anno (1364) fuit tanta frumenti caristia, ut venderetur summa frumenti quindecim solidis. (Walsingham, *Historia Anglicana*, vol. i, Rolls Series.)

15. R. W. Chambers, *Man's Unconquerable Mind*, p. 117.

16. But see T. P. Dunning, *Piers Plowman, an Interpretation of the A Text*, pp. 145–52, where an interesting defence for the priest is advanced; as Father Dunning says, 'the priest is obviously the proper person to interpret the pardon'; but in fact he does not interpret it, he 'impugns it, all by pure reason' (A.VIII. 155), that is, he points out that it is written, not in the form of a pardon, but in the form of a statement of cause and effect, viz. 'if you do well, you will be saved'. Whether the document was a pardon or not, therefore, depends on what is meant by doing well, a matter which the priest omitted to explain and which Langland himself was only able to resolve by writing the B Text, as will be seen.

17. Piers' Pardon is taken verbatim from the 39th verse of the Athanasian Creed (see D. Waterland, *A Critical History of the Athanasian Creed*, ed. J. R. King, 1870), which Skeat, who refers instead to Matthew xxv. 46, and Father Dunning, who refers to John v. 29, seem to have overlooked. The sentence appears to have had some vogue as a catch-phrase about salvation towards the end of the fourteenth century and a little later, as it is used at the climax of the last scene of the *Castle of Perseverance*, viii. 3637–8 (E.E.T.S. Extra Series XCI, *The Macro Plays*).

18. *Man's Unconquerable Mind*, p. 119.

19. This guess is based on the opinion of Skeat who dates the A Text to shortly after 1362 and the B Text to 1376–77. Mr J. A. W. Bennett, following Dr Huppé, advances some reasons for supposing that the A Text 'must have been in process of composition by 1370, even if it was not finished by then' (*P.M.L.A.* lviii, No. 3) and that the B Text was

being written 'between the years 1377 and 1379' (*Med. Æv.*, vol. xii).

20. Attention was first called to these by H. W. Wells in *P.M.L.A.* xliv, No. 1, 'The Construction of Piers Plowman', where relevant quotations from St Thomas (*Summa*, Part III, Quaest. XL. A. I) and from the *Meditationes* are given.

21. As in B.XII. 16.

22. As in A.XI. 136.

23. For a study in identification see *Journal of English and Germanic Philology*, ix, No. 3, 'The Authorship of Piers Plowman', by A. Mensendieck.

24. *A Dialogue between the Resolved Soul and Created Pleasure.*

25. A.XI. 12.

26. For lists of alterations and additions made in the B Text, see E.E.T.S. original series 28, *Piers Plowman A Text* (ed. by Skeat, reprinted 1932), pp. 156–8, and also T. P. Dunning, *Piers Plowman, an Interpretation of the A Text* (1937), pp. 195–6 where some deviations from A are noted in B to support the view that they are by different authors, a view which Father Dunning has recently withdrawn in his extremely interesting article 'Langland and the Salvation of the Heathen', *Med. Æv.*, vol. xii (1943).

27. Dante, *Convivio*, Second Treatise, ch. i. The 'supernal things of eternal glory', so manifestly a part of the B revision, are no doubt the 'mystical developments' to which Dr Mabel Day refers (*Mod. Lang. Rev.* xxiii), in seeking to establish that the B reviser could not have been the author of A. It does not seem impossible that 'the growth of a poet's mind' might include mystical development in the course of the long meditation between the writing of the two texts.

28. In spite of the argument advanced by Mr J. A. W. Bennett, in *Med. Æv.* xii, I cling to this view.

29. 'Throughout we find the Imagination – mediating as the character in Piers Plowman between the senses and the reason.' H. S. V. Jones, 'Imaginatif in Piers Plowman', *J.E.G.Ph.* xiii, No. 4. See also R. W. Chambers, *Man's Unconquerable Mind*, p. 139.

30. I have attempted a more detailed elucidation along similar lines in *Med. Æv.* iv. 2, p. 84, suggesting the identification of Cain with Antichrist, and am indebted to Mr J. A. W. Bennett for reminding me of a passage in *Beowulf* (line 1261 *et seq.*), associating Cain with those ancient giants of evil, of whom Grendel was one, and thought of as the enemy of God and man.

31. B.XIX. 41.

32. For this bracketed emendation, see 'The Text of Piers Plowman' by R. W. Chambers and J. H. G. Grattan, *Mod. Lang. Rev.*, vol. xxvi, No. 1, p. 4.

33. See below p. 174.

34. *Political Songs of England*, Camden Society, 1839, p. 211.

35. A.XI. 40.

36. Ibid., 66.

37. A.XI. 287.

38. Ibid., 295.
39. 'He was familiar with the Pauline distinction of "body, soul, and spirit". He finds such a distinction in the sense of scripture. There too we have a bodily or historic sense, a moral sense, which – perhaps without any very special propriety – he classes with the soul; a higher element, the spiritual meaning.' R. B. Tollington, *Selections from the Commentaries of Origen*, (1929).
40. *Gregory the Great*, by F. Homes Dudden, vol. i, p. 193.
41. *Encyclopaedia of Religion and Ethics*, vol. i, p. 331.
42. *P.M.L.A.*, xlvii, No. 2.
43. Dante, *Convivio*, Second Treatise, ch. i, tr. P. H. Wicksteed.
44. R. W. Chambers, *Man's Unconquerable Mind*, p. 104.
45. *Op. cit.*
46. *P.M.L.A.*, xliv, No. 1, 'The Construction of Piers Plowman', by H. W. Wells.
47. For a detailed demonstration of this see *Med. Æv.* vol. ii, No. 2, 'The Character of Piers Plowman', by Nevill Coghill.

6

God's Wenches and the Light That Spoke*

(Some notes on Langland's kind of poetry)

I.

It was Ymagynatyf who first recognised that Langland wrote poetry and he rebuked him for it. 'Thow medlest the with makynges,' he said, 'and mightest go sey thi sauter.'[1] One may take this as the stricture upon himself of a religiously-minded man, looking back over 45 winters of a life he judged to have been largely wasted, 'for there ar bokes ynowe to telle men what Do-wel is, Do-bet and Do-best bothe'. He had let himself play about with poetry, only to form an incurable and time-consuming habit that led nowhere. He might have been better employed.

And indeed there were books enough about the good life and the way of salvation. What was unique in Langland's was the way it was 'made'. There had been dream-visions, allegories, pilgrimages, delineations of the seven sins, discussions of the Three Lives, satires and complaints before: nor was the rumbling grumble of alliteration anything new: in fact there had been almost everything that seems to make his poem. Yet it is unmatched because of the quite peculiar workings of his mind – the workings of *Ymagynatyf*, if by that phantom we may designate Langland's modes of memory,[2] association of ideas and images, sense of perspective, and feeling for words.

He had many of the gifts that great poets commonly have:

English and Medieval Studies Presented to J. R. R. Tolkien on The Occasion of his Seventieth Birthday (London: Allan & Unwin, 1962).

magnitude of design, passion, intuitions of things natural and supernatural, moral intensity, an instinctive ease in seeing one thing in terms of another, luck if not cunning in language, an obsessive theme. There are passages when his genius seems to fail him, as he flounders in the troublesome debates in which his quest involves him: but that is neither here nor there. What matters is that he has a great poet's stunning-power, and there are elements in it that I seem to meet nowhere but in him. They are not easy to account for, or even to describe, for this very reason; he breaks all convention and cannot readily be accommodated by the accepted language of criticism.

First among his unique creative gifts is a huge fluidity: *Piers Plowman* flows with powerful ease, up and down through time and space, with sudden tides that take unforeseeable directions without a word of warning: they carry the reader, sometimes protesting, from inner to outer worlds, natural and supernatural, with the arbitrary energies of a dream that has its secret purposes and destinations. In the end a reader perceives something of their organic shape, though no map that he can make of them is entirely satisfactory. To give example of the mobility of which I am speaking, the poem opens with the world at work in a field, moves swiftly to Westminster and back, undertakes a pilgrimage, but pauses to plough what is said to be a half-acre but seems to be another image for the working world. The Dreamer then awakes in the Malvern Hills, and turns inward into the life of the mind, moves once more to the life of London, then to the life of Nature in this middle-earth, and after many encounters in other places for the most part nameless, finds himself between Jericho and Jerusalem, stands at Calvary, descends into Hell, and returns thence to his cottage in Cornhill in time for Easter Mass. Beyond that it moves into an indeterminate Christendom, centred by implication in Rome, but yet is soon without a centre of any sort and is seen as a devastated area with no other confines than the world itself. In the course of this astonishing pilgrimage of his in space, the Dreamer is present at the coronation of Richard II, confers with Abraham and Moses, is an eye-witness of the Crucifixion, and of the Harrowing of

Hell, and after watching the building of Holy Church, sees it torn down by Antichrist. Present, Past and Future are as instantly present to him as are the varied regions of his search, and though there is no logical pattern in these swift movements, there is a cogency in each as it happens. The fluidity and freedom of these shifting tides of dream result in a total form which could only come from a poet of archetypal or myth-creating power. However we analyse the detail of its structure, it has organic shape – the shape is of a spiritual hunger of search for some great epiphany that will show us what we are seeking, in a dream: the epiphany is granted and the Dreamer stumbles upon glory: but when it has been given into his hands to hold for ever, it is taken from him by an enemy and he is left in desolation and awake, with all his journey still to do. This is surely the shape of a universal experience.

Piers Plowman is often described as an allegory, even as the greatest of English allegories,[3] and that will do well enough for ordinary purposes: no one will be greatly misled. But the poem is so exceptional in its modes of vision that when we look at it closely we are forced to revise this general account of it and consult our definitions. The most trenchant and authoritative description of allegory I know is that of C. S. Lewis, where he is speaking of the equivalences or correspondences, perceived by a poetic mind, between material and immaterial things:

> This fundamental equivalence between the immaterial and the material may be used by the mind in two ways. . . . On the one hand you can start with an immaterial fact, such as the passions which you actually experience, and can then invent *visibilia* to express them. If you are hesitating between an angry retort and a soft answer, you can express your state of mind by inventing a person called *Ira* with a torch and letting her contend with another invented person called *Patientia*. This is allegory. . . . But there is another way of using the equivalence, which is almost the opposite of allegory, and which I would call sacramentalism or symbolism. If our passions, being immaterial, can be copied by material inventions, then it is possible that our material world in its turn is the copy of an invisible world. . . . The attempt . . . to see the archetype in the copy, is what I mean by symbolism or sacramentalism.[4]

Pure allegory of this kind is nowhere better seen than in the *Psychomachia* of Prudentius, which Lewis instances. It must be among the finest of the mechanical operations of the spirit. As it is all of a piece throughout, a single quotation will suit my present purpose: it is from the passage that describes the battle between *Pudicitia* and *Sodomita Libido*.[5]

> And now, at hand, next on the grassy field,
> Steps Virgin Chastity with shining shield,
> Whom Sodom-Lust, with home-grown torches girt,
> Assaults with flaming sulphur, pitch and dirt,
> And at the Maid's chaste eyes she seeks to poke
> Her flaming pine, to blast them with foul smoke.
> Yet with a stone the Virgin's fearless hand
> Strikes down the She-wolf's arm and furious brand.
> Thus from her sacred face the flames she smote,
> Then with a sword she cut the Harlot's throat.

Piers Plowman is a world and an age away from the *Psychomachia*. Gone are the modish rhetoric and the august Vergilian background, gone the notion of the soul as an orderly battlefield for the passions, where decisive victories in epic style smash, rather than probe, its problems. Who now can feel the manifold of moral tensions in any sort of temptation, sexual or other, in terms of a straight fight between two strapping amazons, whose sex is predetermined by purely grammatical considerations?

Perhaps Prudentius and his early readers felt it so, but for us these equivalences no longer suffice: imagination must take some wider cast, like that of Flaubert's who, in bodying forth the temptations of St Anthony,[6] anticipated those of Gide:[7]

> J'ai repoussé le monstrueux anachorète qui m'offrait, en riant, des petits pains chauds, le centaure qui tâchait de me prendre sur sa croupe, – et cet enfant noir apparu au milieu des sables, qui était très beau, et qui m'a dit s'appeler l'esprit de fornication.

Prudentius, however, was more concerned to tell us that Lust was bad than to tell us what it was like, and consequently the more his 'equivalence' is elaborated, the more it disappears. And this is true of his whole poem. With sturdy Latin steps he follows the *ignis fatuus* of a literary formula, little thinking that it is the poet's business to show us the forms of things unknown, and rakes round the shelf-access of his mind for images already invented. As all are known, so all are predictable, and we watch the outcome of their battles with that yawning expectation commonly accorded to a *bombe surprise*: it is cold, tasteless and inevitable.

Langland's personified figures are of a different kind and, at their best, give no sense of having been fabricated: *Glutton* sounds as if he had been seen not once but many times in some Colwall pub, and *Coveytise* at any Winchester fair:

> And thanne cam Coueytise, can I hym noughte descryue,
> So hungriliche and holwe sire Heruy hym loked.
> He was bitelbrowed and baberlipped also,
> With two blered eyghen, as a blynde hagge:
> And as a letheren purs lolled his chekes,
> Wel sydder than his chyn: thei chiueled for elde:
> And as a bondman of his bacoun his berde was bidraueled.
>
> (B.V. 188–94)

and later,

> 'Repentedestow the eure', quod Repentance, 'ne restitucioun
>   madest?'
> 'Yus, ones I was herberwed', quod he, 'with an hep of chapmen,
> I roos whan thei were arest, and yrifled here males.'
> 'That was no restitucioun', quod Repentance, 'but a robberes
>   thefte,
> Thou haddest be better worthy be hanged therfore
> Than for al that that thow hast here shewed.'
> 'I wende ryflynge were restitucioun', quod he, 'for I lerned neuere
>   rede on boke,
> And I can no Frenche in feith, but of the ferthest ende of
>   Norfolke.'
>
> (B.V. 232–9)

Where did Langland hear this enchanting joke? Could he have invented it? It has the ring of natural authenticity. And who was *Sir Hervy* that looked so hungerly and hollow that he gave Langland an idea of covetousness? Skeat notes that by Skelton's time the name had become traditional for a picklock, and quotes '*Haruy* Hafter, that wel coude picke a male'.[8] But perhaps Skelton found the name in Langland, and Langland found it in life: Sir Hervy might have been some famished, covetous priest he knew, for Proust tells us that a creative writer uses all his acquaintance in imagining a character:

... il n'est pas un geste de ses personnages, un tic, un accent, qui n'ait été apporté à son inspiration par sa mémoire, il n'est pas un nom de personnage inventé sous lequel il ne puisse mettre soixante noms de personnages vus, dont l'un a posé pour la grimace, l'autre pour le monocle, tel pour la colère, tel pour le mouvement avantageux du bras, etc.[9]

Yet it we doubt the historicity of Sir Hervy, there is always *Lady Meed*. Nowhere is she called Alice Perrers in the poem, but it is hardly possible that this woman did not sit (in Langland's mind) for her portrait as the *Radix Malorum*, married to a fiend and feoffed with the seven sins. For Langland she symbolised Graft.

Whether we call *Lady Meed* an allegorical or a symbolic character, she is, as imagery, simple enough, such as another poet, even a Prudentius, might have 'invented'. But unique in Langland's 'making' of personified abstractions is the character of Piers himself. The equivalences are kept shadowy and changeable: *Piers* is not a plain label like *Pudicitia*.

Only gradually do we become aware of the significances the name includes and it is worth remarking that those who know the poem best differ among themselves over shades of meaning in him – a sure sign (since no one attributes this to incompetence in Langland) that Piers is a living character that can be argued over like Falstaff, and not an unmistakable abstraction like *Sodomita Libido*, whose nature is not in doubt, in spite of her grammatical sex. The meanings in Piers are the central meanings of the entire poem and we see them dissolve into one another at every fresh epiphany, with accumulated and ascending richness. The solid, simple farmer, honest worker, faithful son of the Church, who alone knows the way to Truth, returns long after as the Good Samaritan, a figure for Charity, and is seen at last in Christ, or Christ in him: into these meanings we must also pour others which Langland found in the gloss and adumbrated in his retelling of this parable: the man who fell among thieves is Fallen Man himself. The Priest and the Levite that passed by on the other side are the Patriarchs. The Good Samaritan is Christ in his humanity. To this gloss, Langland added identifications: the *patres antiqui* of Hugh of St Victor[10] were

to Langland Abraham and Moses, emblems of Faith and
Hope: what else then could the Good Samaritan be but an
emblem of Charity? All these meanings pass into Piers when
we hear of the entry of Jesus into Jerusalem, to joust in Piers'
arms, *humana natura*, and when Christ rises in triumph out of
Hell, he still has some touch of Piers about him:

> 'Is this Iesus the Iuster?' quod I, 'that Iuwes did to deth?
> Or is it Pieres the Plowman? . . .'
>
> (B.XIX. 10–11)

Later still we are told that Jesus, while on earth, lived the lives
of Do-wel, Do-bet, and Do-best:[11] so these meanings, which
are the quest-meanings of the whole poem, also pass into
Piers and we are brought to realize that he has stood for them
throughout and is their human custodian, the builder of
Christ's Church and House of Unity. If we are to 'lerne to
loue and leue of alle othre', which is the last advice of
Kynde,[12] and sums the whole moral content of the poem, and
of Christianity, we must seek Piers. No wonder, where so
many significances crowd in, if critics differ in their emphasis
when they interpret it! What I would at present stress,
however, is not the *meaning* but the '*making*' of Piers: we
recognise in him at first an allegorical figure, a visible,
invented personification for an abstraction that we may call
'Do-wel'. Next, an abstraction still personified, he teaches the
Dreamer about the Tree of Charity. Then we see him
identified with the Good Samaritan who is a figure from
parable, not allegory, and in company with Abraham and
Moses, who are neither abstractions nor fictions but historic
people, used as symbols of Faith and Hope. Then he is
Christ's humanity, visible and historical; the sum of Charity
seen in person. When we look to our definitions, we see that
all that is finest and most central in this figure is 'made' by a
coalescence or fusion of allegory, parable and symbol, and
that is the poetic fact that volts it with imaginative power,
unmatched in its own region of discourse. Langland is a
visionary poet trying to discern the shape and meaning in our
mortal predicament, through whatever kind of imagery rises
to and is accepted by his mind, not an allegorical versifier at
work upon a tidy little scheme, according to known rules.

We can see this same principle (the fusion of allegory and symbol) giving vigour to his sense of landscape, and even of action. To consider landscape first, the poem opens with one of the most memorable in English poetry: it was once believed to be an allegorical scene, invented to suit the poet's didactic intention. To the east, on high, a Tower of Truth. Below and to westward, a Dungeon of Care: in between, a fair field, full of folk. In these every reader can recognise an allegory of Heaven, Earth and Hell, a fabricated theatrical set. But now it chances that this landscape has been identified and is as visible and as visitable as it ever was, in the Malvern Hills.[13] There stands the Herefordshire Beacon, high to the east; below it lies the dungeon-site of Old Castle, a little to the west: in between them the rolling fields of Colwall parish. These were the *visibilia* which came, for Langland, to symbolise our human situation and the choice between one or other of the eternities before us: many a church in Langland's time had a like image of Doom over its chancel arch: but Langland saw it in his native countryside. Yet from this symbolising mountain in his poem there descends to the Dreamer a Lady, 'in lynene yclothid', who is an allegory, a figure invented to stand for Holy Church. An allegory has issued from a symbol.

This same mixture of kinds can be seen in actions as well as in people and places. Another of the memorable moments in the poem is the action of Kynde when he 'comes out of the planets' at the call of Conscience to protect the House of Unity, attacked by Antichrist and the Seven Sins. It is hardly possible to imagine an occasion that could sound more obviously allegorical: this is the action taken by Kynde:

> Kynd Conscience tho herde, and cam out of the planetes,
> And sent forth his foreioures, feures, & fluxes,
> Coughes, and cardiacles, crampes, and tothaches,
> Rewmes, and radegroundes, and roynouse scalles,
> Byles, and bocches and brennyng agues:
> Frenesyes, and foule yueles, forageres of kynde,
> Hadde yprikked and prayed polles of peple,
> That largelich a legioun lese her lyf sone.
> There was – 'harrow and help!, here cometh Kynde
> With Deth that is dredful, to vndone vs alle!'

> (B.XX. 79–88)

Skeat in fact believed this to be an allegory, invented to show how Nature will fail man and may even prove his enemy in his hour of need:

> Conscience supposes that Nature, for love of Piers the Plowman, will assist men against spiritual foes. But the result is represented as being very different; for Nature also becomes man's enemy, afflicting him with various bodily diseases.... Yet Nature is, at last, man's true friend: see line 109.[14]

When we take up this reference, we find line 109 to be as follows:

> And Kynde cessede tho to seon the peuple amende.
>   (C.XXIII. 109: B.XX. 108)

But Skeat's interpretation is mistaken. Langland was not inventing an allegory to show the caprices of Nature, but showing how Nature serves God by putting the fear of death into man, if he cannot be brought to repent by any other means. Langland believed that he had witnessed a similar occasion in his own life-time – in January 1362, to be precise[15] – and had no need to invent an allegory: he recorded a fact and interpreted it as a symbol, '*in tokenynge of drede*, That dedly synne *at domesday* shal fordon hem alle':

> He preued that thise pestilences were for pure synne,
> And the southwest wynde on Saterday at euene
> Was pertliche for pure pryde, and for no poynt elles.
> Piries and plomtrees were puffed to the erthe,
> In ensample, ye segges, ye shulden do the bettere.
> Beches and brode okes were blowen to the grounde,
> Torned vpward her tailles in tokenynge of drede,
> That dedly synne at domesday shal fordon hem alle.
>   (B.V. 13–20)

Kynde, an allegorical figure, performs a symbolic action: he is coming to man's rescue on the Day of Antichrist by warning him of death. When he sees that the warning has been effective, he relents.

II.

If I have laboured this matter of allegory and symbolism, it is not to deny the dichotomy, but to show that Langland, at his most Langlandian, and at the top of his powers as a poet, obtains his effects by blending or fusing them in his imagery: he may not have done this on purpose, but it was the way his mind worked. This is one of the things that distinguishes his poem from a merely allegorical work, like *Sawles Warde*, *The Abbey of the Holy Ghost*, *La Voie du Paradis*, *The Castle of Love*, and so on. As it seems certain that Langland read and used this last-mentioned poem in one of its many versions, it is of interest to notice the things in it that attracted him and what he did to turn them into poetry.

The Castle of Love is like something pinned out on a board, a blue-print for a poem of piety. It begins with a versified account of the Creation and the Fall of Man and ends with the Incarnation and Passion of Christ, the Harrowing of Hell, the Resurrection and the Ascension. Inserted in this cosmic story, after the account of Adam's expulsion from Eden, there comes the parable of the King who had a Thrall that did amiss, and was put in prison: the King has four daughters who are concerned at this: two of them, Mercy and Peace, plead for the Thrall's release: their sterner sisters, Righteousness and Truth, demand his continued detention. The King, however, also had a son, and he, by offering to take the Thrall's place, promises to pay the needed ransom:

> I sal take the clething of that wretchid prison
> And priuily for him sal I paye ransoun:
> Of his kynde wil I become
> And for him wil y take dome....
> On this maner sothfastnes and mercy
> Sal sone be made gode frendes verraly:
> Also pece and rightwisnes
> Thai sal kis with gret swetnes.[16]

This parable, which is much in the manner of those in the *Gesta Romanorum*, is glossed in the expected way, and the poem makes, as it were, a fresh start and proceeds to the invention from which it takes its name, by plunging into

allegory. A Castle is prepared for the King's Son and we are
told it is the body of the Virgin Mary:

> This is the Maydenes bodi so freo;
> Ther neuer nas non bote heo
> That with so fele thewes iwarned wes
> So that swete mayden Marie wes.[17]

The castle is built on a rock – two versions go so far as to call
it a 'cragg' grey and hard[18] – which is the Virgin's heart! Here
indeed is a call upon us for the suspension of our disbelief.
The Castle has four crenellated turrets (the Four Cardinal
Virtues), three baileys (Maidenhood, Chastity and Espousal),
and seven barbicans (Meekness, Charity, Abstinence,
Chastity, Poverty, Patience and Ghostly Joy). From the
midst of the highest tower there springs a well that fills all the
ditches. It is the well of Grace.

After its exposition of the allegory, the poem returns to the
outer narrative (following from the Fall) of the Redemption,
by a brief account of the Incarnation and Passion of Christ
and the Harrowing of Hell. It ends with the Resurrection and
Ascension: the story is closed with a brief prayer.

Out of this rigid, frigid affair, Langland seems to have
picked some elements in the structure of his poem, enough,
indeed, to make me feel certain that he knew it in one of its
several versions. He was struck by the image of an allegorical
castle, for instance, and used it twice in his own work. On one
occasion he too made it serve as an allegory for the human
body when he tells us of the *Castle of Caro*, the home of
Anima. But instead of pursuing it into crenellations, baileys,
barbicans and other allegorical absurdities, or basing it upon
a heart of rocks, he leaves it airy and elemental. In this passage
there is no touch of symbolism: it is purely in the tradition of
Prudentius, except that instead of epic machinery he employs
romance machinery, with a touch of medieval science:

> Of erthe and eir it is mad, medlit togideris:
> With wynd and with watir wittiliche enioynede.
> Kynde hath closid thereinne, craftily withalle,
> A lemman that he louith lik to hymselue.
> *Anima* heo hatte: to hire hath enuye
> A proud prikere of Fraunce, *Princeps huius mundi*,

> And wolde wynne hire awey with wyles yif he mighte.
> Ac Kynde knowith this wel and kepith hire the betere....
>
> (A.X. 3–10)

These are correspondences that work by light suggestion, rather than by didactic enumeration, and they are helped by the ease and elegance of the alliteration and rhythmic variableness: all the thoughts make part with the rest of Langland's poem, particularly the association of Kynde with the Creator, and the cunning of his creation, of which we hear much more later:

> He is the pyes patroun and putteth it in hire ere,
> That there the thorne is thikkest to buylden and brede....
>
> (B.XII. 227–8)

Princeps huius mundi throws in a neat allusion to the Gospels, yet one in keeping with the general feeling of gallantry and panache that the imagery calls for, as well as with the serious under-thought. This is how an allegorical idea can be put to a fanciful, poetic use, without disaster.

But Langland was also able to use it, crenellations and all, in a more visionary way: it comes immediately after a passage in which his fancy had failed him – the description of the pilgrimage to Truth through the Ten Commandments. A journey through a landscape can be made to correspond with a pilgrimage in moral life, as Bunyan's more successful imagery shows, but obedience to the Commandments cannot be worked into the scheme, because they are not features in scenery to be passed or by-passed in succession; they are supposed to be with us during the entire journey: for this reason, if for no other, lines like these are otiose, one of fancy's failures:

> Two stokkis there stonde, but stynte thou not there:
> Thei hote stele nought, ne sle nought: strik forth be bothe.[19]
>
> (A.VI. 63–4)

But suddenly we come upon another castle; and here, since it is not an image for a human body, but of the Tower of Truth, the architectural elements are brought into play and make imaginative correspondence:

Thanne shalt thou come to a court, cler as the sonne.
The mot is of mercy the Maner al aboute,
And alle the wallis ben of wyt to holde wil theroute;
The kirnelis ben of Cristendom that kynde to saue,
And boterasid with beleue so other thou best not sauid:
Alle the housis ben helid, hallis and chaumbris,
With no led but with loue and loughnesse, as bretheren of o
    wombe.
The tour there Treuthe is hymself is vp to the sonne:
He may do with the day-sterre what hym dere likith:
Deth dar not do thing that he defendith.
Grace hattith the gateward....

(A.VI. 72–82)

Once again the language leaps easily from one alliteration to another with a varying dance and the opening of the whole poem is recalled in the line 'The tour there Treuthe is hymselt is vp to the sonne'.

In the lines that follow this we have a kind of pun that gives the double significance of God's power over the stars themselves, and of his control over Lucifer, Death, and Hell. With a characteristic turn from the outer to the inner life, we are then admitted by Grace to see that our pilgrimage to Truth is a pilgrimage into our own hearts:

And if Grace graunte the to go in this wise,
Thow shalt see in thi-selue Treuthe sitte in thine herte,
In a cheyne of charyte, as thow a childe were....

(B.V. 615–17)

These are some of the unique ways in which Langland's mind worked in his 'makings' – the unforeseeable turn inwards to find the Kingdom of Heaven within, as well as in a court as clear as the sun, and the touching-off of half-explicit echoes from the Bible or from other passages in his own poem. The chain of charity recalls the bond of peace, and the child-image reminds us that we must become as little children to enter the Kingdom of Heaven. That Truth and Love are naturally seated in the human heart he has told us already: to know it instinctively 'it comseth bi myght, and in the herte there is the heuede and the heigh welle' (B.I. 161–2).

His treatment of the Four Daughters of God gives us another glimpse of *Piers Plowman* in the 'making'. In *The*

Castle of Love (in whatever version) they are intolerable prigs;
Mercy tells the king her father:

> 'Vnderstond,' quath heo, 'fader myn!
> Thow wost that I am doughter thyn,
> And am ful of Boxumnes,
> Of Milce and of Swetnes,
> And al Ich habbe, fader, of the.'[20]

No Pharisee in the Temple could have spoken better, no, nor
Goneril or Regan.

Langland does not make Daughters of God of these four
phantoms: he simply thinks of them as 'wenches', while
creating for their appearance an atmosphere of darkness
pierced by supernatural light: of all this the Dreamer is an
eye-witness:

> What for fere of this ferly and of the fals Iuwes,
> I drowe me in that derkenesse to *descendit ad inferna*:
> And there I sawe sothely, *secundum scripturas*,
> Out of the west coste, a wenche, as me thoughte,
> Cam walkynge in the wey; to helle-ward she loked.
> Mercy hight that mayde, a meke thynge withalle,
> A ful benygne buirde and boxome of speche.
> Her suster, as it semed, cam softly walkynge,
> Euene out of the est, and westward she loked,
> A ful comely creature: Treuth she highte....
> Eyther axed other of this grete wonder,
> Of the dyne & of the derknesse, and how the daye rowed,
> And which a lighte and a leme lay befor helle.
> (B.XVIII. 110–24)

Here, with the mixture of allegory and symbolism, there is
the further mixture of a homely naturalism with mystery.
What more natural than two wenches meeting when they are
out for a walk? What more mysterious than the light lying
over the darkness of Hell? Mercy and Truth are allegories,
East and West are symbols. The choice of the word *wench* is
the daring of poetry, to startle us with the familiar in the
ambience of the fantastic. It makes a gothic kind of contrast,
like the lewd motif in some misericord, that heightens the
solemnity of a chancel, as if by shock-tactic. The way the
wenches talk is in keeping with this idea: they talk slang:

'That thow tellest,' quod Treuth, 'is but a tale of waltrot:
For Adam and Eue, and Abraham with other
Patriarkes and prophetes that in peyne liggen,
Leue thow neuere that yone lighte hem alofte brynge,
Ne haue hem out of helle. Holde thi tonge, Mercy!'

(B.XVIII. 142–6)

The mixture of high comedy with a high mystery in the conversation of these wenches is of a piece with what we are told of Abraham and Moses when they came upon the man who fell among thieves:

Feith had first sighte of hym, ac he flegh on syde,
And nolde nought neighen hym by nyne londes lengthe.
Hope cam hippyng after, that hadde so ybosted ...;
Ac whan he hadde sighte of that segge, asyde he gan him drawe,
Dredfully, by this day! as duk doth fram the faucoun.

(B.XVII. 57–62)

Within the perfect seriousness of the story, the farce of Hope hopping, of Moses behaving like a duck, of Abraham dodging the encounter by nine ridges of plough-land, makes a homeliness in the holiness, as the wenches and their colloquialisms do in the mystery. It brings things down to earth. This may perhaps be the best way of approaching the supernatural; it is at least a good way: we may see it in a modern example:

Vladimir: There's a man all over for you, blaming on his boots the faults of his feet. (*He takes off his hat again, looks inside it, feels about inside it, knocks on the crown, blows into it, puts it on again.*) This is getting alarming. (*Silence. Vladimir deep in thought, Estragon pulling at his toes.*) One of the thieves was saved. (*Pause.*) It's a reasonable percentage....[21]

While he gives humanity to the Four Daughters by slang, Langland gives transcendence to Christ by thinking of him as a voice in a light: light speaks in a darkness that comprehends it not:

'What lorde artow?' quod Lucifer, '*quis est iste?*'
'*Rex glorie*', the lighte sone seide,
'And lorde of myghte & of mayne and al manere vertues: *dominus virtutum:*

> Dukes of this dym place, anon vndo this yates,
> That Cryst may come in, the Kynges sone of Heuene.'
> And with that breth helle brake, with Beliales barres:
> For any wye or warde, wide opene the yatis.
> Patriarkes and prophetes, *populus in tenebris*,
> Songen seynt Iohanes songe, *ecce agnus dei*.
> Lucyfer loke ne myghte, so lyghte hym ableynte.
> And tho that owre lorde loued, into his lighte he laughte.
>
> (B.XVIII. 314–24)

Between the comedy that gives animation to the four wenches and the mystery of light that gives transcendence to Christ comes the strangest figure in the whole poem, a Book, seen as a person. The Book is the Bible and, so far as that goes, is not an invention: it speaks an astonishing prosopopeia, some of the most visionary lines in the poem: it appears from nowhere and disappears as soon as it has said its say, like a mystical Jack-in-the-Box: the Dreamer sees that it has something comic and treats it with the same earthly nonchalance as he treats God's wenches and at the same time with even more poetry in what it is given to say. It is a perfect illustration of the grotesque in medieval art: partly ridiculous, partly sublime, even a little mad, by our standards, perhaps:

> Thanne was there a wighte with two brode eyen,
> Boke highte that beupere, a bolde man of speche.
> 'By Godes body,' quod this Book, 'I wil bere witnesse,
> That tho this barne was ybore, there blased a sterre . . .
> And alle the elementz,' quod the Boke, 'herof bereth witnesse,
> That he was God that al wroughte, the walkene firste shewed:
> Tho that weren in heuene token *stella comata*,
> And tendeden hir as a torche to reuerence his birthe:
> The lyghte folwed the Lorde into the lowe erthe. . . .
>
> (B.XVIII. 228–39)

In all that I have discussed in Langland's way of 'making' there is a sense of the union of opposites, whether in space and time, allegory and symbol, familiar and fantastic, comic and sublime: it also has some of that solidity which Bunyan, in *The Author's Apology for his Book* that prefaces *The Pilgrim's Progress*, thinks fitting to religious poetry:

> Solidity indeed becomes the Pen
> Of him that writeth things divine to men.

The divine is apprehended as reality through every image he could find or invent in his material and mental world, and he brings them all together in the only context that can effortlessly hold such contradictions, the context of dreams. What he achieves is best expressed in terms of what Blake has to say of allegory and vision that is to be found among his additions to a catalogue of his pictures for the year 1810, and which therefore antedates the publication of Coleridge's more famous utterance on what is virtually the same theme, in the thirteenth chapter of the *Biographia Literaria*. Indeed it not only antedates, but goes beyond it: for although Coleridge makes a similar distinction between a work of fancy and one of imagination (and they might both have used Prudentius as an example of the former and Langland as an example of the latter) yet Blake adds an assertion that the Imagination shows us truth, a step which Coleridge is not so incautious as to take. It shows us something about the nature of reality. For this further claim he might again have instanced Langland, had he known his poetry, with even more commendation than he gives to Bunyan, when he says:

> Vision or Imagination is a Representation of what Eternally Exists, Really & Unchangeably. Fable or Allegory is Form'd by the daughters of Memory. Imagination is surrounded by the daughters of Inspiration, who in the aggregate are call'd Jerusalem. Fable is allegory, but what the Critics call The Fable, is Vision itself. The Hebrew Bible & the Gospel of Jesus are not Allegory, but Eternal Vision or Imagination of All that Exists. Note here that Fable or Allegory is seldom without some Vision. Pilgrim's Progress is full of it ... but Allegory & Vision ought to be known as Two Distinct Things, & so call'd for the Sake of Eternal Life.[22]

Falstaff thought of the sun as a fair hot wench in flame-coloured taffeta: and I think Langland would almost have been capable of such a flight of fancy: but he would more readily have echoed Blake in saying:

> 'What,' it will be Question'd, 'When the Sun rises, do you not see a round disk of fire somewhat like a Guinea?' O no, no, I see an Innumerable company of the Heavenly host crying, 'Holy, Holy, Holy is the Lord God Almighty.' I question not my Corporeal or Vegetative Eye any more than I would Question a Window concerning a Sight. I look thro' it & not with it.[23]

It is perhaps necessary to add that Langland was a Christian poet (in fact the greatest of English Christian poets) and that he was not writing, nor did he wish to write, 'pure poetry' (if there is such a thing). The tides that move in his writing are religious, which means that not all his powers are amenable to 'aesthetic' principles. To be able to release the forces of Christian feeling in poetry is not a common gift, as any one can see who reads *Hymns Ancient and Modern*. Not everyone that says 'Lord, Lord' can do it: but Langland could, and to read him as 'pure poetry' is like trying to read the Bible as merely literature, to hear the *Sanctus* of the *Mass in B Minor* as merely music, or to take a Grünewald altarpiece from its altar and put it in a museum – that is, it is better than not reading it at all. In thinking of these things it is well to ponder a phrase from the hymn, which, according to the *Apocryphal Gospel of St John*,[24] was sung by Jesus and his disciples at the Last Supper, before they went out into the Mount of Olives:

> Divine Grace is dancing,
> Dance ye all!
> Ye who are not dancing
> Know not what we are knowing.

NOTES

1. B Text, Passus XII, 16–18.
2. Cf. H. S. V. Jones, 'Imaginatif in Piers Plowman', *J.E.G.P.*, xiii (1914), 583–8.
3. C. S. Lewis, *The Allegory of Love* (Oxford, 1936), p. 158.
4. Ibid., pp. 44–5.
5. Prudentius, *Psychomachia*, lines 40–50:
   exim gramineo in campo concurrere prompta
   virgo Pudicitia speciosis fulget in armis,
   quam patrias succincta faces Sodomita Libido
   adgreditur piceamque ardenti sulpure pinum
   ingerit in faciem pudibundaque lumina flammis
   adpetit, et taetro temptat subfundere fumo.
   sed dextram furiae flagrantis et ignea dirae
   tela lupae saxo ferit inperterrita virgo,
   excussasque sacro taedas depellit ab ore.

tunc exarmatae iugulum meretricis adacto
transfigit gladio.

(Loeb edn [Cambridge, Mass., 1949], i. 282)

6. *La Tentation de Saint Antoine* (Paris, 1954), p. 14.
7. *Si le grain ne meurt* (Paris, 1928), p. 345.
8. W.W. Skeat, *The Vision of William concerning Piers the Plowman* (Oxford, 1886), ii. 81, note to C.VII. 197.
9. *Le Temps retrouvé* (Paris, 1927), pp. 54–5.
10. See the passage from *Allegoriae in novum testamentum* quoted by D. W. Robertson and B. F. Huppé, *Piers Plowman and Scriptural Tradition* (Princeton, 1951), pp. 207–8.
11. See B.XIX. 104–85:

In his iuuente this Iesus atte Iuwen feste
Water into wyn tourned, as holy writ telleth,
And there bigan God of his grace to Dowel.
For wyn is lykned to lawe and lyf of holynesse....

[Cf. Walafridus Strabus on John ii.7: 'Christus ... maluit de aqua vinum facere, ut doceret se non solvere legem, sed implere, nec in Evangelio alia facere vel docere quam quae prophetia praedixit.' (Migne, *Patr. Lat.*, cxiv. 363.)]

And whan he was woxen more, in his moder absence, ...
... he conforted carful, & caughte a gretter name,
The whiche was Do-bet, where that he went....
... 'And blessed mote thei alle be, in body & in soule,
That neuere shal se me in sighte, as thow doste nouthe ...
Beati qui non viderunt, et crediderunt, etc.'
And whan this dede was done, Do-best he taughte,
And yaf Pieres power and pardoun he graunted
To alle manere men mercy & foryyfnes....

12. B.XX. 207.
13. A. S. Bright, *New Light on Piers Plowman* (London, 1928), p. 45.
14. *Op. cit.*, ii. 277, note on C.XXIII. 80.
15. *Op. cit.*, p. 64, note on C.VI. 117.
16. Monk of Sawley's version of Grosseteste's *Chasteau d'amour*, printed in *The Minor Poems of the Vernon Manuscript*, Part I, ed. C. Horstmann (*E.E.T.S.* 98, 1892), p. 416, ll. 291–300.
17. Ibid., Vernon Version, p. 374, ll. 761–4.
18. *Cursor Mundi*, Göttingen and Cotton versions, ll. 9885–6 (*E.E.T.S.* 59, 1875), pp. 568–9.
19. Quotations from the A Text are taken from the edition by G. Kane (London, 1960), with spelling slightly modified.
20. Vernon version, ll. 325–9.
21. S. Beckett, *Waiting for Godot* (London, 1956), p. 11.
22. *The Writings of William Blake*, ed. G. Keynes (London, 1925), iii. 145.
23. Ibid., p. 162.
24. The passage here quoted is taken from the version made by Gustav Holst for his *Hymn of Jesus*. See also M. R. James, *The Apocryphal New Testament* (Oxford, 1955), p. 253.

7

Wags, Clowns and Jesters*

Among the less exalted orders of the Shakespearian populace there are three that tend to shade off into a kind of class, whose main functions, mannerisms and idiosyncrasies are easy to recognise, though they tend to merge and mingle, or at least to overlap: they are the Wags, the Clowns and the Jesters.

Mainly they are meant to be funny, whether as wits or butts or both: but they have other functions and qualities too. Time has dealt unkindly with many of their jokes, and some have not survived the footnotes that expound them. Not their jokes only, but their very being, in some cases, may call for explanation. We still meet with rustics in the modern world, with clown-policemen and bull-calf recruits; a yokel needs no footnote. But where are now the pert boys whom Shakespeare shows us paging their young masters from Verona to Milan, from Pisa to Padua, and throwing out a barrage of waggery in chop-logic, cross-purpose, paronomasia and arch commment upon the love-affairs of their betters? And where are the professional fools, those privileged jesters, men like Will Sommers, who called Henry VIII 'Harry' to his face, and could make him roar with laughter on damp days?

Some pictures of the Jesters remain. Richard Tarlton was a snub-nosed smiler, with wide-set eyes, a curly moustache and a little chinbeard; he could play tabor and pipe together, a difficult art. Watteau has left us the melancholy face of Gilles, Court Jester to the King of France, and there is, I learn from Professor Davis, an epitaph in Beckley Church to the last of

---

More Talking of Shakespeare ed. John Garrett (London: Longmans, 1959).

all the Jesters, Dicky Pearce, the Earl of Suffolk's Fool, who died in 1728. It is ascribed, for what good reason I do not know, to Jonathan Swift:

> Here lies the Earl of Suffolk's Fool
>   Men call'd him Dicky Pearce:
> His folly served to make men laugh
>   When wit and mirth were scarce.
>
> Poor Dick, alas! is dead and gone,
>   What signifies to cry?
> Dickys enough are left behind
>   To laugh at by and by.[1]

Wags and Jesters are now denizens of a museum world and there they lead their fancy-dress existence; it may well be that this is a factor which helps us to achieve that never-never-landish state of mind suited to a comedy of Shakespeare's golden world, a state in which it is easy to cross the frontiers of Illyria or Arden, and bid lullaby to our social consciences for an hour or two, for the refreshment of their foolery.

What a fantastic foolery it is! It has an extravagance in which, for once, Ben Jonson has outdone Shakespeare, who has nothing to match the macabre trinity of twisted creatures or grotesques, Nano the dwarf, Castrone the Eunuch, and Androgyno the Man-Woman, who are Volpone's household monsters, his kept Fools. Each of them is a museum piece, a creature of great rarity, quaintness and cost: their collective function in the play is more than that of entertaining their master: it is to appear as further items in, and emblems of, his inordinate wealth and connoisseurship. They are the *trouvailles* of a collector.

When we first meet with them, whether in the text or on the stage, we have to open our mouths wide to swallow them; we teach ourselves to accept them as a deliberately stomach-turning Jonsonian hyperbole, in scale with the huge scope of his satire, with the allegorical stature of Volpone himself. And yet I can recall a paragraph in a newspaper, at the time when Benito Mussolini was waging war in Abyssinia: it described the vast and curious wealth of a certain Abyssinian Prince, Ras Tafari, a cousin of the Emperor. Among his more fabulous possessions, he also kept a little human zoo; it contained a monk, a eunuch and a hermaphrodite. It would seem that Ben Jonson's fantasies are not entirely out of this world.

Half-wittedness, deformity and abnormality seem to have been (historically speaking) the usual qualifications for the Fools or 'naturals' that, from time to time, were kept for a whim, or for the amusement of great households – a use for the village idiot.

At what time cunning, intelligence and talent took over from cretinism in the making of the Court Fool, it is hard to say. The Fool by Nature and the Fool by Art have always existed, and which is the more in vogue will depend on the taste of the age. In a civilised Court, like that of Richard II, we find that entertainment came from poets like Chaucer and Gower, and from tregetours such as those we read of in the *Franklin's Tale*. In a semi-barbarous Court, like that of Henry VIII, we find Will Sommers. It is hard to understand how educated people could relish the company of a freak of nature, and keep him, so to speak, as a pet. Shakespeare lifted the whole company of such Fools out of the slough of imbecility; his jesters have wit, pithiness; they can dance and sing and extemporise, their presence has point. It seems to say, 'as, in the midst of life, we are in death, so, in the midst of sanity, we are in folly.'

But no actual Tudor Fool I ever heard of had such gift or quality. A good loud laugh or an agreeable gibe was as much as could be hoped for from Sommers, or even perhaps from Tarlton, except when he took to his tabor and pipe. If Will Sommers had no better jokes than those that Armin records of him, what are we to think of the taste and intelligence of Henry VIII?

We read in Armin's *Nest of Ninnies*, that the king, when sad, would cheer himself up by rhyming and riddling with this melancholy moron. The stooping, hollow-eyed figure would squinny at his monarch: ' "Now tell me," says Will, "if you can, what it is that, being borne without life, head, lippe or eye, yet doth runne roaring through the world until it dye?" "That is a wonder," quoth the King, "and no question; I know it not." "Why," quoth Will, "it is a fart." At this the King laught hartely and was exceeding merry.'

Richard Tarlton's verbal gifts seem to have been very little better, such, at least, as have come down to us in *Tarlton's Jests* and *News Out of Purgatory*; yet Fuller tells us that, 'when Queen Elisabeth was serious, dare not say sullen, and out of humour, he could undumpish her at his pleasure'. But he brought a frown to her face when he said of Sir Walter Raleigh, 'See, the Knave commands the Queen.' He was famous for his powers of extemporal rhyme, like Touchstone: but alas his published vein is no better than what one would expect to find in a ballad sold at a fair by Autolycus. Here is a sample:

> By rushing rivers late,
>   In Bedford town, no nay,
> Ful many a woeful state
>   May yeeld to fast and pray.
>
> At twelve oclock at night
>   It flowed with such a hed,
> Yea, many a woeful wight
>   Did swim in naked bed.
>
> Among the rest there was
>   A woful widow sure,
> Whome God did bring to passe
>   The death she did procure.
>
> Widow Spencer by name
>   A sleep she being fast,
> The flood so rashly came
>   That she aloft was cast.
>
> Which seeing started up,
>   Regarding small her pelf
> She left beside her bed,
>   And so she drowned herself.[2]

And so on for 36 verses. Contrast them with Touchstone's lilting extemporisations:

> If the cat will after kind,
> So, be sure, will Rosalind. . . .

But before I go on to Shakespeare's imagination of Jesters, let me show you a few more authentic Tudor ones, for it is hardly possible to realise how much Shakespeare transfigured the whole tribe, if one does not know how raw his raw material was.

There was Jack Oates, Fool to a countrified knight.[3] Oates was a 'natural' given to almost senseless rages and jealousies whenever attention was paid to any entertainer other than himself. He broke a fiddle on a fiddler and beat up a bagpiper and burnt his bagpipes, not out of musical feeling, but out of envy. But his vendetta with the cook was crazier and more malicious. Sir William was particularly addicted to quince pies, and so, acting on an imperfectly thought-out plan to get the cook into trouble, Oates stole a quince pie. But it was too hot to hold, so the Fool jumped into the moat to cool it. Sir William's first reaction was to roar with laughter and sack the cook (presumably for having allowed the theft of the pie; he seems to have been almost as big a fool as Oates himself), but on learning that there was malice behind the incident, he 'bid the Cook enjoy his place againe'. Oates's best recorded joke is that he ran in to his master and some assembled guests, to announce that a country-wench in the servants' hall had eaten garlic, and 17 men had been poisoned kissing her.

Then there was Jemy Camber, a fat Scotch dwarf, said to have been a yard and a nail high, and two yards round, with a small head, long hair, one ear bigger than the other, flaming eyes, a flat nose, a wide mouth, few teeth, short legs, pretty little feet and enormous hands. He seems to have been more butt than wit: '"No," says Jemy, "the sun blowes very colde." "No," says the King, "the wind shines very hot." So simple hee was that he knew not whether it was the sunne or the winde made him sweat.'

Perhaps Edward Atienza had read this account of Jemy Camber in Armin's *Nest of Ninnies* when he contrived to perform Lavache in *All's Well That Ends Well* as a tubby dwarf – a miracle of costume, make-up and acting – at Stratford in 1955. There is, of course, no suggestion in Shakespeare that Lavache was a dwarf, but he is described as suffering from another inconvenience which he certainly shared with Jemy, namely a pressing sexual appetite.

'My poor body, Madam, requires it,' says Lavache when asking permission of the Countess to marry, 'if I may have your ladyship's good will to go to the world, Isbel the woman and I will do as we may.' Jemy Camber was sub-intelligent and could never so have expressed himself; nevertheless he got quite a long way towards seducing the laundress. She, however, was too much for him. She stuffed a heap of nettles under her bed; then, having lured him in beside her, she knocked the wall with her hand, as if someone were at the door. Jemy, terrified at being caught in the act, dived naked under the bed and found himself among the nettles.

One might think I had chosen my illustrations from specially oafish jests and jesters, but they are a disappointing lot; even Henry Pattensen, household Jester to Thomas More, was a crude-witted fellow; jokes about the size of a nose were about his level. Only More's charity can explain Pattensen's membership of the household.

What a world away from all such dolts and deformities are the Fools in Shakespeare! What a civilisation breathes from Arden and Illyria, compared with what issues from Hampton Court! Armin's book shows us something of the actuality of Jesterdom, Shakespeare shows us jesters in the ideal, not what they were, but all they could never be.

Yet it was Armin who made this possible. Not his book, but himself, as an actor; *for* him, *through* him, Shakespeare created the witty Fool, the singing Fool, the fey, the tragic Fool. Armin joined Shakespeare's Company just before the turn of the century, in 1599; and from that moment began Shakespeare's vision of the Fool and his high art.

For the moment, however, let me return to the Wags and the Clowns. As I have already said, the three sub-categories of comic actor merge into one another in some of their tricks; what distinguishes the Wag is to strut along behind or beside his master. Some are blockish like the Dromios; some, like Launce and Speed, are fond of their own wit and every ready to risk their bottoms for their tongues. The secret of their comedy is simple: word-play and horse-play. A good friendly knockabout or thrashing of the 'knock-me-on-the-door' style, for instance, is after all what everyone enjoys.

It may have been John Lyly who taught Shakespeare the dramatic charm of this master-to-boy relationship, from which it is so easy to create dialogue, catechism-wise when all else fails. Lyly's boys seem all to be in the top form of some

Prep. School to Parnassus; they have been taught to utter in imagery. Here, for example, is young Halfpenny, in *Mother Bombie*:

Halfpenny: Nay then, let me come in with a dream, short but sweet, that my mouth waters ever since I waked. Methought there sate upon a shelf three damask prunes in velvet caps and pressed satin gowns, like judges; and that there were a whole handful of currants to be arraigned of a riot, because they clung together in such clusters: twelve raisins of the sun were impannelled in a jury, and, as a leaf of whole mace, which was bailiff, was carrying the quest to consult, methought there came an angry cook, and gelded the jury of their stones, and swept both judges, jurors, rebels and bailiff into a porridge-pot; whereat I being melancholy, fetched a deep sigh that waked myself and my bed-fellow.

This is excellent fooling. Youngest and smallest of Shakespeare's Wags, in a vein even more delicate and poetical, is Moth, servant to Don Adriano de Armado. Their happy sparring-partnership, so full of affectation, and, which is more, of affection, is a large part of the verbal magic of the play:

Armado: Warble, child; make passionate my sense of hearing.
Moth
(singing):   Concolinel....
Armado: Sweet air! Go, tenderness of years; take this key, give enlargement to the swain, bring him festinately hither; I must employ him in a letter to my love.
Moth: Master, will you win your love with a French brawl?
Armado: How meanest thou? brawling in French?
Moth: No, my complete master; but to jig off a tune at the tongue's end, canary to it with your feet, humour it with turning up your eyelids, sigh a note and sing a note, sometimes through the throat, as if you swallowed love by singing love, sometime through the nose, as if you snuffed up love by smelling love ... with your arms crossed on your thin belly-doublet like a rabbit on a spit.... These are complements, these are humours, these betray nice wenches....
Armado: How hast thou purchased this experience?
Moth: By my penny of observation.

Lovely nonsense of this kind is a subliming of Lyly's dialogue, and indeed of the 'conceit' itself; the speakers feed each other with question and answer, and their relationship, of master and boy, is as if mellowed out of that between Sir Tophas and Epiton in Lyly's *Endymion*. An impudent variation of it is seen in Falstaff and his page:

Falstaff: Sirrah, you giant, what says the doctor to my water?
Page: He said, sir, the water itself was a good healthy water; but, for the party that owed it, he might have more diseases than he knew for.

This is a *visual* as well as a *verbal* use of the relationship – the enormous Falstaff, the infinitesimal page; verbally, it is amusing to see the first comic (might I say Dickensian?) use of the word *party* that I know of.

The main of Shakespeare's serving-boys are yokels in the egg, peasants like the Dromios, not gentry-pages like Moth; they are meant to be funny, not poetical; but they shade upwards socially, via Launce and Speed, to Biondello and to Tranio, who is well-enough bred to pass for his master Lucentio. But it would seem that there was a limit, even for Shakespeare, to what could be done with comic serving lads by way of stage effect; perhaps he found he was repeating himself; the soliloquies and name of Launce have much in common with those of Launcelot. The species seems to disappear from Shakespeare's work towards the turn of the sixteenth century; chronological order in this matter is not certain, but perhaps the last of the comic pages were the two imps who appear out of nowhere in the forest of Arden, sing 'It was a lover and his lass . . .', and vanish as suddenly as they came.

But the Clown class goes right through Shakespearian comedy: and not only through the comedies, but through the histories and the tragedies. One of his first and most memorable is a tragic clown. He comes in at the height of the agony in *Titus Andronicus*, when the storm of passion is frothed with hysteria. Titus is as mad as the sea, but the tide is beginning to turn; hitherto he has only suffered, now he is beginning to act. As if to mark this moment, Shakespeare brings in a clown carrying a basket of pigeons, and the tension seems to be released a little; at last there will be something to laugh, or at least to smile, at. Titus mistakes the clown, in his crazy way, for a messenger from Jupiter: 'Shall I have justice? What says Jupiter?' 'Jupiter' however is a new word to the simpleton; he mixes it up, in baleful ignorance with 'Gibbet-maker': 'O! the gibbet-maker? He says he hath taken them down again for the man must not be hanged till the next week.' It is grim word-play, the beginning of Shakespearian malapropism, but grimmer is to come.

Titus:	Why, didst thou not come from heaven?
Clown:	From heaven! alas! sir, I never came there. *God forbid I should be so bold to press to heaven in my young days.*

Could there have been, when this was first produced, experienced Shakespearian playgoers, they would have scented irony in airs such as these. Titus sends the fellow with a letter, demanding justice, to his enemy, the Emperor Saturninus: 'And when you come to him, at the first approach you must kneel; then kiss his foot; then deliver up your pigeons; and then look for your reward.' The simpleton moons off on his errand, the scene changes to the Emperor's court.

Tamora:	How now, good fellow! wouldst thou speak with us?
Clown:	Yea, forsooth, an your mistership be emperial.
Tamora:	Empress I am, but yonder sits the Emperor.
Clown:	'Tis he. God and Saint Stephen give you good den. I have brought you a letter and a couple of pigeons here. (*Saturninus reads the letter.*)
Saturninus:	Go, take him away, and hang him presently.
Clown:	How much money must I have?
Tamora:	Come, sirrah, you must be hanged.
Clown:	Hanged! By'r lady, then I have brought up a neck to a fair end. (*Exit, guarded.*)

Here is Shakespeare's first juxtaposition of madman, fool and death; his first use of comedy to heighten horror with surprise. The mention of Saint Stephen may put the fancy into one's mind that this clown is a first martyr to irony. But he has the last word: '*I have brought up my neck to a fair end.*' These effects are above what can be achieved with Wags. It is the *simplicity*, not the waggishness, of the clown that touches the scene with tragic feeling in its unique blend of lunacy and evil and rustic innocence.

Shakespeare's last tragic clown, if the clown that brings the asp to Cleopatra be he, is also a death-clown, also a simpleton; and in this case, that shimmers with ironies even more intense, his simpletonism is underlined by his attempts at waggery: 'You must not think I am so simple but I know the devil himself will not eat a woman.' He, too, has the last word in the interchange: 'I wish you joy of the worm.'

Apart from their vacuous innocence, these two tragic clowns have no 'character'. They do not need it. But most of the great clowns in Shakespeare are highly individual; they are among the most humanly perceived of all the members of their little worlds. One has only to think of Bottom and his companions.

It may be that we have to thank Will Kempe for this; we know, from the 1599 quarto of *Romeo and Juliet*, that he played Peter: from the Folio we know he played Dogberry too. If we unbridle our imagination a little, we may see him as a chief stimulus to Shakespeare's comic invention until Robert Armin took over from him, about 1599. Whatever quirks of individuality Shakespeare invented to give scope to the antics of Kempe, all the clowns have the great foundation-stone we have already noted, of simpletonism. Bottom is a simpleton who is also a genius. Suppose him, for a moment, anything but the pure innocent he is; suppose him a knowing wag; how intolerable would his relation with Titania become! But, as with the clown with the asp, such waggery as he has is the index of his innocence: 'And yet, to say the truth, reason and love keep little company together now-a-days. The more the pity, that some honest neighbours will not make them friends.' Bottom and the clowns of his class have, in their making, a hint of the aphorism of St Augustine that Langland quotes in *Piers Plowman*: '*Ecce ipsi idioti rapiunt celum, ubi nos sapientes in inferno mergimur.*' See! very fools take Heaven by assault, where we, the wise, are sunk into the pit.

On this foundation of innocence, Bottom's genius as an artist is superimposed. I believe it was Mr J. B. Priestley who first noted that Bottom was essentially an artist, among companions whose only thought was for sixpence a day from the Duke. But Bottom cares about *style*; he knows how to distinguish – 'in the *true* performing' – between the 'condoling' style of the lover and the cat-tearing manner needed for the part of Ercles. His first thought is his make-up: 'Well I will undertake it. *What beard were I best to play it in?*' and he rattles off half a dozen plausible alternatives from a glowing imagination. When, later, problems in production arise, he overflows with exciting suggestions, and he rejects the proposal of Quince that the Prologue shall be written in the trite metre of 'eight and six', preferring the full dignity of octosyllabics: 'Let it be written in eight and eight.' Certainly style is a great preoccupation with him, and inventiveness his special talent. One would like to see a tapestry woven by Bottom the Weaver.

Dull and Elbow, the constables in *Love's Labour's Lost* and *Measure for Measure*, are simpletons, both of them, too; but they have no genius. They have character, however, far beyond what is needed for their minimal plot-function. Dull is a model of obstinacy well-based in ignorance. 'I said the deer was not a *haud credo*; 'twas a pricket,' he asserts to Holofernes, and he can hold his own in a debate:

Holofernes: ... The allusion holds in the exchange.
Dull: 'Tis true indeed; the collusion holds in the exchange.
Holofernes: God comfort thy capacity! I say the allusion holds in the
              exchange.
Dull: And I say the pollution holds in the exchange. ...

Elbow, whose plot-function is the arrest of Pompey and Mistress Overdone, is a product of the same constabulary, an adept in word-mismanagement; but his endearing incompetence as an officer is used not only to make us smile, but to show the patient tact of Escalus, who, after a tiring morning with him and Pompey Bum, sees that Elbow will have to be replaced and manages to make arrangements for this without hurting his feelings. The patient justice and good feeling of Escalus are, in turn, juxtaposed to the contemptuous attitude of Angelo, who cannot be bothered with such matters and has left them, with a sneer, to Escalus to handle. Thus the insufficiency of a comic Constable is used by his creator to show the insufficiency of a protagonist.

The idea 'that out of the mouths of babes and sucklings hast thou ordained strength', however, is more directly presented to us through Dogberry, Verges and the Messina Watch in *Much Ado About Nothing*. Once again we have a feast of malapropism and a good deal of ordinary clowning ('We will rather sleep than talk; we know what belongs to a Watch'); on top of that there is a sudden overflow of character in Dogberry's last speech which instantly places him as a person – that is, as more than a Constable, in the social context of Messina: 'I am a wise fellow; and, which is more, an officer; and, which is more, a house-holder; and, which is more, a pretty a piece of flesh as any in Messina; and one that knows the law, go to; and a rich fellow enough, go to; and a fellow that hath had losses; and one that hath two gowns, and everything handsome about him.'

Pompey Bum, and his fellow-pander, Boult, in *Pericles*, are spirits of another sort, and yet the same actor may play them; they are in the Kempe tradition. To them are also allowed supererogatory moments of intimacy, brief glimpses of disarming candour, touches of grace. Pompey is brought to admit that his profession 'does stink in some sort': Boult, about to make the old and obvious joke about roses and prickles, suddenly stops short and says, 'O! sir, I can be modest.' Lysimachus retorts, 'That dignifies the renown of a bawd.'

Clowns make a class but Jesters are only a guild; that Shakespeare would ever have thought of that guild as a rich mine of drama without the advent of Robert Armin, seems unlikely. Yet his first Jester had been created some years before Armin replaced Kempe, and he sprang out of the Wag tradition, the tradition of the imp-servant in mischievous mood. It was Puck, court-fool to fairyland: 'I jest to Oberon, and make him smile. ....'

The boy who played Moth could no doubt have played Puck too, but Touchstone is imagined for a matured actor: breathlessness and brio will carry Puck through his part, but Touchstone calls for timing. His lines are a study, an *étude*, for a professional, full of antitheses, alternatives, conditionals and qualifications: 'By my knavery, if I had it, then I were; but if you swear by that that is not, you are not foresworn; no more was this knight, swearing by his honour, for he never had any; or if he had, he had sworn it away, before he ever saw those pancakes or that mustard.' This and so many of his speeches depend for their effectiveness on infinitesimal changes of tone and tempo. Shakespeare seems to have discovered Armin's range gradually; it looks as if he did not at first know that he could sing, for the songs in *As You Like It* go to Amiens and the pages; but what he seized upon was the power of pulling off a set-piece in prose: and that means timing, and cadencing – the precise degree of emphasis required for the two demonstratives, for instance, *those* pancakes and *that* mustard. Touchstone is a shallower, or at least a less complex character than Feste; he is the jester of prepared witticisms, the raconteur with a repertory. The story of Jane Smile, and the recital of the Seven Degrees of the Lie have evidently been made perfect by many previous repetitions. One feels he may even have tried out his dialogue with Corin on some previous occasion too, with some other shepherd, the reasons he gives fall so pat; court versus country was a stock debate, and Touchstone was prepared for it; indeed he initiates it. He is playing on home ground.

Touchstone: Wast ever in court, shepherd?
Corin: No, truly.
Touchstone: Then thou art damned.
Corin: Nay, I hope –
Touchstone: Truly, thou art damned like an ill-roasted egg, all on one side.
Corin: For not being at court? Your reason.
Touchstone: Why, if thou never wast at court, thou never sawest good manners; if thou never sawest good manners, then thy manners must be wicked; and wickedness is sin, and sin is damnation. Thou art in a parlous state, shepherd.

There is no bitterness in Touchstone: bitterness (mild though it be) in *As You Like It* is given to Jaques. Touchstone is there to be a blithe wit, and he knows it; he takes pleasure in it; he is a great exhibitionist. His name, no doubt, is chosen to tell his function – a debunker of romantic nonsense, whose triumphant common sense leads him to espouse Audrey. Jaques never made a worse guess than when he hazards that their loving voyage 'is but for two months victual'd'. An audience may well imagine it will outlast that of Rosalind and Orlando, even in that romantic world. Professor Hotson has reminded us that Armin had been apprenticed to a jeweller, and that may have given Shakespeare a hint for the Fool's name: for a touchstone is 'a piece of black quartz or jasper, used for testing the quality of gold and silver alloys, by the colour of the streak produced by rubbing them upon it'.

Feste does not seem to rely on set-pieces, but on extemporal wit; he has a repertory not of jokes, but of songs. He is a great reader of character; the first service he does for the audience in this regard is to make them realise that the Countess's 'mourning' for her brother is simply a mask she has assumed, in order to keep the Duke Orsino at arm's length. No one but Feste perceives this; he not only perceives it, but thinks the best way back into her favour is to tease her about the very man for whom she is so ostentatiously in grief:

Feste:	I think his soul is in hell, madonna.
Countess:	I know his soul is in heaven, fool.
Feste:	The more fool, madonna, to mourn for your brother's soul being in heaven. Take away the fool, gentlemen.
Countess:	What think you of this fool, Malvolio? doth he not mend?

But a melancholy, not unlike the melancholy given to Jaques in *As You Like It*, is in *Twelfth Night* allowed to tinge the wit of Feste; undaunted co-operative jollity, such as we see in Touchstone, is exchanged for touches of controlled, critical derision: 'Vent my folly! he has heard that word of some great man, and now applies it to a fool; vent my folly!' He is also coldly, wittily *mercenary*; no one ever hears Touchstone ask for money, but Feste is an adept:

Clown:	Would not a pair of these have bred, sir?
Viola:	Yes, being kept together and put to use.
Clown:	I would play Lord Pandarus of Phrygia, sir, to bring a Cressida to this Troilus.
Viola:	I understand you, sir: 'tis well begg'd.

Above all he is malicious, a grudge-bearer, who has it in him to gird at Malvolio, tormented and defeated as he has been; but the whirligig of time brings its revenges even to Feste, for, at the end, he is left out of things. When all the rest have moved off to the joyful *solemnitas* of their journey's end, Feste, who has no Audrey to serve his turn, who does not even seem to have a turn to serve, is left alone to sing his melancholy song of the wind and the rain, the song he has in common with the Fool in *Lear*. Feste seems to me the most complex of all the Armin Fools, the subtlest and bawdiest and coldest, the most attractive, the most musical, the most talented; he has it in him to glitter in the golden world, and yet to throw across it the long and deepening shadow.

Having drifted into the romantic way of thinking about Touchstone and Feste – as if they were real people, not characters in a play – let us note that this is what the old magician so unfailingly contrives, and his spell is a simple one; he gives his characters more character than they actually need for the purposes of their play. This is the bamboozling touch, that makes one think it is life, not a play; for in life the characters of men and women have similar surprises for us. Let us therefore, for a moment, submit to the illusion, go the whole hog; the truth is that Touchstone could easily become rather a bore, but Feste never. You would be lucky if Feste even liked you. But then, of course, you could always buy his liking – or a perfect imitation – and if you went on buying it, it would stay bought.

One has to try to keep one's head over Shakespeare's greatest Fool, the Fool in *Lear*; for, as Granville-Barker has warned us, it is possible to etherialise him to such a point that any actor would be a disappointment in the part. There are three things about him that differentiate him from all the other Jesters in the canon. First, he is a half-wit; that is, he is in the tradition of the 'natural' which, as we have seen, is the historic Tudor household-fool tradition, the village idiot taken into the family. Lear's Fool is an idiot of genius, just as Bottom is a simpleton of genius. Secondly he is a fierce critic of his master – no other 'allowed Fool' is allowed so much, because no other is a half-wit – and thirdly he is in total dependency on Lear; and this is also the effect of his native imbecility. He must be protected.

Lear's Fool thus does two things for an audience, both of which stem from his helpless, feeble-minded nature. It enables him to satisfy one of the strongest of an audience's wishes during Acts I and II, which is to hear someone give the insensate King a piece of their minds, for his treatment of Cordelia and trust of Goneril and Regan. It is true that Kent's gruff, bluff rebukes offer some expression to the indignation of an audience; but Kent cannot hit the King where it hurts most, because Kent's attack is *from outside*. Kent's attack can be repelled, and is so. Kent is banished. But the Fool is *inside*, under Lear's guard.

Because he is a helpless dependant, the Fool's attack cannot be repelled; he is inside Lear's armour, grafted to his compassion. He can, of course, be threatened with the whip, but what good is that? Lear would only be whipping himself for having heard and rebelled against the truth, as excellent a whipping as he advises later to the rascal beadle. The Fool's crazy versicles, riddles and proverbs sting Lear inwardly, and therefore give an 'I could have told you so' satisfaction to an audience; these are the satisfactions for which the Fool is so much beloved:

Fool: The reason why the seven stars are no more than seven is a pretty reason.
Lear: Because they are not eight?
Fool: Yes, indeed: thou wouldst make a good fool.

The second great thing he does for us is to make visible the charity of Lear. This again is a consequence of the Fool's helplessness, of the *nuncledom* of their relationship.

Come on, my boy. How dost, my boy? art cold?
I am cold myself. Where is this straw, my fellow? . . .
Poor fool and knave, I have one part in my heart
That's sorry yet for thee. . . .

The action that must go with these lines makes one perceive the sincerity of Lear's prayer for the misery of others, the naked wretches, wherever they may be, that bide the pelting of the pitiless storm. His new-found charity and humbleness of heart are made manifest, are actable, are *seen*, in his tenderness towards the Fool. Seeing is believing.

That yet a fourth Fool, wholly different from all the others, and almost as dominating a figure, should have followed is one more example of a dramatic invention that seems never to repeat itself; the singing rogue-fool Autolycus, who has in his time been a gentleman and worn velvet, and is now reduced to the theft of lesser linen from farmers' wives, has to be considered. He is there to contribute an explosion of energy and rejuvenation at the very moment when *The Winter's Tale* needs the vigorous impulse of a new start. So he comes in singing, '*When daffodils begin to peer*'.

He has, of course, an infinitesimal part in the plot by which Camillo helps the escape of Florizel and Perdita; Florizel borrows his clothes. This could easily have been contrived in some other way, and it seems probable that Shakespeare made that rather mechanical use of Autolycus, to give countenance to his presence in the play, for a further, more significant purpose. Autolycus, it seems to me, is there not only for his energy but also for the stiffening of *roguery* he gives to what, without him, might have been indicted of pastoral sentimentality. Shepherd and shepherdess idealism and the pure airs of the country are all very well, but Shakespeare had always taken care to moderate such raptures. Silvius and Phoebe are brought to their senses even in Arden; Touchstone shows William off, and gets Audrey. One is kept down to earth. This earthiness is what Autolycus exists to provide, and with his earthiness he brings his country music; it has all the air of an Armin part.

Trinculo is the last and most deboshed of the race of Jesters. He is as different from those that preceded him as they are from each other; he seems only there to be bullied, to sink in the esteem of Caliban, to be jester to a drunken butler. He can just manage to sing a catch, but he seems to have no other talent; if he were not listed as 'a Jester' in the cast-list at the end of the play in the Folio, one might almost take him for a Clown, and a cowardly one. Unlike most of his fellow-fools in other plays, he has sunk into the sub-plot; he is even less than Lavache, the Fool in *All's Well*.

Trinculo, like the others, however, fits into his own play. Touchstone would have made rings round Caliban; Feste would have deserted Lear. Only Lavache, Jester to the old Countess of Roussillon, has moments which seem to qualify him for something better than his part and play. His actual function is to be a time-sandwich, that is, to keep a scene going which has no other purpose than to indicate a lapse of time between the scene before and the scene to follow, or to deliver a letter from one part of France to another. He has two or three creative touches lavished and lost upon him, for in spite of them he never comes into full view as a character. He builds no sympathy for Helena, as Lear's Fool does for Cordelia. He does little for the old Countess and nothing for Bertram. He is unimportantly rude to Parolles on two occasions, but whenever the play gets going, he is forgotten, or laid aside as not-for-the-moment necessary.

And yet this character which barely exists is given a lovely snatch to sing, one that deepens the enigma of what Shakespeare thought about the tale of Troy, which haunted him so long:

> Was this fair face the cause, quoth she,
>   Why the Grecians sacked Troy?
> Fond done, done fond,
>   Was this King Priam's joy?
> With that she sighed as she stood,
> With that she sighed as she stood,
>   And gave this sentence then;
> Among nine bad if one be good,
> Among nine bad if one be good,
>   There's yet one good in ten.

and he has one speech that rings strangely in the mouth of a jester: 'I am for the house with the narrow gate, which I take to be too little for pomp to enter; some that humble themselves may; but the many will be too chill and tender, and they'll be for the flowery way that leads to the broad gate and the great fire.'

'A shrewd knave and an unhappy' is Lafeu's wise comment on Lavache. He is an extreme example of what one finds in so many of Shakespeare's creations – there is more to them than they actually need for the plays in which they appear – they spill over into life.

NOTES

1. Samuel Palmer, *Epitaphs and Epigrams* (London 1869).
2. Tarlton's *Jests and News out of Purgatory*, ed. J.O. Halliwell, (Shakespeare Society, 1844).
3. See *Fools and Jesters*: with a reprint of Robert Armin's *Nest of Ninnies*, with an Introduction by J.P. Collier, (Shakespeare Society, 1842).

8

Six Points of Stage-craft in *The Winter's Tale**

It is a critical commonplace that *The Winter's Tale* is an ill-made play: its very editors deride it. A recent apologist, S. L. Bethell, after posing the question 'Why is his dramatic technique crude and apparently incoherent?'[1] answers with the bold suggestion that Shakespeare was trying to be funny: instancing several examples in the Florizel–Perdita–Camillo–Autolycus–Shepherd–Clown sequences of IV, iv, he concludes: 'surely this is a deliberately comic underlining of a deliberately crude technique. Considering now the play as a whole, are we not justified in suspecting a quite conscious return to naïve and outmoded technique, a deliberate creaking of the dramatic machinery?'[2]

These conjectures may seem valid in the study, but have no force on the stage. Shakespeare's stage-craft in this play is as novel, subtle and revolutionary as it had been a few years before in *Antony and Cleopatra*, but in an entirely different way: just as he had then found the technical path to an actual and life-sized world – to the drums and tramplings of the Roman Empire – so, in *The Winter's Tale*, he hit upon a means of entry into the fabulous world of a life standing (as Hermione says) in the level of dreams.[3]

Stage-craft is a word for the mechanics in the art of telling a story, through actors, on some sort of stage, *with a certain effect*. It must inventively use the facilities available to it. No one was more inventive than Shakespeare: deftness and dexterity of this kind mark all his work, and his surprises (so

---

Shakespeare Survey, No. 11, (1958).

often, afterwards, felt to be 'inevitable') recall those in Beethoven, of whose last quartets the composer Balfour Gardiner said once to me, with a sigh of envy, 'Ah, the desolating old monkey! Never without a fresh rabbit to pull out of his hat!'

Six main charges of creaking dramaturgy have been made against *The Winter's Tale*, severally, by Bethell and the Cambridge editors. Let us consider them one by one, with this thought in mind, that if Shakespeare has demonstrably told his story in certain rather unusual ways, he may well have had some special, and perhaps discernible, intention in doing so: the careful consideration of how a contrivance works may often guide us to an understanding of its purpose.

THE SUPPOSED SUDDENNESS OF THE JEALOUSY OF LEONTES

In *Pandosto* (we shall use Shakespeare's names) Leontes' jealousy is made slow and by increase plausible. Shakespeare weakens the plausibility of it as well by ennobling Hermione – after his way with good women – as by huddling up the jealousy in its motion so densely that it strikes us as merely frantic and – which is worse in drama – a piece of impossible improbability. This has always and rightly offended the critics.... (Sir Arthur Quiller-Couch)[4]

Then suddenly with no more hint of preparation – and no hint at all on the psychological plane – Leontes' jealousy comes full upon him. (S. L. Bethell)[5]

In an appendix devoted to this subject Bethell adds the conjecture that if Shakespeare had intended Leontes to be jealous from the start he would have brought him on alone 'to deliver an appropriate soliloquy'.[6] This would indeed have been 'a naïve and outmoded technique', one at least as old-fashioned as that which, long before, had so brilliantly opened *Richard III*. But in *The Winter's Tale* Shakespeare went about his business with new subtlety of dramatic invention. To understand it we must begin at the opening scene, a dialogue between Archidamus and Camillo, asking ourselves certain questions in dramaturgy.

What is the reason for this dialogue? What information

does it convey? What is it supposed to do to an audience? At first sight it seems to resemble the opening scenes of *King Lear* and *Antony and Cleopatra*: just as Kent and Gloucester prepare us for the division of Lear's kingdom and introduce the Bastard, just as Philo and Demetrius announce Antony's dotage and prepare us to see him enter as a strumpet's fool, so Archidamus and Camillo prepare us to witness a kingly amity between Sicilia and Bohemia, his guest, and to introduce us to Mamillius. There is no other point in the little scene:

Cam.:   Sicilia cannot show himself over-kind to Bohemia. They were
          trained together in their childhoods; and there rooted betwixt
          them then such an affection, which cannot choose but branch
          now . . . they have seemed to be together, though absent, shook
          hands, as over a vast, and embraced, as it were, from the ends of
          opposed winds. The heavens continue their loves!
Arch.:   I think there is not in the world either malice or matter to alter
          it. You have an unspeakable comfort of your young prince
          Mamillius. . . .

                                                        (I.i.23–38)

Now whereas Kent and Gloucester, Philo and Demetrius, prepare the audience for what it is about to see (technique of gratifying expectation raised), Camillo and Archidamus prepare it for what it is about *not* to see (technique of the prepared surprise): directed to expect a pair of happy and affectionate friends, the audience is startled by seeing exactly the opposite: the two monarchs enter separately, and one, perceived to be the other's host, wears a look of barely controlled hostility that may at any moment blacken into thundercloud. The proof of this is in the dialogue, which contains all the stage-directions necessary; Polixenes leads in with his elaborate lines:

> Nine changes of the watery star hath been
> The shepherd's note since we have left our throne
> Without a burthen: time as long again
> Would be fill'd up, my brother, with our thanks;
> And yet we should, for perpetuity,
> Go hence in debt: and therefore, like a cipher,
> Yet standing in rich place, I multiply
> With one 'We thank you' many thousands more
> That go before it.

                                                        (I.ii.1–9)

Polixenes is an artist in the language of court compliment, at once flowery and formal, like Jacobean embroidery. All the flourish of his opening lines conveys no more information than this: '*I am visiting the King and have been here nine months.*' His closing lines, however, make it certain that he is standing beside Hermione (she is perhaps upon his arm?) and addressing her. With self-deprecating paronomasia, and a bow no doubt, he pays her compliment:

> And therefore, *like a cipher,*
> *Yet standing in rich place....*

To a visiting King there can be no richer place than next to the Queen. This Queen, however, has something specially remarkable about her: she is *visibly pregnant,*[7] and near her hour, for a day later we hear the First Lady tell Mamillius:

> The queen your mother rounds apace.
>
> (II.i.16)

This fact about her has been grasped by the audience at her first entry, because they can see it is so; they hear the visiting King say he has been there nine months; who can fail to wonder whether the man so amicably addressing this expectant mother may not be the father of her child? For what other possible reason can Shakespeare have contrived the conversation so as to make him specify nine changes of the inconstant moon? These things are not done by accident; Shakespeare has established a complex situation with the same inerrant economy, swiftness and originality that he used to open *Hamlet* or *Macbeth*.

How then is Leontes to bear himself? Again the clue lies in the dialogue, in the calculated contrast between the flowery language of Polixenes and the one-syllabled two-edged utterances of his host. To the airy conceits of his boyhood's friend, Leontes replies with ironic brevity, sprinkled with equivocation:

> Stay your thanks awhile;
> And pay them when you part.
>
> (I.ii.8)

To these lines Dover Wilson offers the illuminating note: 'Though very gracious on the surface, this remark, Leontes' first, is ominous ... "Praise in departing", a proverbial expression, meaning "wait till the end before praising".'[8] The *équivoques* of Leontes continue to alternate with the flourishes of Polixenes, mannerly on the surface, menacing beneath:

> We are tougher, brother,
> Than you can put us to't.
>
> (I.ii.15)

> Tongue-tied, our queen? speak you.
>
> (I.ii.27)

'Our queen' are cold vocables for married love and 'tongue-tied' is a familiar epithet for guilt. It is clear that Leontes, as in the source-story which Shakespeare was following, has long since been jealous and is angling now (as he admits later) with his sardonic amphibologies, to catch Polixenes in the trap of the invitation to prolong his stay, before he can escape to Bohemia and be safe. All this, as Dover Wilson's note points out, is easy for an actor to suggest, facially and vocally, and it is the shock we have been prepared to receive by the conversation of Archidamus and Camillo. We have witnessed a little miracle of stage-craft.

EXIT PURSUED BY A BEAR

The stagecraft is justifiably described as crude or naïve. We have the frequently remarked *Exit, pursued by a bear* ... (S. L. Bethell)[9]

Now let us take Antigonus and the deep damnation of his taking off. The child Perdita is laid on the seashore. . . . All we have now to do as a matter of stage-workmanship is to efface Antigonus. But why introduce a bear? The ship that brought him is riding off the coast of Bohemia and is presently engulfed with all her crew. The clown sees it all happen. Then why, in the name of economy, not engulf Antigonus with the rest – or better still, as he tries to row aboard? If anyone asks this editor's private opinion, it is that the bear-pit in Southwark ... had a tame animal to let out, and the management took the opportunity to make a popular hit. (Sir Arthur Quiller-Couch)[10]

Let us note the mild self-contradiction contained in the above; if the appearance of a bear at this point would make 'a popular hit' it would be a very good piece of stage-workmanship, supposing it to be consistent with the story to be told, as it demonstrably is.

> ... nor can it be disputed that tame bears (very tame) were seen upon the stage at this period. The popular *Mucedorus*, for example, was revived in 1610 or 1611, and a new scene was written ... in which the clown, in attempting to escape from a white bear, is actually made to tumble over her on the stage.... After this it can hardly be doubted that Antigonus was pursued by a polar bear in full view of the audience at the Globe. (J. Dover Wilson)[11]

Now the polar bear is an extremely dangerous beast, even if bred in captivity, and albino brown bears are of the utmost rarity, though it is true a pair was born at Berne in 1575. A brown bear could, of course, be painted white, but brown bears are cross and unreliable;[12] even if they were as mild as milk they could not be counted on for a well-timed knock-about routine such as is needed with Antigonus. On the other hand it is easy, even for a modest acrobat, to personate a bear, with an absolutely calculated degree of comic effect: he has only to be able to walk on all fours without flexing his knees and rise then on to his 'hind legs' for an embrace. There is of course no difficulty in making a bear-costume. Real bears are neither so reliable, so funny, nor so alarming as a man disguised as a bear can be; the practical aspects of production make it certain that no Harry Hunks or Sackerson was borrowed for *The Winter's Tale* from the bear-pit next door. We are back, then, at Q's question '*Why introduce a bear?*'

If we appreciate the problem in dramaturgy that faced Shakespeare at this turn in his story, the answer is clear enough: it was a *tour de force*, calculated to create a unique and particular effect, at that point demanded by the narrative mood and line of the play. It is at the moment when the tale, hitherto wholly and deeply tragic, turns suddenly and triumphantly to comedy. One may modulate in music from one key to another through a chord that is common to both; so, to pass from tragedy to comedy, it may not be unskilful to build the bridge out of material that is both tragic and comic at the same time.

Now it is terrifying and pitiful to see a bear grapple with and carry off an elderly man to a dreadful death, even on the stage; but (such is human nature) the unexpectedness of an ungainly animal in pursuit of an old gentleman (especially one so tedious as Antigonus) can also seem wildly comic; the terrible and the grotesque come near to each other in a *frisson* of horror instantly succeeded by a shout of laughter; and so this bear, this unique and perfect link between the two halves of the play, slips into place and holds.

There are those who will say this is a piece of far-fetched, subjective interpretation; but that is how the scene works on the stage, as Shakespeare foresaw that it would; he deliberately underlined the juxtaposition of mood, achieved by the invention of the bear, in the speeches he put into the mouth of the Clown, grisly and ludicrous, mocking and condoling, from one sentence to another:

> O, the most piteous cry of the poor souls! Sometimes to see 'em, and not to see 'em; now the ship boring the moon with her main-mast, and anon swallowed with yeast and froth, as you'ld thrust a cork into a hogshead. And then for the land-service, to see how the bear tore out his shoulder-bone; how he cried to me for help and said his name was Antigonus, a nobleman. But to make an end of the ship, to see how the sea flap-dragoned it: but, first, how the poor souls roared, and the sea mocked them; and how the poor gentleman roared and the bear mocked him, both roaring longer than the sea or weather.... I have not winked since I saw these sights: the men are not yet cold under water, nor the bear half dined on the gentleman: he's at it now.

(III.iii.88–110)

If Shakespeare did not mean it that way, why did he write it that way? So far from being crude or antiquated, stage-craft such as this is a dazzling piece of *avant-garde* work; no parallel can be found for what, at a stroke, it effects: it is the transformation of tragedy into comedy: it symbolises the revenge of Nature on the servant of a corrupted court: it is a thundering surprise; and yet those Naturals that are always demanding naturalism cannot complain, for what could be more natural than a bear? That this scene is a kind of dramaturgical hinge, a moment of planned structural antithesis, is certain from the dialogue; we are passing from tears to laughter, from death to life:

Now bless thyself: thou mettest with things dying,
I with things new-born.

(III.iii.115)

FATHER TIME

In this play of ours, having to skip sixteen years after Act 3, he desperately drags in Father Time with an hour-glass ... which means on interpretation that Shakespeare, having proposed to himself a drama in which a wronged woman has to bear a child, who has to be lost for years and restored to her as a grown girl, simply did not know how to do it, save by invoking some such device. (Sir Arthur Quiller-Couch)[13]

Time the Chorus is not central at all but a necessary mechanism of the plot ... (S. L. Bethell)[14]

Both critics essentially regard Time as a mechanism for over-leaping sixteen years and therefore necessary to the plot. But in fact, if that is all he is there for, he is redundant. His choric soliloquy makes three plot-points: first, that we are to slide over sixteen years, second, that Leontes has shut himself away in penitence for his great sin, and, third, that we are about to hear of Florizel and Perdita. As all these points are clearly made in the scene immediately following (between Camillo and Polixenes, IV.ii), Time and his speech, so far as mere plot is concerned, could be cut without much loss; but the loss to the theme and quality of the play would be enormous, for Time is absolutely central to both and if he were not a character in the play, it would be necessary to invent him. His function is as follows: he shows us we are being taken beyond 'realism' into the region of parable and fable, adumbrated in the title of the play. Time stands at the turn of the tide of mood, from tragedy to comedy, and makes a kind of pause or poise at the play's centre; coming to us from an unexpected supernatural or mythological region, yet he encourages us (in spite of that solemnity) to enter with confidence, by the easy-going familiarity of his direct address, into that mood of comedy initiated by the no less unexpected bear. The same unique imagination envisaged both Time and bear for the great moment necessary to the narrative and to the theme it bears, when the hour-glass turns and the darkness passes. To take a further step in the defence of Time's presence in the play will perhaps lead me into the subjective interpretations I believe myself so far to have avoided; but the risk must be taken. Few will deny that the central theme is the sin of Leontes, which has its wages in the death, and seeming death or dispersion of all that he loves; but, under the guidance of Paulina, this sin is long and truly repented, and the self-inflicted wound, given, as Camillo says, by one who is 'in rebellion with himself' is healed. But repentance and healing both take *time*; Time is the tester:

> I, that please some, try all.

> (IV.i.1)

Time is at the heart of the play's mystery; why should his visible presence offend? We do not take offence at Time with his hour-glass in a Bronzino or a Van Dyck; why then in Shakespeare? He who holds too tenaciously in the study of Shakespeare to 'realism' and the Unities, has left the punt and is clinging to the pole.

THE CRUDE SHIFTS TO CLEAR STAGE IN THE FLORIZEL–PERDITA–CAMILLO–AUTOLYCUS SEQUENCE

The stage-craft is justifiably described as crude or naïve ... there is a patch of astonishingly awkward management towards the end of Act IV, scene iv, beginning at the point where Camillo questions Florizel and learns he is determined to 'put to sea' with Perdita (IV.iv.509). Then we have:

Flo.:   Hark, Perdita (*drawing her aside*) (*To Camillo*) I'll hear you by and by.
Cam.:   He's irremovable, Resolved for flight. Now were I happy, if His going I could frame to serve my turn.

IV.iv.514–17

The conversation of Florizel and Perdita is required only to cover Camillo's explanation of his motives and this explanation is given to the audience in soliloquy, with more than a tinge of direct address. (S. L. Bethell)[15]

There is nothing in the least awkward, crude or naïve about

this stage-craft. As for direct address, its use has been among the chief glories of drama from Aeschylus to T. S. Eliot; let us, then, in considering Shakespeare, for a moment free ourselves of the limitations of the proscenium arch and its attendant fads, one of which is the denigration of soliloquy. It will be safer, too, to eliminate the stage-directions offered in the extract quoted, for they do not appear in Folio; we may have to replace them, but with a difference.

Next, let us consider the context. Perdita has said nothing for thirty lines; her last speech was one of sad resignation to fate:

> How often have I told you 'twould be thus!
> How often said, my dignity would last
> But till 'twere known!
>
> (IV.iv.484–6)

Now she stands anxiously by, listening to her headstrong lover at odds with one who is (to her) an elderly stranger of grave authority, a friend and servant of the dreaded King himself; the Prince is wildly asserting that he is ready to be wiped out of the succession for her sake; she hears him end brusquely with a less than civil defiance of Camillo's kindly counsel:

> What course I mean to hold
> Shall nothing benefit your knowledge, nor
> Concern me the reporting.
>
> (IV.iv.513–15)

Camillo replies with a mixture of rebuke and pleading:

> O my lord!
> I would your spirit were easier for advice,
> Or stronger for your need.

What if we suppose that Perdita, in sympathy with the caution of Camillo, makes some impulsive gesture towards him, at this point, to show her feelings? And why should not such a gesture be the cue for Florizel to swing round on her with his 'Hark, Perdita' (as who should say, in a mood of bravado, 'Now you listen to me, my girl!'), and take her a few steps upstage for a brief private colloquy, to divulge to her the plan he is keeping so secret from Camillo? To whom, over his shoulder, he throws:

> I'll hear you by and by.

This would lead very simply and convincingly to Camillo's

> He's irremovable,
> Resolved for flight. . . .

Stage-directions such as these I have suggested are certainly no less authorised by the text than those in the extract quoted by Bethell; candid consideration may even judge them more in harmony with the line and feeling of the scene; and so, nearer to Shakespeare's intention. Be that as it may, no audience would be aware of any awkwardness or difficulty.

But Bethell does not base his case on a single instance:

A little later the device is repeated; Camillo has disclosed his plan and ends:

> > For instance, sir,
> > That you may know you shall not want, one word. (*They talk aside*)
> > (*Re-enter Autolycus*)
> Aut.:   Ha, ha! what a fool Honesty is! etc.

>   (IV.iv.604)

At the end of his speech we have another stage-direction: *Camillo, Florizel, and Perdita come forward*. There is no natural occasion for this 'talk aside' since all three are engaged in it; its only purpose is to allow Autolycus his direct address to the audience on the gullibility of rustics. Worst of all is the device to allow Camillo a last explanation to the audience in an aside. Florizel exclaims:

> O Perdita, what have we twain forgot!
> Pray you a word. (*They converse apart*)
> We never hear what they have forgot . . . (S. L. Bethell)[16]

Let us take these points one by one, first eliminating all the stage-directions quoted by Bethell, for they are the inventions of editors. We can invent our own if we need them. Folio reads (Camillo speaking):

That you may know you shall not want: one word,
Enter Autolycus

Aut.:   Ha, Ha, what a Foole Honestie is?

There is a colon in Camillo's line (transformed by Bethell into a comma). What is it there for? It is there to indicate a sudden pause; the cautious Camillo, in mid-sentence, has *heard* the approach of Autolycus, laughing, like a Jaques (*As You Like It*, II.vii). He stops, looks round behind him, sees the intruder, frowns and draws his companions aside to conclude their highly secret colloquy in a corner, leaving the centre of the stage to the still laughing Autolycus. There is nothing very awkward or archaic in that.

Next comes the question what it is that Florizel and Perdita have forgotten; no doubt Bethell is right in supposing this a simple dodge to give Camillo a soliloquy, but no producer would find the smallest difficulty in masking that basic fact, and no audience would even be aware that he had done so; Shakespeare left many such stage-directions to our common sense. At this point upon common sense we must rely, for there are no pointers in Folio, which reads:

Flo.:   *O Perdita*: what haue we twaine forgot?
Pray you a word.

'Pray you a word' clearly must be addressed, not to Perdita, but to Autolycus, so as to draw him away as well, and leave Camillo isolated for his direct address. Therefore what they have forgotten concerns Autolycus too.

Now we have just witnessed a hasty exchange of garments between Florizel and Autolycus; nothing is easier than to suppose that Florizel, having left something that he and Perdita value in the garments he has given to Autolycus, and suddenly remembering, takes the rogue aside with Perdita to recover it. What could this 'something' be? Perhaps the betrothal flowers she had given her lover earlier in the scene, or some fairing bought from Autolycus – it does not matter what, *so long as the audience sees and recognises it*; for if the audience can see what it is that the lovers have forgotten, there is no reason why they should be told what it is.

THE MESSENGER-SPEECHES IN V.ii

> But the greatest fault of all, to our thinking – worse even than the
> huddling up in Act I – is the manner in which the play mishandles
> Leontes' recognition of Perdita. ... If, having promised ourselves a
> mighty thrill in the great master's fashion, we really prefer two or three
> innominate gentlemen entering and saying, 'Have you heard?' 'You
> don't tell me!' 'No.' 'Then you have lost a sight' – why that is the sort of
> thing we prefer and there is no more to be said. (Sir Arthur Quiller-
> Couch)[17]

It *is* the sort of thing we prefer; in practice this scene is among
the most gripping and memorable of the entire play. Whoever
saw the production of it by Peter Brook at the Phoenix
Theatre in 1951–52 will remember the excitement it created.
I know of at least two other productions of the play in which
this scene had the same effect, and generated that mounting
thrill of expectation needed to prepare us for the final scene.
No doubt Shakespeare could have handled the matter just as
rousingly in the way sighed for by Q, if he had so wished.
Instead he decided on a messenger-speech scene for several
voices (an unusual experiment) and made a masterpiece of it.

Bethell holds a different view from Q and believes that
Shakespeare used this technique so as to have a last fling at
court jargon. His comment on the scene runs thus: 'This can
only be burlesque; Shakespeare had always enjoyed a thrust
at such affectation, and a straight line runs from Don Armado
through Osric to these gentlemen in *The Winter's Tale*.'[18] But
there is no such 'straight line'. Don Armado is a fantastical
foreigner and his language reflects it; Osric, the subtlest of
Claudius's emissaries, emits a smoke-cloud of words with the
intent to blind Hamlet (as he successfully does) into thinking
him of no account; whereas he is the bearer of his death-
warrant.[19] The Three Gentlemen of *The Winter's Tale* are
neither Armados nor Osrics; they talk the same dialect of
early seventeenth-century refinement and wit as is used by
Archidamus and Camillo in Act I, scene i, and by Polixenes
(though he speaks it in verse) in Act I, scene ii.

There may be a case to be made against the Metaphysicals
and their wit, but I do not believe that Shakespeare was here
making it; we, if we admire Donne and Crashaw, should not
gird at the conceits of the Three Gentlemen. Let us consider

their situation; never in the memory of court-gossip has there been so joyful and so astounding a piece of news to spread; they are over the edge of tears in the happy excitement and feel a noble, indeed a partly miraculous joy, for the oracle has been fulfilled; so far as they can, they temper their tears with their wit. What could be a more delightful mixture of drollery and tenderness, or more in the best 'Metaphysical' manner than

> One of the prettiest touches of all and that which angled for mine eyes, caught the water though not the fish, was when, at the relation of the queen's death, with the manner how she came to't bravely confessed and lamented by the king, how attentiveness wounded his daughter; till, from one sign of dolour to another, she did, with an 'Alas,' I would fain say, bleed tears, for I am sure my heart wept blood. ...
>
> (V.ii.89)

Could Donne have found a better hyperbole than 'wounded', or Crashaw a more felicitous conceit for eyes and tears?

THE STATUE SCENE

Of all Shakespeare's *coups de théâtre*, the descent of Hermione from her pedestal is perhaps the most spectacular and affecting; it is also one of the most carefully contrived and has indeed been indicted for its contrivance: 'Hermione's is not a genuine resurrection ... The very staginess of this 'statue' scene acknowledges the inadequacy of the dramatic means' (S. L. Bethell).[20] These dramatic means (Bethell seems to argue) are inadequate to certain religious ends he senses in the play. I had hoped in this essay to avoid those private, still more those metaphysical interpretations, to which even the best of us are liable; but since, by drawing attention to the fineness of Shakespeare's stage-craft in this scene, I may be aggravating the charge of staginess, let it be admitted certainly that Hermione is not a Lazarus, come from the dead, come back to tell us all; that she is *believed* dead is one of those errors which Time makes and unfolds.[21] The spiritual meaning of the play in no way depends on her being a Lazarus or an Alcestis. It is a play about a crisis in the life of

Leontes, not of Hermione, and her restoration to him (it is not a 'resurrection') is something which happens not to her, but to *him*. He had thought her dead by his own hand ('She I kill'd')[22] and now finds her unexpectedly alive in the guardianship of Paulina. (So a man who believed himself to have destroyed his soul by some great sin might, after a long repentance under his Conscience, find that the very Conscience had unknown to him kept his soul in being and could at last restore it to him alive and whole.) That is the miracle, it seems to me, for which Shakespeare so carefully prepared.

It had to be a miracle not only for Leontes, but for the audience. His first dramaturgical job, then, was to ensure that the audience, like Leontes, should *believe her dead*. For this reason her death is repeatedly reasserted during the play by a number of characters, and accepted by all as a fact. Shakespeare's next care was to give credentials to the statue. The audience must accept it *as a statue*, not as a woman; so the Third Gentleman names its sculptor, an actual man, Giulio Romano; a novel trick to borrow a kind of authenticity from the 'real' world of the audience, to lend solidity to the imaginary world of the play; it seems to confer a special statueishness. For the same reason Paulina warns Leontes that the colour on it is not yet dry.

But above all Shakespeare stretched his art in creating for his 'statue' a long stillness. For 80 lines and more Hermione must stand, discovered on her pedestal, not seeming to breathe; that is, for some four long minutes. Those among the audience who may think her a living woman, encouraged by Paulina's promise to 'make the statue move indeed', must be *reconvinced against hope that she is a statue* if the miracle is really to work excitingly for them. So when at last Hermione is bidden to descend Shakespeare does not allow her to budge; against all the invocations of Paulina, he piles up colons, twelve in five lines; it is the most heavily punctuated passage I have found in Folio. It can be no other than his deliberate contrivance for this special effect; only at the end of the long, pausing entreaty, when the suspense of her motionlessness has been continued until it must seem unendurable, is Hermione allowed to move:

            Musick; awake her: Strike:
      'Tis time: descend: be Stone no more: approach:
      Strike all that looke vpon with meruaile: Come:
      Ile fill your Graue vp: stirre: nay, come away:
      Bequeath to Death your numnesse: (for from him,
      Deare Life redeemes you) you perceiue she stirres. ...

There is nothing antiquated or otiose in stage-craft such as this.

NOTES

1. S. L. Bethell, *The Winter's Tale: A Study* (1946), p. 47. This important work is a contribution to the imaginative and philosophical understanding of the play; although in my essay I have only quoted from it to disagree, the disagreements are largely of a technical kind on relatively minor matters.
2. Ibid., pp. 49–50.
3. III.ii.78.
4. Sir Arthur Quiller-Couch and John Dover Wilson, *The Winter's Tale* (Cambridge, 1931, reprinted 1950, p. xvi). This work hereafter in these notes will be referred to as *W.T.* (Camb.).
5. Bethell, *op. cit.*, p. 78.
6. Ibid., p. 122.
7. A point also noted by Miss M. M. Mahood, in her *Shakespeare's Wordplay* (1957), p. 147, in discussing the first line spoken by Polixenes.
8. *W.T.* (Camb.), p. 131.
9. Bethell, *op. cit.*, p. 48.
10. *W.T.* (Camb.), p. xx.
11. Ibid., pp. 156–7.
12. I am indebted to Mr R. B. Freeman, Reader in Taxonomy, University College, London, for reference to Marcel A. J. Couturier, *L'Ours brun, Ursus arctos L.* (1954), published by the author at 45 Rue Thiers, Grenoble, Isère, from which this information about bears is taken.
13. *W.T.* (Camb.), p. xix.
14. Bethell, *op. cit.*, p. 89.
15. Ibid., pp. 48–9.
16. Ibid., pp. 48–9.
17. *W.T.* (Camb.), p. xxiii.
18. Bethell, *op. cit.*, p. 42.
19. I accept the account of Osric's character put forward by Richard Flatter in his *Hamlet's Father* (1949), pp. 119–20.
20. Bethell, *op. cit.*, p. 103.
21. IV.i.2.
22. V.i.17.

9

Two Small Points in *Measure for Measure*[*]

Professor Leech, ever persuasive, has laid his finger on a fault in Shakespeare's comic Dukes:[1] they are a vacillating lot, he tells us, their minds are very opals. And he has assembled a fair show of them at their tricks; they culminate in his old enemy,[2] the Duke in *Measure for Measure*, in one flagrant instance; for this Duke (on top of all else that he is accused of) appears flatly and absolutely to change his mind, on a matter of life and death, within six lines and for no reason.

Folio is clear enough on the point and all editors, I think, have followed its text here without question, in spite of this preposterous behaviour in the Duke. The relevant passage begins on page 77 of Folio and concludes on page 78:

(Page 77)
Bar.:   I sweare I will not die to day for anie mans perswasion.
Duke: But heare you:
Bar.:   Not a word: if you haue anie thing to say to me, come to my
         Ward: for thence will not I to day.

                                                                    Exit

                        Enter Prouost
Duke: Vnfit to liue, or die: oh grauell heart.
                        G₃   After
(Page 78) After him (Fellowes) bring him to the blocke.
Pro.:   Now Sir, how do you finde the prisoner?
Duke: A creature vnpre-par'd, vnmeet for death,
         And to transport him in the minde he is,
         Were damnable.

Review of English Studies New Series. XVI (1965).

But for the single line

> After him (Fellowes) bring him to the blocke

the Duke would be perfectly consistent.

Let us consider a little what has happened in the scene before, and what is happening in this scene; the essence of the action is that the Provost has at last had explicit orders from Angelo for the immediate execution of Barnardine:

> *Whatsoeuer you may heare to the contrary, let Claudio be executed by foure of the clocke, and in the afternoone Bernardine* ... IV.ii.122

There is to be no more of Barnardine's nonsense. The Duke has added his own authority to that of Angelo: 'Call your executioner, and off with *Barnardines* head' (IV.ii. 214). The Duke has promised to visit Barnardine 'to give him present shrift', and has been warned by the Provost that he is a pretty tough character. The Duke comes in, in the following scene, while Abhorson and the more timid Pompey are endeavouring to carry out the orders given them (off-stage) by the Provost, to have Barnardine's head off. The Duke has never been seen in the company of Abhorson before and there is no reason to suppose that the Executioner thinks more of him than that he is a wandering Friar, a 'ghostly Father', as he calls him; in other words a person of no authority over him, or the prison and its prisoners, in the dispatch of an executioner's duty. Yet, within ten lines or so the Duke is apparently ordering him about with his 'After him (Fellowes) bring him to the blocke'. Bearing these points in mind, let us return to the Provost and to his entry at the point shown in our quotation from Folio. What does he see as he comes in? He sees Barnardine strolling back to his ward, completely master of the situation, and Abhorson, Pompey and the Duke standing by, nonplussed. It was exactly the sort of situation the Provost had led the Duke to expect: he was accustomed to it. And so he instantly assumes full authority and takes control with a smart word of command 'After him (Fellowes) bring him to the blocke'. For the line is obviously his, not the Duke's. Having issued this order, he then turns, with a touch of 'What did I tell you?' to the Duke, and says 'Well Sir, how do you finde the prisoner?' This reading makes sense both of the Provost's exactly placed entry in the Folio text, and of his position of authority, as well as of the Duke's attitude towards Barnardine. All that has happened is that the speech-heading has slipped a line, and this could easily be due either to a compositor's mistake at the turn of the page, or to an imperfect alignment of speech-headings in the copy before him.

The strategy of the scene, behind all this, is of some interest. It is to empty the stage for the crucial interview that is to follow immediately between the Duke and the Provost. For it is in this scene that the Duke unmasks himself to the Provost; this is clear enough from a gesture hinted in the dialogue (ever the proper place to look at for stage-directions as to gesture). Once again, let us look at the situation. The Provost knows himself to be in great danger from Angelo should he disobey him, yet is sufficiently assured by the Duke's signet which he has recognised (IV.ii. 202) to propose the substitution of Ragozine for Claudio (IV.iii. 69–72). At the same time he is still in grave doubt what he should do about Claudio, whose continued existence may well be discovered; Barnardine is in any case to die:

Pro.:   This shall be done (good Father) presently;
              But *Barnardine* must die this afternoone,
              And how shall we continue *Claudio*,
              To saue me from the danger that might come,
              If he were knowne aliue?

The Duke brushes his fears aside, overruling him with:

          Let this be done,
          Put them in secret holds, both *Barnardine* and *Claudio*,
          Ere twice the Sun hath made his iournall greeting
          To yond generation, you shal finde
          Your safetie manifested.

To this the Provost surprisingly replies, 'I am your free dependant'. What does *free* mean? How is he *dependant*? What are we to infer from this contradiction in terms? It makes best sense if we take *free* in the sense of its sixth meaning in *O.E.D.*, namely 'Released from ties, obligations, or constraints upon one's action'. In other words, the Provost is saying that he feels himself to be *free* (from his obligations to the Deputy Angelo) because he now knows himself to be *dependent* on the higher authority of the Duke. We may, therefore, somewhat firmly conjecture the following stage-directions, as they might appear in Shavian style:

[Duke]   ... you shall find
                    Your safety manifested. (*He turns back the cowl of his Friar's habit, revealing who he is*)
Provost: (*Falling on one knee and kissing his hand.*) I am your free dependant.

Were he not to unmask himself at this point, the Provost would have no better reason than he had before, for obeying the Duke in a matter far more dangerous than that to which he before had grudgingly consented, though it was 'against his oath'. That the Duke does bring the Provost into his secrets is certain from what he tells Friar Peter at the beginning of IV.V, the next scene in which we see him, for he says, 'The Prouost knowes our purpose and our plot.' For the Duke to unmask himself as suggested gives a visual foretaste of this important turn of the story, and prepares the audience more richly for the Provost's part in the *dénouement*.

NOTES

1. C. Leech, 'Shakespeare's Comic Dukes', *Review of English Literature*, V, No. 2 (1964), 110–14.
2. See C. Leech, 'The "Meaning" of *Measure for Measure*', *Shakespeare Survey*, iii (1950), 66–73.

10

The Basis of Shakespearian Comedy*

I.

The Comedies of Ben Jonson are clearly no laughing matter if
we compare them with those of Shakespeare. A harsh ethic in
them yokes punishment with derision: foibles are persecuted
and vices flayed; the very simpletons are savaged for being
what they are, and it is seldom that any but a minor character,
if that, gives proof of a nobility or grace of nature. The
population of his Comedies in part accounts for this; they are
a congeries of cits, parvenus, mountebanks, cozeners,
dupes, braggarts, bullies and bitches. If we are shown virtue
in distress, it is the distress and not the virtue that matters.
All this is done with an incredible, stupendous force of
style.

In Shakespeare things are different. Princes and dukes,
lords and ladies jostle with merchants, weavers, joiners,
country sluts, friendly rogues, schoolmasters and village
policemen, hardly one of whom is lacking in, or incapable of,
a generous impulse. The very butts can think nobly of the
soul and have everything handsome about them. Shakespeare
will not punish even a Barnadine.

In all this it is easy to discern the promptings of two
opposed temperaments in the use of comic form by these
writers; so much so that it hardly makes sense to speak of

Essays and Studies (1950). (The substance of a lecture delivered in 1949 at
Stratford-upon-Avon at the invitation of Mr John Garrett, to whom it is
affectionately dedicated.)

'comic form' as if it were a single thing of which both had the same theoretical conception, to the discipline of which both were in voluntary and agreed subjection. And because it does not seem to make sense, it is often supposed that Shakespeare wrote under no discipline of form, that he followed no particular and definable tradition of Comedy, but was simply fancy's child; for what definable form could include *The Comedy of Errors*, *A Midsummer Night's Dream*, *Measure for Measure* and *The Winter's Tale*?

It is the purpose of this essay to show that Shakespeare was not simply following the chances of temperament in designing his Comedies, but that he was following a tradition that evolved during the Middle Ages from the same parent-stock of thought as that from which evolved the contrary tradition followed by Ben Jonson. That parent-stock is to be found in the writings of the Latin grammarians of the fourth century AD, namely Evanthius, Diomedes and Donatus.

These have left us a handful of dry and cursory generalisations derived by an inductive, Aristotelian, method from such Comedies as they knew or had heard of. They noted what comedy had been, rather than what it ought to be, and we may be grateful to them for that. But it must be said that they lacked the large lucidity and comprehensiveness of Aristotle in his analysis of the opposite form of Tragedy.

From their barely coordinated jottings I have taken the following paragraphs, omitting nothing that seemed to further the present inquiry.[1]

Evanthius
...As between Tragedy and Comedy, while there are many distinguishing marks, the first is this: in Comedy the characters are men of middle fortune, the dangers they run are neither serious nor pressing, their actions lead to happy conclusions; but in Tragedy things are just the opposite. Then again (be it noted) that in Tragedy is expressed the idea that life is to be fled from, in Comedy, that it is to be grasped. Lastly that all Comedy is made up of feigned actions, but Tragedy is more often fetched from historical belief. Comedy is divided into four parts, a Prologue, a Protasis, an Epitasis and a Catastrophe; the Prologue is so to speak the preface to a certain story ... the Protasis is the first act and beginning of the drama, the Epitasis is the growth and progress of the confusions and as I might say of the knot of the whole misunderstanding, and the Discovery is the turning round of things to happy issues, made clear to all by a full knowledge of the actions....[2]

Diomedes
... Comedy differs from Tragedy in that in Tragedy heroes, generals and kings are introduced, in comedy humble and private people. In the former, grief, exile and slaughter; in the latter, love-affairs and the abduction of maidens. Then in the former there are often and almost invariably sad endings to happy circumstances, and a Discovery of former fortune and family taking an ill turn ... for sad things are the property of Tragedy.... The first comic poets were Susarion, Myllus and Magnes; these offered plots of the old kind, with less skill than charm ... in the second age were Aristophanes, Eupolis and Cratinus, who pursuing the vices of the principal characters composed very bitter Comedies. The third age was that of Menander, Diphilus and Philemon, who palliated all the bitterness of Comedy and followed all sorts of plots about agreeable mistakes...[3]

Donatus
... Comedy is a tale containing various elements of the dispositions of town-dwelling and private people, to whom it is made known what is useful in life and what contrary and to be avoided...[4]

It is convenient at this point to rearrange these platitudes (in the light of later developments) into two groups that will be found to correspond with the Jonsonian and Shakespearian forms of Comedy, and that may be named the Satiric and the Romantic. The evolution that justifies this rearrangement will later appear.

The Satiric

Concerns a middle way of life, town-dwellers, humble and private people. It pursues the principal characters with some bitterness for their vices and teaches what is useful and expedient in life, and what is to be avoided.

The Romantic

Expresses the idea that life is to be grasped. It is the opposite of Tragedy in that the catastrophe solves all confusion and misunderstanding, by some happy turn to an agreeable issue. It has great variety of plot which may include a light touch of danger from which there is a happy issue. It commonly includes love-making and the abduction of virgins.

Common to both kinds

The plots are not historical but imaginary.

I do not know of any account or even mention of comic form between the fourth and twelfth centuries. Boethius defined Tragedy but not Comedy; after him there yawned the Dark Ages. Unless I am mistaken the next allusion to either form occurs in the *Ars Versificatoria* of Matthieu de Vendôme (*c.* 1150). In true Boethian style he describes a vision of Philosophy accompanied by Satire and Comedy (different beings it would seem), and this is all he says of the latter:

Tertia surrepit Commoedia, cotidiano hiatu [*habitu* in a preferable reading], *humiliato capite, nullius festivitatis praetendens delicias.*[5]

This appears to be an allegorical way of saying that the start of a Comedy lacks the lofty style of Tragedy and seems beset with dangers that promise no happy outcome. If this be the meaning it fits well enough with what Vincent de Beauvais and Dante have to say of Comedy, to whose accounts we may now turn.

Vincent de Beauvais flourished a century later than Matthieu de Vendôme and his aphorism on the nature of Comedy is quoted by Sir Edmund Chambers in the second volume of his work *The Medieval Stage* (p. 209 n.):

Commoedia poesis exordium triste laeto fine commutans.
Comedy is a poem changing a sad beginning into a happy ending.

Evanthius and Diomedes, as we have seen, contrasted Comedy and Tragedy in a general way. It was left to the logical and systematic mind of the Middle Ages to sharpen the point of this opposition. If Boethius was right in defining Tragedy as a story in which a flourishing prosperity was cast down by the deeds of fortune to a miserable end,[6] then (they thought) Comedy must be precisely the reverse, a story that started in sorrow and danger and, by a happy turn of fortune, ended in felicity. It was a tale of trouble that turned to joy.

This simple formula is the true basis of Shakespearian Comedy. It is not, however, so simple as it looks. It was claimed to be not merely the shape of comic form but also the shape of ultimate reality. That, at least, was the claim that Dante made for it and in virtue of which was fashioned the greatest of all imaginative and philosophical structures in

poetry, *The Divine Comedy*. The story of the Universe was to
be a Comedy as defined.

As well as a lofty poet, Dante was a lofty lecturer, and in
dedicating the *Paradiso* to Can Grande he set forth a lengthy
and explicit account of how his Comedy was to be
understood. It contains two passages of special interest to this
inquiry, one dealing with comic form itself and its supposed
origins, the other with the various planes of meaning upon
which it may be proper to interpret a Comedy. I shall later
attempt to apply both passages to the understanding of
Shakespeare. In setting them forth I have reversed the order
in which they occur in Dante's epistle, so that I may deal with
the question of form, which is the easier, first. The more
difficult question of allegory will be considered later.

Dante: Epistle to Can Grande

10. The title of the book is: 'Here begins the Comedy of Dante
Alighiere a Florentine by nation, not by manners.' As a note to which it
should be known that the word Comedy derives from *comos*, a village,
and *oda*, a song, whence Comedy, a sort of rustic song. Comedy is
moreover a kind of poetical narrative, differing from all others. It differs
therefore from Tragedy in its matter thus, that Tragedy is calm and
noble to start with, but in its ending or outcome stinking and terrifying
(*foetida et horribilis*); and it is named for that reason after *tragos*, that is, a
goat, and *oda*, a goatish song, so to speak; that is, it stinks like a goat, as
appears by Seneca in his Tragedies. Comedy on the other hand begins
with the harshness of some affair (*asperitatem alicuius rei*) but its matter
ends happily (*prospere*) as appears by Terence and his Comedies ...
similarly it differs in its manner of speech; Tragedy, lofty and sublime;
Comedy negligent and humble ... and hence it appears that the present
work is called a Comedy. For if we look at the matter, it stinks and is
terrifying to begin with, being *Infernus*; in the end it is happy, pleasing
and to be desired (*prospera, desiderabilis et grata*), being *Paradisus*.

This shows what the vision of genius can make of a truism,
even when it is expressed in lecturer's language. It transforms
the simple formula of Vincent de Beauvais into a true and
total picture of ultimate reality. Dante, however, did more
than this for our comprehension. He laid it down how his
Comedy was to be *understood*; here he was only explaining for
the benefit of Can Grande principles also laid down in the first
Chapter of the Second Treatise of the *Convivio*; and there
these principles are stated to be valid for all poetry, not

merely for his own. These are terms in which he expounds them to Can Grande:

> 7. . . . Be it known that the meaning of this work is not single (*simplex*), indeed it can be called *polysemos*, that is of several meanings; for there is first the meaning to be had from the letter; another is to be had from what is signified by the letter. And the first is called the literal (meaning); the second, however, is called the allegorical, or the moral, or the anagogical. This method of analysis, that it may seem the clearer, may be considered in these verses: '*In exitu Israel de Aegypto, domus Iacob de populo barbaro, facta est Iudaea sanctificatio eius, Israel potestas eius.*' Now if we only look at the letter, the meaning to us is the exodus of the Children of Israel from Egypt, at the time of Moses; if to the allegory, the meaning to us is our redemption made through Christ; if to the moral meaning, there is signified the conversion of the soul from the grief and misery of sin into a state of grace; if to the anagogical, the departure of the holy soul from this servitude of corruption into the liberation (*libertatem*) of eternal glory. And although these mystical senses are called by various names, they can all be generally called allegorical, since they differ from the literal or historical. In view of these things it is clear that the subject should be double (*duplex*) round which should flow alternate meanings.[7]

Dante has thus taken over and expanded (but with what enlargement!) the hints of the fourth-century grammarians, including the hint that love is a theme in Comedy. In the *Divine Comedy* it is the theme of themes, though it is no longer merely human love but love absolute, the power and the glory of God, seen by created souls as the Beatific Vision, for which indeed they were created.

Chaucer knew and quoted from the *Divina Commedia*, but, allegorist though he was, there is nothing to show he knew, or anyhow cared, about anagogy. Except for the problems of predestination he had few metaphysical interests. I should suppose it impossible to illuminate any passage in Chaucer by using a Dantesque technique of interpretation, though it is easy and even necessary to illuminate Langland so. Whether such a technique can in any way be usefully applied to Shakespearian Comedy has still to be argued; meanwhile we have reached the point at which Chaucer's grasp of the nature of comic form has to be considered.

He only uses the word 'comedye' once:

> Go, litel book, go, litel myn tragedy,
> Ther god thi makere yit, or that he dye,
> So sende myght to make in som comedye!
>
> (*Troilus & Criseyde*, Bk. V, 1786–88)

In this passage the word is manifestly used in antithesis to Tragedy, and we know what Tragedy signified to him, for we know what Boethius had said of it. Would that he had said something of Comedy! We can at least infer what Chaucer thought of it from a few sentences he placed in the mouth of his Knight. The occasion is when the Knight has interrupted the Monk's long spate of Tragedies, all fitting the Boethian formula more or less. The Knight objects that such stories are painful to him; he would prefer to hear the opposite kind of story. And then he gives what amounts to a definition of comedy. It is in line with what we have seen so far of the medieval tradition:

> I seye for me, it is a greet disese
> Wher-as men han ben in greet welthe and ese,
> To heren of hir sodeyn fal, allas!
> *And the contrarie is Ioye and greet solas,*
> *As whan a man hath been in povre estaat*
> *And clymbeth up, and wexeth fortunat,*
> *And there abydeth in prosperitee,*
> Swich thing is gladsom, as it thinketh me.

Chaucer's follower and admirer Lydgate returned to the Vincentian definition, *tout court*. It was the standard medieval view:

> A Comedy hath in his gynnynge, A pryme face a maner complaynynge, and afterwarde endeth in gladnesse.
>
> (*Chron. Troy*, II, xi)

II.

The Renaissance view of Comedy was entirely different. Its only concern is ridicule. It offers no antithesis to Tragedy as such, and indeed the ends of either form are often alike, namely ethical, both in theory and practice. There may be calamity at the end of *Sejanus* and laughter at the end of

Volpone, but both laughter and calamity are punitive and deterrent. Note that the theory does not suggest a narrative line, as did the medieval theory.

That punishment is the proper object of Comedy is the almost unanimous opinion of English Renaissance critics. Here is a selection of their opinions:

George Whetstone: *Dedication to Promos and Cassandra*, 1578.
... I deuided the whole history into two Commedies, for that, *Decorum* vsed, it would not be conuayed in one. The effects of both are good and bad: vertue intermyxt with vice, vnlawfull desyres (yf it were possible) queancht with chaste denyals: al needeful actions (I thinke) for public vewe. For by the rewarde of the good the good are encouraged in wel doinge: and with the scowrge of the lewde the lewde are feared from euill attempts ...

Thomas Lodge: *Defence of Poetry*, 1579.
... their matter was more pleasaunt (i.e. than that of tragedies) for they were suche as did reprehend, yet *quodam lepore* ... (i.e. with a certain charm).

Sir Philip Sidney: *An Apologie for Poetrie* (c. 1583, printed 1593).
... Comedy is an imitation of the common errors of our life, which he representeth in the most ridiculous and scornefull sort that may be; so that it is impossible that any beholder can be content to be such a one.

Now, as in Geometry the oblique must bee knowne as wel as the right, and in Arithmetick the odde as well as the euen, so in the actions of our life who seeth not the filthines of euil wanteth a great foile to perceiue the beauty of vertue. This doth the Comedy handle so in our priuate and domestical matters, as with hearing it we get as it were an experience, what is to be looked for....

George Puttenham: *The Arte of English Poesie*, Ch. XIV, 1589.
... but commonly of marchants, souldiers, artificers, good honest housholders, and also of vnthrifty youthes, yong damsels, old nurses, bawds, brokers, ruffians, and parasites, with such like, in whose behauiors lyeth in effect the whole course and trade of mans life, and therefore tended altogither to the good amendment of man by discipline and example. It was also much for the solace and recreation of the common people by reason of the pageants and shewes. And this kind of poeme was called *Comedy*....

Sir John Harrington: Preface to the Translation of *Orlando Furioso*, 1591.
... The Comicall, whatsoeuer foolish play-makers make it (poetry)

offend in this kind (i.e. by lewdness) yet being rightly vsed, it represents them so as to make the vice scorned and not embraced ...

Against this chorus of Renaissance moralising one voice at least proclaimed the more generous but vulnerable view of the Middle Ages that Comedy was there to please and give us joy:

> William Webbe: *A Discourse of English Poetrie*, 1586.
> ... The Comedies, on the other side (i.e. as opposed to Tragedies), were directed to a contrary ende, which, beginning doubtfully, drewe to some trouble or turmoyle, and by some lucky chaunce alwayes ended to the joy and appeasement of all parties.

*   *   *

Such, then, are the two theories of Comedy, the Romantic and the Satirical, twinned out of the late Latin grammarians to attain their different dramatic maturities in the Elizabethan Age. The older tradition was for Romance, the new world was all for Punishment. For the new world had to face the onslaught of Puritanism. If the right of poetry to exist at all was to be successfully defended, ethical weapons had to be used. '*Ioye and greet solas*' had nothing to do with it. Faced by a choice in such matters, a writer is wise if he follows his temperament. Ben Jonson knotted his cat-o'-nine tails. Shakespeare reached for his Chaucer.

III.

It is true that he did not do so immediately. His first thoughts in Comedy were for Plautus. Yet anyone caring for poetical forms who compares *The Comedy of Errors* (1592–3) with the *Menoechmi* will find significant differences in the shapes of the two plays. It is not simply a matter of the doubling of the pairs of twins by the exuberant Elizabethan. It is a matter of a change of *venue*, of quality, and of catastrophe. He *medievalised* the story; he invented a beginning and an end for it, starting in trouble and ending in joy.

Few comedies, one might suppose, could reach a prosperous conclusion that started with a man being seriously led out to execution. Yet this is what happens to the Merchant *Egeon* in the first scene of *The Comedy of Errors*; and *Egeon* is the father of the Antipholus twins, a major character in fact. This gambit is not in Plautus, and the style in which it is introduced is as high as tragedy could wish it to be. Execution on *Egeon* is deferred; but it is not remitted. He remains (albeit off-stage) in anticipation of immediate death until the last scene. That death is then about to be inflicted on him when from an improbable Abbey (in Ephesus) an even more improbable Abbess appears and is most improbably discovered to be *Egeon's* long-lost wife, and the means of his deliverance. She also is Shakespeare's invention, and turns the catastrophe to general joy.

These modifications in Plautine structure can hardly have come about by accident or whim. And if by whim, how is it that the new shape should correspond so exactly with the medieval view of what is proper to comic form?

This new shape brings with it an incidental feature in play-construction, in the conventions rather than in the form of English Comedy. It fills the stage with the whole happy cast at the catastrophe. In the *Menoechmi* the play closes with the twins and their servant only on stage. Shakespearian and almost all subsequent comic drama in England closes with a stage cram full of happy people; the whole world of the play has been led into delight, and with it the whole audience.

The changes in venue and structure go with a change in quality. It is not simply that there is a general coarseness and selfishness in Plautine's personal relations that is not to be found in Shakespeare. There is a specific and medieval delicacy injected into *The Comedy of Errors* by the invention of a romantic sub-plot – the love-affair between Antipholus of Syracuse and Luciana. Save for the greater lyrical fluency of Shakespeare it is Chaucerian, and its sentiments are those of *amour courtois*:

> Teach me deere creature how to thinke and speake:
> Lay open to my earthie grosse conceit:
> Smothred in errors, feeble, shallow, weake,
> The foulded meaning of your words deceit:
> Against my soules pure truth, why labour you,
> To make it wander in an vnknowne field?

> Are you a god? would you create me new?
> Transforme me then, and to your powre Ile yeeld....

Love as the centre and solvent of all troubles could not absolutely govern this Comedy of mistaken identity, but it thrust its way into it and coloured the conclusion.

The Taming of the Shrew was Shakespeare's next and indeed last venture[8] into a kind of Comedy not mainly romantic. In this play the dangers are not so sharp at the beginning, the joy not so general at the end. The characters are all from the middle and lower ranks of society and the love-element seems at first nearer to the *raptus virginum* of Diomedes than to the exalted professions of courtly love and medieval tradition.

And yet the theme has a Shakespearian softness of treatment very far removed from the harsh correction of vice and folly recommended by the Renaissance critics and practised by Ben Jonson. *The Taming of the Shrew* has often been read and acted as a wife-humiliating farce in which a brute fortune-hunter carries all, including his wife's spirit, before him, to the general but vicarious joy of hen-pecked husbands. Yet it is not so at all. True, it is based on the medieval conception of the obedience owed by a wife to her wedded lord, a conception generously and charmingly asserted by Katerina at the end. But it is a total misconception to suppose she has been bludgeoned into it. Indeed if either of them has triumphed in the art and practice of matrimony it is she.

Let us in the first place consider *why* she is a shrew; Shakespeare has made perfect preparation for this aspect of her character. She is a girl of spirit, yet has to endure a father who has openly made a favourite of her sly younger sister, and who is willing, even more openly, to sell his daughters to the highest bidder. We can see the sort of man he is from the marriage-market scene (II.i). We see, too, what sort of girl her petted sister is, with her pretended submissions and *minauderies* which culminate first in a clandestine and double-faced elopement, then in a contempt of her husband's authority and prestige. Thus environed, what choice has Katerina but to show her disdainful temper if she is to keep her self-respect?

Petruchio is a self-admitted fortune-hunter, but he is also a good-natured, vigorous, candid and likeable chap. No doubt whatever is left that he admires Katerina for herself on sight. Though he is loud-mouthed and given to swaggering, he is not contemptible; the companions of Beowulf would have approved of him. *Beot he gelaeste*. To Katerina he must moreover seem her one hope of escaping from that horrible family. The defensive technique of shrewishness was no final solution to her troubles. It was too negative. Yet she had adopted it so long that it seemed to have become second nature to her.

It is this which Petruchio is determined to break in her, not her spirit. And he chooses a technique of practical jokes to do so.

At first she does not see the point, for his Hotspur manners are too violent. Still she senses, while resenting, his claim to love her, oddly though it conflicts with his boisterous and not very kindly behaviour:

> And that which spights me more than all these wants,
> He does it under name of perfect loue.

It is not until he positively declares that the sun is the moon that the joke breaks upon her in its full fantasy, and it is then that she wins her first and final victory by showing she has a sense of fun as extravagant as his own, and is able to go beyond him; so, entering the joke, she addresses the ancient Vincentio as if he were a

> Yong budding Virgin, faire, and fresh, & sweet

and when Petruchio whirls about once more with a

> Why how now *Kate*, I hope thou are not mad,
> This is a man old, wrinckled, faded, withered,
> And not a Maiden as thou saist he is.

she reaches her top triumph of wit, proving herself more than his match in spirit with this disclaimer, and blaming the sun (or should it have been the moon?):

> Pardon old father my mistaking eies,
> That haue bin so bedazzled with the sunne....

After that, victory is all hers, and like most human wives that are the superiors of their husbands she can afford to allow him mastery in public. She has secured what her sister Bianca can never have, a happy marriage; and her solution is not far from that imagined by Chaucer for Dorigen and Arveragus in the *Franklin's Tale*. She will certainly run him in private, though her honour in public must of course depend on his:

> Save that the name of soveraynetee,
> That wolde he have for shame of his degree.

I have touched on these two early plays because neither of them, at first sight, seems to fall into the 'Romantic' class. Shakespeare's instinct for romance can nevertheless be seen at work not only on a Plautine plot, but also on a Comedy of middle life, enlarging both towards a conformity with that view of Comedy held by Vincent and Dante and Chaucer; he may have taken it from the last of these if he needed any source more specific than a general, anonymous medieval tradition. His debt to Chaucer cannot, I think, be certain until the great year of *A Midsummer Night's Dream* (1595-6).

IV.

Dante, as I have said, saw the formula for Comedy as the pattern or picture of ultimate reality, and applied it to the state of the soul after death. That application may be extended to include life on earth; there was trouble in Eden, the knot was untied on Calvary, there is bliss in Heaven. The course of human life well lived is a Comedy as defined. These realities, then unquestioned, could be figured in an earthly tale that followed the same pattern. Any human harmony achieved out of distress can awaken overtones of joy on higher planes. At least they imply an assertion that the harmonious is the normal, the attainable, that heaviness may endure for a night but joy cometh in the morning. Life is a union in love, not a battle of self-interest waged by the rules of an expedient ethic. Its greatest and characteristic triumph is positive joy, not a negative correction of vice and folly. The medieval formula for Comedy leads to the Beatific Vision, the

Renaissance formula leads no further than the Day of Judgment, and is principally preoccupied with punishing the goats. The Christian vision sees love the cause and crown of life, the classical sees a useful morality, which will do to go on with. The best pagan faith offers Justice; Christianity, Mercy and Forgiveness.

In a spirit of conformity with these opposites stand the Comedies of Jonson and Shakespeare respectively. Almost all in Shakespeare are built up on a love-story, often indeed on a group of love-stories; lovers are united, faults are pardoned, enmities are reconciled. All this might be thought intolerably sentimental if it were merely a question of sentiment, not a whole and serious view of the real nature of life. Shakespeare's comic vision is not a sickly indulgence or 'an escape from reality', but the firm assertion of basic harmony.

Out of this settled and traditional view he began early to create his 'Comedy of the golden world' as it has been called. *A Midsummer Night's Dream* is its first full expression, and perhaps the most delicate. It is a picture of a world with no ill-will. If his comedies had never enlarged this picture to include the melancholy and the sinful, he might well be indicted of leading an escape from unpleasant facts into some Tudor Garden of the Rose. It is a proof how strongly he held to a view of life as harmony that he learnt later how to stretch Comedy to contain sorrow and evil, and yet to show them capable of resolution in love and joy. *Measure for Measure* and *The Winter's Tale* are the extreme examples of this vision and power.

If we follow the chronology of his plays worked out by Sir Edmund Chambers, *Love's Labour's Lost* preceded *A Midsummer Night's Dream* by at least a year. *Love's Labour's Lost* does not follow the medieval pattern of comic form, though it is 'romantic' rather than 'satirical' in quality, being the story of five or six love-affairs (if we may include the passions of Don Adriano and of Costard). Yet in its very refusal of the pattern it admits the pattern:

> Our woing doth not end like an old Play:
> Iacke hath not Gill: these Ladies courtesie
> Might wel haue made our sport a Comedie.

In its exuberance of language, lordliness and buffoonery, it seems the work of a young *Avant-gardiste*, newly confident of and revelling in his powers. He will show the world what wit and rhetoric can do, he will defy convention, bring death into the last Act of a Comedy and separate his lovers for a year. His confidence was justified; quality could make a Comedy though form was standing on its head. He did not, however, repeat the experiment, and Puck is allowed the reassertion of orthodoxy:

> *Iacke* shall haue *Iill*, nought shall goe ill,
> The man shall haue his Mare againe, and all shall bee well.

V.

I have tried so far to show Shakespeare's dependence on, or agreement with, a medieval conception of Comedy as a story starting in trouble, ending in joy, and centred in love; and I have suggested some of the philosophical implications of this picture of life and their conformity with a medieval and Christian understanding of reality. I have exampled the opposed 'corrective' view of Comedy favoured by Renaissance critics, a view which owes nothing in form to the Middle Ages but goes back to Donatus and his fellows directly. This was the classical Jonson's style, in whom there are no memorable love-stories, if any that could be dignified by the name at all. The only thing he seems to have taken from the Middle Ages was the doctrine of the Humours.

I would like now to consider two of the consequences that follow from what I have advanced and concern the opposite techniques followed by Shakespeare and Jonson in the imagining and writing of a play. To do this I must go back to Chaucer.

When Chaucer prayed for the strength to write a Comedy before he died, he was not asking for the strength to write a play, but a *story*, or a collection of stories. The definition *Commoedia poesis exordium triste laeto fine commutans* indicates the shape of a *narrative*. There is nothing (as I have already noted) in the Renaissance definitions of Comedy to suggest that a strictly narrative interest is of noteworthy importance in writing a comedy.

Here again Shakespeare's affinity to the medieval tradition can readily be seen, for we can trace his ceaseless search for stories that could be told on a stage. He gutted Chronicles, novels, legends and romances; he went to Gower and Plutarch, to Chaucer and Lydgate, to Cinthio and the *Gesta Romanorum*. Like Chaucer he never troubled to invent a plot if he could find one invented by somebody else. A good story was the first necessity in imagining his plays.

Ben Jonson worked differently. Satire was his object and he therefore had to begin with a *character* (or a group of characters) fitted to his lash. He then placed them in a certain situation calculated to show them at their worst, and by a prodigious intellectual mastery contrived the complete series of their logical developments into successive scenes, working from his data to his QED with the stunning ingenuity of a master in algebra. By doing so he almost in some cases achieved a story. *Volpone* and *Epicoene*, by dint of the unanswerable logic he shows in the deployment of his data, very nearly achieve a narrative interest separable (in a sense) from the humours they were written to flay. The same is but barely true of *The Alchemist*, but not at all of *Bartholomew Fair*, which has nothing in it that could be fairly dignified by the title of a tale.

The effect of this, as has been often noted, is that none of the characters show development. They were not meant to; they were complete at the start. x and y do not change their values in an equation. To write thus is to forfeit every element in dramatic surprise except that which Jonson's unforeseeable ingenuity of logical manipulation could contrive. No one could foresee the *dénouement* of *Epicoene*, because no one but Jonson would remember that one of the data to be manipulated was the convention that gave him a boy to act the part of a girl. The stunning surprise that results from this brilliant conjuring trick is only damped by the sense that we have been fooled as much as poor Morose was. Ben Jonson has withdrawn his confidence from us; Shakespeare always lets us into his secret and shows us the disguiser assuming his (or her) disguise.

If we now consider the Shakespearian method of first seeking a *story*, we shall gain some insight into his craft in delineating character. It is a truism that his characters are 'round' where Jonson's are 'flat', that they have changes of mood and motive, that they develop and surprise us. And the surprise is always such that in the very moment of surprise we feel we should not have been surprised. For these reasons his people seem 'natural' to us, like people that we know, like ourselves. This is never so in Jonson.

It will in no way diminish the marvel of Shakespeare's psychological insight if it can be partly explained by his habit of first finding a *story*. Stories, as can be seen from folk-tale, exist largely in their own right as narrative shapes and hardly depend at all (save in a rudimentary way) on 'character'. Their interest is 'What happened then?' Thus the episodes in a continuous tale, being told for their own sake, may often lead the protagonists into moods, situations and activities in which if their 'characters' were defined and fixed they could not behave in the way demanded by the story. Shakespeare, starting with a story, had to imagine people to fit it, variable, fluid and many-sided natures containing cross-currents and inner contradictions. If Hamlet is to have an opportunity of killing Claudius at his prayers, then even the villain Claudius must be capable of trying to pray. No one could imagine Volpone praying, but then his nature does not emerge from the story, but the story from his nature.

Or consider Anthonio in *The Merchant of Venice*. Why is he pictured as a melancholy man? Because every aspect of the story that concerns him demands that he should be one. The story demands that he shall lose a friend he loves to a lady he has never seen, and that he shall pay for the wooing. Such a man with such a friend is commonly more loving than beloved, and that is a melancholy thought. Moreover, love him as he may, he can see that he has a bad influence on Bassanio and makes a high-falutin sponge of him, a kind of liar; for which he rebukes him:

> You know me well, and herein spend but time
> To winde about my loue with circumstance

Bassanio's bombast is again called forth by the presence of

Anthonio at the trial scene

> Good cheere *Anthonio*, What man, corage yet:
> The Iew shall haue my flesh, blood, bones, and all,
> Ere thou shalt loose for me one drop of blood.

It is a lie. Had he meant what he said he had only to draw his rapier on Shylock and hang for murder. Anthonio answers with the melancholy submission of a man who knows his love is misdirected:

> I am a tainted Weather of the flocke,
> Meetest for death

The nature of the story demands it. So, too, the nature of the story demands his resigned attitude towards Shylock when the bond falls due. If he had shown more fight at the trial, if he had been a Gratiano, it would have robbed Portia of her full triumph in snatching victory from an accepted defeat. The story demands it shall be Portia's scene, and Portia's scene it is. The narrative line determines the psychological line, and narrative is of the romantic and not the satirical tradition.

VI.

I now come, with diffidence, to the most conjectural part of this essay, namely the development of a theme which of its nature can only be treated with the dangerous help of subjective intuition; but I will cling to such facts as I can. The first is the fact of the medieval tradition of allegory, an account of the nature of which I have quoted from Dante. I will not pretend that Shakespeare read either the *Epistle* to *Can Grande* or the *Convivio*. But I think it reasonable to suppose that an age that had produced *The Faerie Queene* felt more at home in allegory than we do. It was an age that found no difficulty in accepting *The Song of Songs* as a figure of the love of Christ for His Church, and the act of holy matrimony as a signification of that same love. Thinking in allegory is to us an unaccustomed habit of mind, but to those in a medieval tradition, second nature. It only means a habit of power to draw simultaneous meanings on parallel planes of experience. In proportion as materialist ways of life encroach upon us, other more spiritual planes withdraw and are lost to view. Ceasing to think of them, we lose the faculty to do so and at last deny that such a faculty can have had genuine part in a poetry which we think can be well enough understood without it.

Yet in recent years much has been done to enlarge our apprehensions of imagery in poetry, especially in the poetry of Shakespeare. For the most part this new study of imagery has been devoted to the study of the *detail* of poetry; that *a narrative itself, taken as a whole, may be an image* is an idea that has received too little attention.

Let us, however, begin with a detail, taken from *Cymbeline*. It is from the speech of Posthumus (V.3) describing a panic flight in battle; he interjects this parenthesis about panic:

> ... (Oh a sinne in Warre
> Damn'd in the first beginners) ...

How easily familiar with Christian thought an audience must have been to catch this fugitive allusion to Adam and Eve, those 'first beginners' in the sin that brought damnation in its train! Yet it is there, and can allude to nothing else. It is to be caught as an overtone in an exciting battlepiece, packed with other imagery. Indeed there is hardly a speech in all Shakespeare that contains such a mass of unexpected images, continued through nearly forty lines. Every listener was expected to listen on many planes of allusion, that is, of meaning.

What is true of the detail of this poetry I hold to be often true of the narrative as a whole. If we apply Dante's injunctions we shall many times get a result. It may be objected that such results are so highly subjective, so far-fetched, so liable to contrary interpretations, that we can never be sure; and it is an objection that has much validity. But it is also to be answered that no effort to interpret (let us say) *Volpone* on a figurative or allegorical plane will have any success whatever. It means no more than it says directly, it alludes to nothing. There are, of course, some Shakespearian

Comedies that may resemble *Volpone* in this, *The Taming of the Shrew* or *Much Ado About Nothing* for example. Yet there are others which seem to invite a figurative as well as a naturalistic understanding; among them I would list *The Merchant of Venice*, *Measure for Measure*, *The Winter's Tale* and *The Tempest*. To analyse all these à la Dante would take this essay on too wide a course, and I hesitate which to choose for a demonstration.

It has been my fortune, at one time or another, to produce all these plays, and in doing so I have been made aware of the presence of other planes of meaning than those immediately manifested in the 'story'. Spiritual parallels suggest themselves. When this happens to a producer the newly discerned 'meaning' must be rigorously tested against the manifest meaning as a whole, for fear someone may say with Horatio "Tis but our fantasy'. But when the new meaning is confirmed by such a test it will be found to make practical demands on the technique of production, if no part of it is to escape unexpressed.

Of the four plays I have mentioned I choose the easiest (*The Merchant of Venice*) and the most difficult (*The Tempest*) to illustrate what I mean by Shakespeare's use of narrative imagery, and how he can give simultaneous meaning on other than naturalistic planes of interpretation. We will find ourselves led back into medieval tradition and a Christian concept of the universe.

In the case of *The Merchant of Venice** we are first confronted with a producer's problem. Is he to understand the play as pro-Jew or anti-Jew? Can he please his own prejudices in the matter? When he looks at the facts, this is what he finds.

The title-page of the second quarto of *The Merchant of Venice*, dated 1600, reads: 'The most excellent Historie of *The Merchant of Venice*. With the extreame crueltie of *Shylocke* the Iewe towards the said Merchant, in cutting a iust pound of his flesh'.

This announcement seems to justify a producer in supposing that the play was intended to be sold as a piece of

---

*Nevill Coghill discussed this case in similar terms in 'The Governing Idea. Essays in Stage-Interpretation of Shakespeare', *Shakespeare Quarterly* (1948).

anti-Semitism, and the almost contemporary Lopez scandal is generally quoted in support of this view. Yet even this title-page, by the use of the word 'just' (intended no doubt to mean 'exact') may raise thoughts about justice in the producer's mind. Should he, however, stifle such thoughts and proceed to a full-blooded Jew-baiting production (à la *Jew of Malta*) he may at a pinch be able to bring it off by ruthless distortion and insensitiveness to detail. In the trial scene he will have to disregard the noble dignity and unimpeachable logic of the supposed 'villian' and on several other occasions during the action he will find himself forced to underplay a sympathy for Shylock which is manifestly in the text:

Shylock: Faire sir, you spet on me on Wednesday last;
              You spurn'd me such a day; another time
              You cald me dog: and for these curtesies
              Ile lend you thus much moneyes.
Ant: I am as like to call thee so againe,
              To spet on thee againe, to spurne thee too.

Or,

Hath not a *Iew* eyes? hath not a *Iew* hands, organs, dementions, sences, affections, passions, fed with the same foode, hurt with the same weapons, subiect to the same diseases, healed by the same meanes, warmed and cooled by the same Winter and Sommer as a Christian is: if you pricke vs doe we not bleede? if you tickle vs doe we not laugh? if you poison vs doe we not die?

These passages cannot be harmonised with a governing idea of anti-Semitic feeling. They would rend the unity of such a production.

On the other hand, to regard Shylock as the wronged hero of an oppressed race, falling with final grandeur through a wily woman versed in legal trickery makes nonsense of the last Act of the play: for how can a Comedy of rings and nuptials be clapped on to so tragic an event without laying the producer, not to say the author, open to the charge of heartless levity, and a gross breach in the unity of design?

If then the production of *The Merchant of Venice* is attended by certain incompatibilities of meaning whether we produce it on pro-Jew or anti-Jew prejudices, should we not think it possible that neither kind of production was intended

by Shakespeare? Might it even be that the fundamental
notion of the play was to be found in a region far above and
beyond race feeling?

Is there any other notion that can give the play a genuine
unity? What is it really *about*?

I believe that to answer these questions we must return to
the Middle Ages and to one of its traditional themes. The best
expression of the theme I have in mind is to be found in *Piers
Plowman*. In that poem, Truth (God) sends Piers a Pardon, in
two lines:

> *Et qui bona egerunt, ibunt in vitam eternam*
> *Qui vero mala, in ignem eternum.*

In the first version of the poem (the 'A Text') this 'pardon'
remains an unexplained enigma. In what sense can it be a
'pardon'? It states a proportionate requital, an eye for an eye.
It shows *Justice* in God, but not *Mercy*.

The second version of the poem (the 'B Text') was written
to elaborate and explain the seeming paradox of the 'pardon'.
It does so by adding the whole story of the Incarnation,
Passion and Descent into Hell, the picture of God's love to
man. For in demanding an exact payment for all sin, He paid
it Himself, and His payment is available to all who are willing
to acknowledge their debt (*'redde quod debes'*) in confession
and obedience to His Church.

Now God's right thus to despoil the Fiend of his prey
(sinful man) is very closely argued by four characters in the
poem (B XVIII). They are the four daughters of God, Mercy
and Truth, Righteousness and Peace. Briefly their argument
is this: under the Old Law God ordained punishment for sin,
eye for eye and tooth for tooth in Hell. But under the New
Law, God underwent and paid that punishment Himself on
Calvary, and He has therefore bought back and redeemed
'those that he loved' with a perfect *Justice* that is also a perfect
Mercy. God is Truth, but He is also Love. The New Law
does not contradict but complements the Old.

Almost exactly the same argument is conducted by the
same four daughters of God at the end of *The Castle of
Perseverance*, a morality play written in the early fifteenth

century. In this the protagonist, *Humanum Genus* has died in sin and so his soul comes up for judgment. Righteousness and Truth demand his damnation, which the play would show to be just. Mercy and Peace plead the Incarnation, and *Humanum Genus* is saved. The play ends with *Te Deum Laudamus*.

Now if we follow this Christian tradition of a former age as a pathway into Shakespeare it will lead us to an understanding of *The Merchant of Venice* that will solve the dilemma I have stated. It is a presentation of the theme of justice and mercy, the Old Law and the New. Seen thus it puts an entirely different complexion upon the opposition of Jew and Gentile. The two principles for which, in Shakespeare's play, respectively they stand are both *inherently right*, and they are only in conflict because, whereas God is absolutely just as He is absolutely merciful, mortal and finite man can only be relatively so, and must arrive at a compromise. In human affairs either justice must yield a little to mercy or mercy to justice, and the former solution is the more Christian. The conflict between Shylock and Anthonio is thus an *exemplum* (to use medieval terminology) of this traditional theme.

As I am here considering what Dante would have called the allegorical meaning of the play, let me stress that I am not saying it is the 'only' meaning. The play will stand on the natural plane well enough (if we allow impossibilities such as choice-by-caskets and young women disguised as lawyers to be 'natural'). All the characters can be shown to have a determinable human psychology consistent with themselves and with the story, as I have tried to show in the case of Anthonio. If I use the word 'allegory' in connection with Shakespeare I do not mean that the characters are abstractions representing this or that vice or virtue (as they do in some allegories, say *The Roman de la Rose* or *The Castle of Perseverance* itself). I mean that they contain and adumbrate certain principles, not in a crude or neat form, but mixed with other human qualities; but that these principles taken as operating in human life, do in fact give shape and direction to the course, and therefore to the meaning, of the play.

Let us return to the Trial scene. The principle here mainly adumbrated in Shylock is justice, in Portia, mercy. He stands, and says he stands, for the Law, for the notion that a man must be as good as his bond. It is the Old Law. As *Piers Plowman* has it:

> ... the olde lawe graunteth
> That gylours be bigiled . and that is gode resoun.
> *Dentem pro dente, & oculum pro oculo.*

Before Shylock's uncompromising demand for justice, mercy is in the posture of a suppliant refused. Thrice his money is offered him and rejected. He is begged to supply a surgeon at his own cost. But no, it is not in the bond.

From the technical point of view the scene is constructed on a sudden reversal of situation, a traditional dramatic dodge to create surprise and *dénouement*. The verbal trick played by Portia is not a part of her 'character', but a device to turn the tables and show justice in the posture of a suppliant before mercy. The reversal is instantaneous and complete, as it is also unexpected for those who do not know the story in advance. Portia plants the point firmly:

> Downe, therefore, and beg mercy of the Duke.

And, in a twinkling, mercy shows her quality:

> Duke: That thou shalt see the difference of our spirit,
>   I pardon thee thy life before thou aske it:
>   For halfe thy wealth, it is *Anthonio's*,
>   The other halfe comes to the generall state,
>   Which humblenesse may driue vnto a fine.

Out of this there comes the second reversal. Shylock, till then pursuing Anthonio's life, now has to turn to him for favour; and this is Anthonio's response:

> So please my Lord the Duke, and all the Court
> To quit the fine for one halfe of his goods,
> I am content; so he will let me haue
> The other halfe in vse, to render it
> Vpon his death, vnto the Gentleman
> That lately stole his daughter.
> Two things prouided more, that for this fauour
> He presently become a Christian:

> The other, that he doe record a gift
> Heere in the Court of all he dies possest
> Vnto his sonne *Lorenzo*, and his daughter.

Evidently Anthonio recognises the validity of legal deeds as much as Shylock does, and his opinion on Jessica's relationship with Lorenzo is in agreement with Shakespeare's, namely that the bond between husband and wife overrides the bond between father and daughter. Cordelia and Desdemona would have assented. Nor is it wholly alien to Shylock who is himself a family man. For him to provide for Jessica and Lorenzo is not unnaturally harsh or vindictive.

It is Anthonio's second condition that seems to modern ears so harshly vindictive. In these days all good humanitarians incline to the view that a man's religion is his own affair, that a religion imposed is a tyranny, and that one religion is as good as another, if sincerely followed.

But the Elizabethans were not humanitarians in this sense. Only in Utopia, where it was one of 'the auncientest lawes among them that no man shall be blamed for reasonynge in the mayntenaunce of his owne religion' (and Utopia was not in Christendom) would such views have seemed acceptable. Whether we dislike it or not, Shylock had no hope, by Elizabethan standards, of entering a Christian eternity of blessedness; he had not been baptised. It would not have been his cruelty that would have excluded him (for cruelty, like other sin, can be repented) but the simple fact that he had no wedding-garment. No man cometh to the Father but by me.

Shylock had spent the play pursuing the mortal life of Anthonio (albeit for private motives) in the name of justice. Now, at this reversal, in the name of mercy, Anthonio offers him the chance of eternal life, his own best jewel.

It will, of course, be argued that it is painful for Shylock to swallow his pride, abjure his racial faith and receive baptism. But then Christianity is painful. Its centre is crucifixion, nor has it ever been held to be equally easy for all natures to embrace. If we allow our thoughts to pursue Shylock after he left the Court we may well wonder whether his compulsory submission to baptism in the end induced him to take up his cross and follow Christ. But from Anthonio's point of view,

Shylock has at least been given his chance of eternal joy, and it is he, Anthonio, that has given it to him. Mercy has triumphed over justice, even if the way of mercy is a hard way.

Once this aspect of the Trial scene is perceived, Act V becomes an intelligible extension of the allegory (in the sense defined); for we return to Belmont to find Lorenzo and Jessica in each other's arms. Christian and Jew, New Law and Old, are visibly united in love. And their talk is of music, Shakespeare's recurrent symbol of harmony.

It is not necessary for a single member of a modern audience to grasp this study in justice and mercy by any conscious process of cerebration during a performance, or even afterwards in meditation. *Seeing one may see and not perceive.* But a producer who wishes to avoid his private prejudices in favour of Shakespeare's meanings, in order that he may achieve the real unity that binds a poetical play, should try to see them and to imagine the technical expedients of production by which that unity will be experienced. If he bases his conception on the resolution of the principles of justice and mercy, he will then, on the natural plane, be left the freer to show Christians and Jews as men and women, equally containing such faults and virtues as human beings commonly have.

I now come to *The Tempest* in which almost all critics have seen adumbrations of mystical meaning. I would first like to seize on what little there is in the way of fact to guide an inquiry that must be mainly subjective. What can we *know* that an Elizabethan audience understood in it? Oddly enough two points of first importance that would have been clear to them are least often expressed in modern productions.

The first is that it is, at the start and at the end, a *Ship-play.* To an Elizabethan audience the stage imaginatively, and as I think to some extent visibly, changed into a ship, both in the first scene and during Prospero's Epilogue. The great bare apron was the main deck, the 'inner stage' the cabin, the gallery above it the forecastle and the second gallery above that the masthead, rigging or crow's nest. In the cabin were the royal party; above were the Master, the Boatswain and his men. All this can be seen at once from the text of the dialogue in Act I, scene i by those who ask themselves, 'How was this contrived on an Elizabethan stage?' It is just possible that the 'inner stage' was not used for the royal party, but that they came up from below the main-stage to parley with the Boatswain through the trap-door commonly called the 'grave-trap'. But I prefer to think that for this play at least there was a companion-way or ladder at the back of the inner stage leading up to the gallery, for the colloquy between Gonzalo and the Boatswain. Be that as it may the dialogue makes it quite clear that the audience is looking at a stage representing *a ship that is going away from them*. I think it reasonable to suppose that this effect was visibly enhanced by the spreading of sails, ropes and rigging above in the gallery, all of which at 'We split! We split!' would collapse and disappear, together with the crew. Gonzalo says his last say and also disappears, either down the trap, or into the inner stage, drawing the curtains behind him to close upon the King and his party at their prayers.

At the end of the play, when Prospero comes forth from his cell to speak the Epilogue, the sails are hoisted again; up goes the rigging with the mariners in attendance, and the curtains of the inner stage part to show the whole and happy company as a background to Prospero's speech

> Gentle breath of yours my sailes
> Must fill, or else my project failes,
> Which was to please ...

If, with whatever scenic additions, the stage at the start and finish of the play represents a ship going away from the audience, we only now have to ask 'where was it going?' and the answer must be, at the end of the play, '*Home*'. It is a play about going home. Once this simple fact is apprehended it will be seen that all the action leads to it. 'Home' in this case is called *Millaine* and it is associated in the mind of Prospero with the idea of being ready to die:

> Euery third thought shall be my graue.

In between these two ship scenes, we learn that Prospero has been expelled from his natural inheritance (together with his daughter), for having devoted himself too closely to a kind of knowledge that is itself forbidden, that is, to magical knowledge. And he has to abjure it before he can go home with auspicious gales. He has also to reconcile himself with the enemies he has made.

Now if we take such a story on the natural plane of meaning only it is impossible to account for the deep impression made upon us by the play. Compared with any other play of Shakespeare the sequence of action from scene to scene is tenuously spun; the succession of incidents in the loves of Ferdinand and Miranda, the bewildering of the royal party and the debauch of Caliban is even less integrated into a firm and purposive narrative-line than the actions in *Love's Labour's Lost*. The characters are less sharply observed; villains are merely villainous, comics are merely comic. The story makes no demands on the psychology of Miranda, who is not only simple when compared to an Ophelia, but even when compared to a Viola. As a 'character', Gonzalo is nothing to Polonius. Prospero himself is not psychologically recognisable in the sense that can be claimed for other male protagonists in Shakespeare. The natural plane of interpretation is insufficient to explain the effect the play produces.

In turning to the plane called allegorical by Dante we are in danger from its inherent chartlessness. We must find a discipline for subjective fancy. I propose the discipline of narrative-imagery.

What story then, familiar to Shakespeare and to his audience, does this *Tempest* story of a man and woman exiled from their natural inheritance for the acquisition of a forbidden knowledge resemble? An answer leaps readily to mind; it resembles the story of Adam and Eve, type-story of our troubles. *The Tempest* also contains the story of Prospero and his brother Anthonio, that has something of the primal, eldest curse upon it, something near a brother's murder. There is in Genesis, as well as the story of Adam and Eve, the story of Cain and Abel. But in *The Tempest* there is also a turn in both stories by which there is a repentance and a forgiveness, and a home-coming in harmony. This is the shape of the promise of the New Testament and of the Second Adam. There is the hope of a return to Paradise when we come to die. Trouble will turn to joy.

These simplest and most obvious elements in the Christian story, upon which (but literally and without allegory) the great medieval mystery cycles were built, are, at a distance, mirrored in the story of *The Tempest*, well enough at least to be worth investigating.

Let us then turn to the second point on which an Elizabethan audience would be more instinctively understanding than we are, namely the natures of Ariell and Caliban. Can these be fitted into the suggestion I have put forward?

Medieval science believed, and Marlowe in his poetry reiterated, that the physical body of man is composed of the four elements. Air and fire, earth and water were the constituents of the human frame; everybody knew that. It would have been no great leap of recognition to see in Ariell the elements of air and fire, and in Caliban (at once addressed by Prospero as 'Thou earth, thou!' and constantly mistaken for a fish) the elements of earth and water. These two, Ariell and Caliban, are the only occupants of Prospero's island at his coming thither. Their functions in the play are for Ariell obedience to the will of Prospero in his spiritual designs upon the royal party, for Caliban rebellion against Prospero and a drunken and murderous association with the lower louts, Stefano and Trinculo. They are the images of what is higher and lower in man, the occupants of his body, the servants (both subject to momentary rebellions) of his intellect.

By this account Prospero himself stands for the intellect and Miranda for his soul. The island, which he is shortly to leave, is the form of his body. Caliban is to be left behind and Ariell to be freed; the elements are to return to the elements from which they came.

Miranda is pure where Eve was not; but if she be taken on this plane of meaning to figure the soul of Prospero, it can be seen why she is so. Prospero has not used his forbidden knowledge in sinful ways. He is a magician, but a white one. Yet by being so he has alienated elements in his own nature, and has been cut off from them, particularly from the most royal. His faults have begotten theirs. These are seen in the persons of Alonzo, Gonzalo, Sebastian, Antonio and

Ferdinand, variously disposed towards him. Separated from him by the gulf of the seas, nothing but a tempest can bring them together, and at the moment determined by Destiny (the moment of preparation for death) Prospero commands the tempest to arise, that he may reassemble and set in harmony all the wrongs and enmities that stand between him and wholeness of being. The psychologist Jung would agree.

This harmony is not too facile; its achievement is as grave as the airy texture of the play permits. Prospero has to abjure as well as to rebuke before he can forgive and reunite. These more painful things must not be out-run by the image of happy love. It was a part of Prospero's design that Ferdinand should wed Miranda, that the image of marriage no less than that of music and the blessing of the gods should celebrate the reconcilement of his soul. But this easier image had to be delayed, threatening as it did to accomplish itself too quickly; there were things more intractable to settle first. A wound must heal from the bottom, otherwise there is only a skinning and a filming of the ulcerous place.

It is not until Prospero, in summoning an invisible music, has for the last time exercised his forbidden knowledge and until he has confronted and rebuked the enemy that he can forgive them and show them the image of that forgiveness in the love of Ferdinand and Miranda at their game of chess. Then Stephano and Trinculo can return, chastened, to their proper service, and Caliban, come to his senses, can acknowledge his master and be accepted into grace. In this way the story completes its image of the Old Adam made whole by the New, and of a reconcilement before the return to a lost Paradise.

Shakespeare is too subtle an entertainer to preach openly. I do not even think it was his purpose to do so under a veil. I suppose he took the basis of his vision for granted, what everyone in Christendom knew to be true of life. It was a natural, time-honoured shape, for a story, re-told in contemporary terms. His purpose was (he says) 'to please', and how to please better than by comfortable words and a new fable to body forth the old beliefs in an harmonious world where trouble was an intrusion and joy the goal? He left to Ben Jonson the preaching of a morality that fundamentally presupposes the opposite, namely a world of discordant self-interest in which the most we can hope for is a sort of social prudence, kept in being by the continual castigation of unethical excesses.

Dr Johnson blamed Shakespeare for having in his plays too little regard for 'morality'. But if the kind of happiness to which all his Comedies travel is at all communicated to his readers and audiences, their imaginations, filled by that positive good, are themselves touched through happiness to goodness.

In his earlier Comedies such griefs as there were came from cross-purposes, separations, misunderstanding and the lighter conflicts of temperament. These were sorted out and sealed up with songs, masques and dances, marriages and friendly feelings. Katerina is left at one with Petruchio, Sebastian finds Viola, Benedick and Beatrice change their minds and are happy. The wicked Bastard is eliminated. A Duke and a Countess can stoop to sue a wronged Steward and entreat him to a peace. One might say that anyone can write some sort of Comedy on these terms. It is easy to solve misunderstandings and turn them into joy. It is only with the existence of evil as a real presence in the world that a Comedy on the medieval pattern becomes difficult; it is not so easy to solve in joy the problem of sin. But medieval ways of thinking had an answer for that too, a Christian answer, like Shakespeare's. If there were a breach in nature there was also the power of charity and repentance, of mercy and forgiveness, with laughter on the way. *The Winter's Tale* follows a like pattern; so does *Measure for Measure*.

In recent years Shakespeare has been shown to have many affinities with medieval ways of apprehending human life and the values involved in it. For instance *Troilus and Cressida* cannot be properly understood in terms of Homeric Troy. It stems from the medieval tradition (available to Shakespeare in Lydgate and elsewhere) that we British are Trojans, descendants of Brutus of Troy, and that the Greeks are the enemy. Troilus stands for truth in love, Hector for chivalry in battle. It is a Chaucerian and Malorian piece and the tragedy is that these noble hearts should perish in contention with the scum of the earth, the Macchiavel Ulysses, the braggart Ajax, the gangster Achilles, the bastardly Thersites, and the inconstant Cressida who goes over (in every sense) to the Greeks. Knowledge of the medieval tradition behind Shakespeare has made rubbish of the recent sentimental view of his supposed disgust and disillusion with life, and particularly with sex. However, Shakespeare is the mirror to nature and the first thing a critic sees in a mirror is too often his own wise face. He is thoroughly disillusioned. So Shakespeare must have been.

The English Histories, too, as Dr Tillyard has shown, are steeped and saturated in medieval ways of political and religious thought, and Mr Danby's recent book on *Shakespeare's Doctrine of Nature* takes us back to the same harmonious world into which Shakespeare perceived the entry of that uncovenanted character, the Black Macchiavel, in whom force and fraud are the cardinal virtues, for whom nature is not a harmony but a war.

It cannot, then, be wholly improbable that Shakespearian Comedy comes to us out of a like region and is to be understood in a like manner. Medieval principles of form and interpretation cannot be stretched to account for the works of Ben Jonson (save in respect of the Humours); if, however, they be found to fit the Comedies of Shakespeare, it can hardly be deemed a coincidence.

NOTES

1. *Comicorum Graecorum Fragmenta* ed. Georgius Kaibel, Vol. I, Fasc. Prior, Berlin 1899.
2. ... Inter tragoediam autem et comoediam cum multa tum inprimis hoc distat, quod in comoedia mediocres fortunae hominum, parui impetus periculorum laetique sunt exitus actionum, at in tragoedia contrario ordine res aguntur; tum quod in tragoedia fugienda vita, in comoedia capessanda exprimitur; postremo quod omnis comoedia de fictis est argumentis, tragoedia saepe de historica fide petitur. Comoedia per quattuor partes diuiditur, prologum, protasin, epitasin, catastrophen: est prologus uelut praefatio quaedam fabulae ... protasis primus actus initiumque est dramatis, epitasis incrementum processusque turbarum ac totius ut ita dixerim nodus erroris, catastrophe conuersio rerum est ad iucundos exitus patefacta cunctis cognitione gestorum ...
3. ... Comoedia a tragoedia differt, quod in tragoedia introducuntur

heroes, duces, reges, in comoedia humiles atque privatae (personae), in illa luctus exilia caedes, in hac amores, virginum raptus; deinde quod in illa frequenter et paene semper laetis rebus exitus tristes et liberorum fortunarumque priorum in peius adgnitio ... tristia namque tragoediae proprium ... poetae primi comici fuerunt Susarion, Mullus et Magnes. hi veteris disciplinae iocularia quaedam minus scite ac venuste pronuntiabunt ... secunda aetate fuerunt Aristophanes, Eupolis et Cratinus, qui et principium vitia sectati acerbissimas comoedias composeurunt. tertia aetas fuit Menandri, Diphili et Philemonis, qui omnem acerbitatem comoediae mitigaverunt atque argumenta multiplicia gratis erroribus secuti sunt ...

4. ... Comoedia est fabula diuersa instituta continens affectuum ciuilium ac priuatorum, quibus discitur quid sit in uita utile quid contra euitandum ...

5. Edmond Faral, *Les Arts poétiques du XIIème et du XIIIème Siècle*, p. 153. Paris, 1923 – Thirdly, there stole along Comedy, with daily grin (in work-a-day dress?) and humbled head, bringing the allurements of no gaiety.

6. Boethuis, *De Consolatione*, Book II, Prose 2.

7. Moore e Toynbee, *Opere di Dante Alighierei*, quarta edizione (Oxford, 1924), pp. 415–16.

8. Save for that hurried and exceptional affair *The Merry Wives of Windsor*.

Index